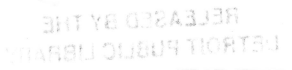

A Brief and Tentative Analysis of Negro Leadership

Ralph J. Bunche, Ph.D.

HOWARD UNIVERSITY
WASHINGTON, D.C.
AUGUST 1940

EDITED AND WITH AN INTRODUCTION BY
Jonathan Scott Holloway

NEW YORK UNIVERSITY PRESS
New York and London

NEW YORK UNIVERSITY PRESS
New York and London
www.nyupress.org

© 2005 by New York University
All rights reserved

SEP 2 7 2005

Library of Congress Cataloging-in-Publication Data
Bunche, Ralph J. (Ralph Johnson), 1904–1971.
A brief and tentative analysis of Negro leadership / Ralph J. Bunche ;
edited and with an introduction by Jonathan Scott Holloway.
    p. cm.
"Howard University, Washington, D.C., August 1940."
Includes bibliographical references and index.
ISBN 0-8147-3664-5 (cloth : alk. paper)
    1. African American leadership.   I. Holloway, Jonathan Scott.
II. Title.
E185.61.B929   2004
324'.089'96073—dc22   2004017816

Frontispiece: Ralph Bunche. (Scurlock Studio Collection, Archives
Center, National Museum of American History)

New York University Press books are printed on acid-free paper,
and their binding materials are chosen for strength and durability.

Manufactured in the United States of America

10 9 8 7 6 5 4 3 2 1

*For my mother, Kay Trent Holloway,
who ignited my passion for history.*

*For my father, Wendell M. Holloway,
who helped me focus this passion
upon political ideology.*

Contents

Acknowledgments

This project represents an evolutionary step in my interest in twentieth-century African American political thought. In my first book, *Confronting the Veil: Abram Harris Jr., E. Franklin Frazier, and Ralph Bunche, 1919–1941,* I examined black radical intellectual ideology during the New Deal. One of these radicals was Ralph Bunche, who, after leaving progressive politics behind in the early 1940s, became best known as an establishment insider and political moderate. In the early 1990s, I came across the carbon-copy set of Bunche's memoranda to Gunnar Myrdal's *An American Dilemma* during archival research in the Bunche Papers at the University of California, Los Angeles. Bunche's two-hundred-page "memo" on leadership intrigued me from the start, although I would do little with it for many years. It has been a delight to revisit that early moment of fascination.

My weeks in the archives, however, did not represent my original engagement with Ralph Bunche. In 1994, six months before I received my doctorate, my parents presented me with a Christmas gift: Margaret Young's *The Picture Life of Ralph Bunche* (Franklin and Watts, 1968), a slender cloth-bound book that was part of a late-1960s and early-1970s series on black leadership designed for the adolescent market. This particular book was about Bunche and his United Nations work. It took a moment, but then I realized that I had seen this text before, roughly twenty-two years earlier. My mother and I read this book together when I was four or five years old. I confess that I did not retain anything about Bunche's life from the book, but I vividly remember its color: what I have always called "United Nations Blue." It is impossible to say, of course, but it may be that my interest in Ralph Bunche—even if I only associated the individual with a particular shade of blue—extends back to that introduction to him in the early 1970s. What is certain is that I owe my love for history to my mother, and she thus deserves the first acknowledgment.

I must also give thanks to my father for the way that he exposed me to the world of politics from an early age. I remember (only with an adult fondness) being dragged along to various meetings or receptions on Capitol Hill. I can still feel the pride when I impressed him with my knowledge, thanks to *Schoolhouse Rock,* of how a bill became a law. I certainly recall being corrected for failing to include the nonvoting delegates to the House of Representatives when I confidently answered that there were 535 members of Congress. And while I still think that it was silly to expect that kind of refined knowledge of a nine-year-old, I do appreciate that my abiding interest in the practice and performance of politics stems from my interactions with my father.

This project, of course, did not emerge wholly from these deep wells of recollection. Rather, the hard work and generosity of many people helped me at every juncture. Octavio Olvera from UCLA's Charles E. Young Research Library Department of Special Collections reproduced the entire carbon-copy manuscript for me (Ralph J. Bunche Papers, Collection 2051, Box 80). That could not have been fun. Simon Elliott, also of UCLA, greatly facilitated the reproduction of a number of the images that you find in the book. Closer to home, Janet Giarratano transcribed the photocopied manuscript. This had to be much less fun, and her interpretive skills in this task are to be admired. Shana Redmond provided critical background research and was an effective sounding board throughout the process. Nilofar Gardezi was my Los Angeles–based quality-control expert. Her ready assistance and sharp archival eye are deeply appreciated. Erin Wood saved me from making numerous mistakes when she served as my second set of eyes during the proofreading process.

At the eleventh hour I enjoyed the opportunity to present some of this work at Northwestern University. Comments and questions that followed my lecture proved to be immensely valuable. In this regard I must thank Dwight McBride, Robert Gooding-Williams, Nancy MacLean, Martha Biondi, and Jeffrey McCune for their contributions.

At the eleventh hour and fifty-ninth minute, I received critical assistance from Nancy Kuhl and John Monahan at Yale's Beinecke Rare Book and Manuscript Library, David Haberstich at the Smithsonian Institution's Archive Center in the National Museum of American History, and Jeff Bridges of the Photographs and Prints Division at the Library of Congress. Hats off to all of them.

Eric Zinner, the editor in chief at New York University Press, and Emily Park, an editorial assistant there, were supportive from the start. Despina Papazoglou Gimbel steered the manuscript through a complicated copyedit, never wavering in her commitment to the text. It has been a joy to work with them on this project from beginning to end. Jerry Watts and Nikhil Singh read the carbon-copy manuscript before it had been transcribed and, despite that burden, still managed to have encouraging things to say about the project. Their constructive criticism was incredibly valuable, and their imprint is found throughout the introduction. Sir Brian Urquhart, the literary executor of Bunche's estate, immediately understood the importance of this work and encouraged its publication. His enthusiastic embrace of the project made life considerably easier for everyone involved.

Finally, I am delighted to report that while I was working on this project, Ellison Holloway joined the family. Every day, he and his big sister, Emerson, make plain how joyful life is meant to be. They are, without doubt, the best teachers I ever had. Although it can go without saying (but never should), all of this would be meaningless without Aisling Colón. I once declared that she was my inspiration. Now I know that she is my distraction, and that I am blessed for it.

Despite all of this friendly meddling, I am alone at fault for any mistakes in the text.

Note on Editorial Policy and Formatting

"A Brief and Tentative Analysis of Negro Leadership" was a rough draft that Bunche cobbled together from interview transcripts, old lecture notes, public talks, and fresh, but raw, commentary. Given this amalgamation and the pace of its production, the memo is fairly littered with typographical errors. These have been corrected for publication.

There are a number of sections in the memo that present ethnographic material on race leadership via field notes. These notes were inconsistently formatted, at times leaving readers to fend for themselves if they wanted to decipher whose voice was speaking at a particular moment. I have changed the presentation of these interviews so that they now share the same format. I have also inserted asterisks (* * * *) between interviews or field notes to clarify a change of speaker and/or interview subject. Bunche often declined to identify certain interview subjects. I decided to adhere to Bunche's decision in these cases rather than to conduct time-consuming investigations that would yield, at best, a name. Elsewhere, Bunche mentioned prominent leaders in passing or only by their last name. I presume Bunche paid fleeting attention to these details, knowing that they would be addressed if and when the memo became incorporated into *An American Dilemma*. Where I felt that more biographical detail was merited, I annotated the text via endnotes that follow the memorandum. Some clarifications of vernacular are also found in these endnotes.

Finally, despite the best efforts of the transcriber, a research assistant, and several other people, there remains a handful of instances where the memo's text is either indecipherable or clearly missing a word. I have exercised an editor's prerogative and have introduced my own best guess at the proper language. My interpretations are found in brackets. Even in light of these various editorial changes, the content of the memo remains unchanged.

. . . leadership itself is a form of escape.
—Ralph Bunche, 1940

Negro Leadership

Chapter I

Introduction

We are lacking in the data necessary to undertake any comprehensive analysis of Negro leadership. Practically nothing of a scientific nature has been written upon the subject and it has been found impossible to devote any considerable time to the task of sifting out leadership materials from the great mass of publications on the Negro—newspapers, periodicals and books. The field workers, in their hurried journeys here and there, did jot down occasional and casual notes on the Negro leadership encountered in the various communities. We also have 50 specially prepared short life histories, written or dictated at our request, by selected Negro leaders and white inter-racial leaders. On the whole, these scattered and sketchy materials do not lend themselves readily to integration in any scientific analysis of Negro leadership. As a matter of fact, I do not consider myself equipped with the tools essential to any such analysis. For these reasons, this treatment of the subject must be viewed as largely impressionistic, based upon my personal observations and opinions as supplemented by the field and other materials at hand.

An effort will be made to indicate what needs to be done on the subject and to suggest where greatest emphasis ought to be placed. In this particular memorandum, emphasis is directed to the social mechanisms by which Negro leaders are chosen and permitted to exercise influence. In my estimation, it is of prime importance to determine how particular individuals have attained the influence and status of leadership. This is no easy task, however, and the necessary data are not readily available. The very nature of the subject implies an analysis of those social factors

First page of the master document. (Ralph J. Bunche Papers, Collection 2051, Department Special Collections, Charles E. Young Research Library, University of California, Los Angeles)

A political cartoon expressing African American frustration over the Carnegie Foundation's choice of a foreigner to study a domestic "problem." (Ralph J. Bunche Papers, Collection 2051, Department Special Collections, Charles E. Young Research Library, University of California, Los Angeles)

Editor's Introduction

The Politics of Escape: Ralph Bunche and Black Leadership in the 1940s

In August 1940, an exhausted Ralph Bunche submitted the last of his four memoranda to Gunnar Myrdal. Less than two years earlier, Myrdal, the Swedish economist whom the Carnegie Corporation had hired to produce the authoritative study of black life in the United States, had asked Bunche to offer analyses of blacks' political ideology, their betterment organizations, and their leadership. Bunche, still teaching in the department of political science at Howard University, produced over three thousand pages of material for his memoranda—most of it written in the first half of 1940. When Myrdal published his findings in 1944 as *An American Dilemma: The Negro Problem and Modern Democracy*, Bunche knew that his was one of the guiding voices in the most important piece of social science literature that had been written on race in America. Despite possessing a general sense that he had been participating in a project of such importance, Bunche could not have known that *An American Dilemma* would play a central role in post–World War II liberal orthodoxies about race and citizenship at least through the mid-1960s.[1]

Just over half of Bunche's contribution was dedicated to his final memorandum, "The Political Status of the Negro." This memo, essentially an examination of black political containment in the South, was edited and published posthumously in 1973.[2] Bunche also authored "Conceptions and Ideologies of the Negro Problem," "Extended Memorandum on Programs, Ideologies, Tactics, and Achievements of Negro Betterment and Interracial Organizations," and "A Brief and Tentative Analysis of Negro Leadership." Until now, none of these other memos has been published.

Of the four memos, Bunche's examination of black leadership is the shortest—thus he is able to rationalize calling a two-hundred-page effort a "brief" analysis. Bunche is on similarly safe ground when he suggests that the memo is also "tentative." His opening lines of the memo confirm as much: "We are lacking in the data necessary to undertake any comprehensive analysis of Negro leadership. . . . it has been found impossible to devote any considerable time to the task of sifting out leadership materials from the great mass of publications on the Negro."[3] While Bunche was a master of self-effacement, requiring that we take his apologia with a grain of salt, his comments do alert the reader that the memorandum is a rough draft.

This roughness, however, enriches the document since it often allows the reader more direct access to the subject matter. Instead of a scholar's constantly distanced and distilled analysis of individual leaders, we get transcriptions, participant observations, and first-person profiles. In short, we get an undiluted ethnography of black leadership. Of course, this means that the reader frequently has to do the work of divining meaning and significance from the manuscript, locating those items of ethnographic value that can be extrapolated to have greater meaning. But this is work that pays off, for it allows us a better purchase on the nature of the dynamics, complications, impediments, and benefits of leading the race in the early 1940s.

One of the most important aspects of this ethnographic approach to black leadership is that Bunche forces us to rethink exactly who were the leaders in the black community. To be sure, he pays careful attention in his memo to the more famous names with which many of us have at least passing familiarity. But by cataloging, in effect, page after page of figures who would only have been known to local communities and by listing still more individuals in his first appendix, Bunche reminds us that "community" and "leadership" are local phenomena. National leaders have a specific role to play in the formation of political or social agendas and in engaging moments of national crisis, but local leaders do the daily work of helping a community simply survive and, hopefully, thrive. It is the local leader, the minister, the principal, the social worker, and the lawyer to whom communities first turn in moments of doubt. Moreover, it is the local leader who creates infrastructures (whether well conceived or not) that allow the national figurehead quick access to local or grassroots community support. Bunche's grounded understanding of who the leaders were in America's black communities takes us a healthy step away from a cult of singularity that often surrounds national black leaders. Hearing this from Bunche in the 1940s tells us that as much as we want and need to know about the A. Philip Randolphs and Martin Luther Kings of this world, we also need to know about the local folk who paved the way for the more famous leaders' various successes.

All of this does not mean that Bunche ignores the more famous figures in black America. Indeed, one of the more appealing aspects of the close-to-the-source character of the memo is that the reader gets to look through Bunche's eyes as he assesses the state of black leadership in America, and the world of possibility for such leaders. This is fascinating in large measure because of who Bunche was. In this memo we get to sift through the thoughts of someone who himself was a prominent figure in black America and who knew well so many of the great African American leaders of the day: W. E. B. Du Bois, Paul Robeson, Mary McLeod Bethune, and Charles Houston, to name just a very few. In this way, Bunche's insights and critiques take on the air of privileged knowledge.

Despite the fact that Bunche's observations are so tantalizing for their proximity to leaders, it is important to note that Bunche's work did not exist in a vacuum. Other scholars, most notably University of Chicago political scientist Harold Gosnell, had produced work on black leadership prior to Bunche's engagement with the Myrdal project. Gosnell's *Negro Politicians* must have been considered the most important text in the field when it appeared in 1935. Other scholars such as sociologists Charles S. Johnson and E. Franklin Frazier were engaged in new research on the black community in *Growing Up in the Black Belt* and *Negro Youth at the Crossways,* respectively. Both of these books were published within a few months of Bunche's delivery of his memoranda to Myrdal. Between Gosnell's 1935 work and Johnson's and Frazier's early 1940s books were sociologist John Dollard's *Caste and Class in a Southern Town* and anthropologist Hortense Powdermaker's *After Freedom.*[4] So, even though it went unpublished until today, Bunche's memo on leadership needs to be understood as part of a larger scholarly conversation about the black community and citizenship. It bears noting that this conversation is what *An American Dilemma* came to dominate over the next generation.

Part of what made Myrdal's book so central to any discussion of black life was the sheer size of the undertaking. What also made the book noteworthy was its great range. Unlike Gosnell's, Johnson's, Frazier's, Dollard's, and Powdermaker's works, *An American Dilemma* was a panoptic rendering of black life in the United States. Indeed, it is this characteristic that highlights the very thing that distinguishes Bunche's memorandum from his peers' published work: although a draft, it attempted a far broader sweep in its effort to understand black leadership and the black community. Perhaps this is what inspired Bunche to make such aggressive swipes at the existing literature on black leadership in the opening and closing pages of his memo. Bunche felt that "nothing of a scientific nature" had been produced on black leadership and that "the studies of Negro leadership [which] have been made . . . are good examples of what Negro leadership studies ought not to be."[5] Bunche was uninterested in the mere identification of prominent blacks and their respective genealogies. What he wanted instead was an interpretive assessment of black leadership, where it came from, and how it maintained itself.

Bunche was skeptical of what he saw. Most black leaders, he was convinced, would never relinquish power once they had their first taste of it. The remnants of his 1930s Marxist leanings also led him to see something more invidious: the insatiable quest for the accumulation of power and the potential for increased wealth that accompanied it only exacerbated class differences within the black community. A slavish devotion to material gain and to class proprieties reinforced a value system that declared that whites belonged on top. Bunche's obviously subjective approach to the topic and his frequent slippage into ad hominem attacks on or dismissals of black leaders ran against Myrdal's desire for something antiseptic and empirical.

While Myrdal probably felt this way from the start of the project, he was certainly further compelled to refrain from the more sensational attacks on individuals and organizations based on his experiences with Walter White and Roy Wilkins of the National Association for the Advancement of Colored People (NAACP) and Eugene Kinckle Jones of the National Urban League (NUL). After Bunche had submitted an early draft of "Conceptions and Ideologies of the Negro Problem," one of the memos preceding "A Brief and Tentative Analysis," Myrdal invited White, Wilkins, and Jones to respond to Bunche's scathing critiques.

The three leaders were apoplectic when they read Bunche's assessments. Together and individually, they implored Myrdal to refrain from publishing what they considered politically biased interpretations. White, for example, lamented that "Ralph has been too long sheltered in

Roy Wilkins. (Photo by Carl Van Vechten, Carl Van Vechten Papers, Van Vechten Trust, Yale Collection of American Literature, Beinecke Rare Book and Manuscripts Library, Yale University)

academic circles." He insisted that Bunche's "field trips as a social investigator" blinded him to what it really meant to live in the black community. Wilkins merely dismissed Bunche as an "arm chair radical" who could "theorize about social movements . . . without any great danger to himself, and without the necessity of having to produce results in any program of social action."[6]

It is safe to say that given this response to the "Conceptions and Ideologies" memo, there are large parts of "A Brief and Tentative Analysis" that Myrdal must have found unusable if only for their tone. In fact, the only discernable presence that Bunche's leadership memo has in *An American Dilemma* is found in the book's chapters on "Accommodating Leadership" and "Compromise Leadership" (the thirty-fourth and thirty-seventh chapters, respectively, out of a total of forty-five). Even then, Myrdal's incorporation of Bunche's ideas on this topic was mostly limited to the occasional uncredited phrase or to nondiscursive citations in the book's endnotes.

Just because Myrdal felt that he could not use Bunche's highly charged observations in the final product did not mean that they were without value. If one can temporarily look past Bunche's frequent dismissals or critiques of so many black leadership types (an issue to which we will return at the end of this introduction), one will find important concepts that undergird Bunche's investigation of black leadership. The most important ideas in this regard concern the central role that "escape" plays in black leadership formation and the extent to which such formation was so often contingent on white approval.

Although Bunche only uses the word (or forms of it) seven times in the entire manuscript, it is evident that "escape" carries great weight for the way that it deepens our understanding of race leadership. Even on its own, "escape" is freighted with meaning. While one typically escapes *from* someone or something, one can just as easily escape *to* someone or something. In this very simple way we can see that "escape" suggests a kind of duality, a literal or figurative movement from one place to another, an either/or proposition. Most often, of course, escape suggests flight, and if there is a good story to be told it is typically found in that sojourn from a difficult situation to one rich with promise. In this regard, we can think of escapes from prisons, from death camps, or from repressive governments. Finally, although it runs the risk of stating the obvious, it is important to remember that "escape" has a special resonance in black America, recalling as it does the legacy of slavery and the abiding determination of those who lived under that system to extricate themselves from it.

But what happens when the escape does not involve such movement, does not involve literally leaving a community or a way of life? What if

Walter White. (Photo by Carl Van Vechten, Carl Van Vechten Papers, Yale Collection of American Literature, Beinecke Rare Book and Manuscripts Library, Yale University)

it only involves leaving a socially constructed circumstance, or, as in the case before us, a racially constructed circumstance? It is here that the implications of "escape" become quite complicated. First of all, when thinking about "escape" and "race" one must contend with the fact that escape suggests a condition that simultaneously reflects desire and denial. The ultimate form of black escape—passing as white—perfectly captures this duality. In such cases, the desire for a better life was fundamentally contingent on one's willingness to deny one's history in perpetuity. If one could not pass as white or was unwilling to pay the cost of that passage, one would be left to wonder if escaping race was even possible. Further complicating matters is the fact that in this country, race has always concerned more than physiognomic features. "Race," in its fullest expression, needs to be understood for the way that its social significance colors, if you will, those other factors that define our lives: class position, wealth or the possibility of attaining it, power, and prestige.

It is clear that being a leader suggests a transcendence over a community of peers and, thus, a transcendence to a place of enhanced material prosperity. It would seem that for black Americans leadership status similarly implies escape from a predetermined set of racially proscribed realities. But the physiognomic stain of race complicates the notion of transcendence/escape. If race is inescapable, if race is accompanied by so many other social realities, what exactly does it mean to be a black leader? What benefits might one accrue from a transcendence that is, at best, a fluttering of clipped wings? To state things in more concrete terms, leadership often comes with material gains that, among other things, also suggest the possibility of moving to nicer neighborhoods. This notion, however, was at best a spirited joke in the 1940s since housing segregation typically circumscribed one's ability to relocate.[7]

Even in light of these qualifications, it is clear that the idea of "escape" resonated with black Americans. Despite the realities that made African Americans circumspect about escape, the idea still suggested the chance to live beyond the sociological and perhaps even psychological confines of race. Bunche addressed this phenomenon with a brusque eloquence: "To the degree that any Negro has attained prominence, to that degree he has thrown off some of the stigma attached to identification with the group labeled as inferior and subordinate. The Negro individual, therefore, who attains prominence, symbolizes the hope of every member of the group for escape from the shackles of the racial curse."[8]

This observation spoke to the irony that was born of the legacies of racialized systems of organizing society and citizenship: escape for black Americans was always accompanied by a burden. Whether one liked it or not, being a leader in black America meant that one was freighted with the weight of group expectation. The black leader, Bunche commented, almost involuntarily "symbolizes the aspirations of the deprived individuals whom he leads or aspires to lead. In a sense, he becomes a symbol of escape or a means of vicarious release, since Negroes can get a 'life' out of seeing 'one of the group' perform at the top of the tent."[9]

Bunche felt comfortable making these observations about the symbolic manifestations of group expectations because he drew on a wide range of field notes and other scholarly work and, perhaps just as important, because he could tap the wellspring of his own experiences with the evocative allure of escape. To this end, an effective place to start talking about the politics of escape and Ralph Bunche is his own life story.

Bunche was born in Detroit in 1903 and lived an almost itinerant lifestyle until his adolescence, moving five times by the time he was twelve as his father took the family with him in his search for stable work. The family relocated to Albuquerque in 1915 with the hopes that Bunche's mother and uncle would recuperate from extended bouts with tuberculosis. The hopes were dashed two years later when Bunche's mother died from the disease and his uncle, still unhealthy and now depressed over his sister's death, committed suicide three months later. To complete the cycle of pain, Bunche could not turn to his father for solace since he had already left the family in his continuing quest for work. Bunche's father never returned. Confronted with this nightmare at the still tender age of fourteen, Bunche moved to Los Angeles, where his grandmother lived. Lucy "Nana" Johnson raised Bunche and became the most adored person in his life—the adult from whom he drew wisdom and the source, he would later claim, of his internal strength.[10]

Just as Bunche pointed to his grandmother as the person who made him what he was, it is clear that the move to Los Angeles was critically important in other ways as well. Unlike the great majority of his future peers in Cambridge, Massachusetts, Washington, D.C., and the New York metropolitan region, Bunche grew up in a fairly integrated environment. Consequently, his sense of what was possible for African Americans was fundamentally different. This did not mean that Bunche was racially unaware. Indeed, Bunche's fair-skinned grandmother was adamant that he develop a strong sense of race pride, and she nurtured in him a commitment to securing full citizenship rights for all blacks. With his grandmother as a guiding force, Bunche acquired practical skills in navigating the semi-integrated world of southern California and also fashioned himself as something of a race leader. He publicly spoke

out against encroaching segregation in Los Angeles and, upon gradua-
tion from the University of California, Los Angeles, wrote a letter to
W. E. B. Du Bois requesting advice on how best to provide "service to
my group."[11]

Bunche's relocation to Los Angeles was also transformative in more
symbolic ways. Given the struggles of Bunche's youth and then the com-
pounded tragedies of his father's flight and his mother's and uncle's
deaths, Bunche's relatives decided that moving further west was an opportunity for a clean break from a troubled past. To that end, they
added the "e" to Bunche's last name.[12] This was, to be sure, the slightest
feint, but it does underscore how people invest great meaning in small
actions. As there are no records that tell us what Bunche thought of the
name change himself, we ought not make too much of this escape to a
new and brighter future. However, the fact that Bunche never changed
his name back lends some support to the idea that he saw little reward
in returning to the birth name that connected him in its literal spelling to
his absent father and difficult youth. If this much is true, we can see in
Bunche's own life the symbolic and highly personal value that accompanied escape.

After college, Bunche moved to the East Coast in order to pursue a
doctorate in political science from Harvard University. He quickly became acquainted with the handful of black graduate and professional
students at the school, a coterie that included people such as economist
Robert C. Weaver and attorneys William Hastie and John P. Davis.
Barely into his twenties, Bunche was now matched with individuals who
would become some of the more important black leaders of the mid-
twentieth century.[13]

During the 1930s, Bunche began teaching at Howard University, organized that school's political science department, received his PhD (thus
becoming the country's first African American to earn a doctorate in political science), was promoted to associate professor, and pursued an aggressive regimen of research, writing, and civic activism. Nearing the end
of the decade, he was already recognized as one of the leading African-
ists in the nation. And while he had not yet managed to rework his dis-
sertation into a book, Bunche published several articles and an extended
essay, all of which demonstrated an abiding commitment to social justice
being achieved through a pursuit of economic goals.[14] In this regard,
Bunche was part of a concentration of scholar-activists at Howard who
were deeply invested in challenging the social construction of race, who

sought to dismantle racial ideology, and who argued that an interracial workers' movement was the logical solution to the deepening economic malaise of the Great Depression.

Bunche, along with Howard colleagues including economist Abram Harris, sociologist E. Franklin Frazier, education specialist Doxey Wilkerson, and political scientist Emmett Dorsey, joined the Howard Teachers Union and through it became involved in campus and community protests. Harris and Frazier most closely matched Bunche's scholar-activist pursuits, and together they used the university's Social Science Division as a platform for antiracialist scholarly activism.[15]

By 1938, Bunche's skills as a researcher and his reputation as a political commentator were well known. It is not surprising, then, that Gunnar Myrdal, who had just arrived in the United States to make the final plans with the Carnegie Corporation for his investigation of the so-called "Negro problem," contacted Bunche and hired him as a member of his core research team. While in New York, Myrdal also hired more than thirty outside consultants to produce independent monographs exploring different aspects of the black experience in the United States.[16] Bunche, like many of his social science peers—white as well as black— was initially unhappy that a foreigner was selected for such an important assignment, skeptical that an outsider could ever sufficiently understand the country's "logic" when it came to race. But after meeting Myrdal, Bunche quickly reassessed his opinion of the Swede.[17] Their mutual respect and their easy comfort with each other were critical since soon after meeting they spent a month on the road together, driving through the deep South conducting research for the project.

There were a number of occasions on their road trip when Myrdal's relaxed manner and his outsider naiveté ran afoul of southern racial mores. Part of this, no doubt, is attributable to his failure to understand the intensity of racial prejudices in the United States. Another part was the result of Myrdal's irreverent sense of humor. Much to Bunche's dismay, for example, Myrdal did not appreciate that asking white women, even in jest, if they secretly desired black men as sexual partners was an invitation to mob violence. Bunche recalled, "I was always on the verge of being lynched because of his playful pranks. We actually had to run for it a couple of times."[18] This is, to be sure, a different kind of escape than the symbolic name changing of Bunche's childhood, but his recollection remains instructive.

In Bunche's comment and in Myrdal's actions we see the different

- *98* -

The following excerpts from a field interview undertaken by
Dr. Myrdal and myself are presented at rather great length, because the
Negro leader interviewed in this Southern seaport provides so excellent
an illustration of the attitudes and techniques of a type of leader whom
most modern Negroes, even cautious ones, would immediately brand as an
"Uncle Tom." We will call him Sam Jones of Seaport, a town along the
southeast coast — not that Jones would feel any self consciousness at
seeing himself identified with the sentiments he expressed. He is
cautious, suspicious, patient and proud of his "quality folks" white
friends, who greatly admire him. Through them he can get things done.
With Negroes he is hard and revengeful and doesn't like to be crossed
by them. He is considerable of an opportunist, a go-between also, and
there is a suggestion of the racketeer in his activities. But he can
get things done, in his way, which is the way of the old school, the not
so very old school of plantation days, whose pattern has been refined by
but not lost to many modern Negro leaders.

Dr. Myrdal and I went to visit Sam Jones about 10.30 on the
evening of October 29,1939. We stopped the car and I suggested that I
go in first to see if he was at home and to allay any fears or suspicions
that he might have if he should see a white man coming to his door. After
some delay, Mr. Jones, a large, fat, pot-bellied, dark brownskinned man
of considerable age came to the door. He was considerably knock-kneed.
He was quite surprised when he saw me and he stood talking to me at the
door without showing any inclination to admit me at first. I told him
briefly that I was engaged in a study of the problems affecting the
Negro, and that I had been told by several of the people whom I had con-

A sample page from Bunche and Myrdal's interview with "Sam Jones, a political stooge." (Ralph J. Bunche Papers, Collection 2051, Department Special Collections, Charles E. Young Research Library, University of California, Los Angeles) kinds of social possibility that accompanied racial identity. Bunche, like so many other blacks who were acquainted with American racial folkways and who also worked in interracial environments, had a refined understanding of the privilege that accompanied Myrdal's ascribed racial identity. The true power of this privilege, however, was not in Bunche's awareness of it but in Myrdal's ignorance of it. This was the ultimate power of privilege: it allowed one to presume access, to presume universal humanity, to presume, in fact, a sense of humor about situations in which there was so rarely humor to be found.

The phenomenon of white privilege plays an important role in Bunche's memo for the way that it relates to the development of a presumptive authority of how life should be lived. In short, as much as one needs to understand the centrality of "escape" when thinking about the politics of black leadership, one must also appreciate the extent to which whites so often exercised control over which blacks became leaders and were thus "allowed" to escape.

The politics of escape and privilege are intertwined in subtle ways. In one extended moment in the memo, however, their interlocked nature is displayed in the least subtle character Bunche describes in the entire memorandum: "Sam Jones," a black leader from an unidentified southeastern coastal town.[19]

Bunche's road trip with Myrdal, it turns out, yielded more than crazed harangues by offended white women and threats on their lives. Indeed, a significant portion of Bunche's analysis of black leadership is devoted to a novelistic account of a several-days-long series of interviews he and Myrdal conducted with Jones. Given the extensive attention that Bunche devotes to his interaction with Jones, it is not surprising to learn that Bunche considered Jones the perfect manifestation of one of the most important leadership types in the black community: the liaison, the professional politician who was little more than a stooge for powerful whites. It is a type of leader for whom Bunche made clear his disdain.

Bunche's introductory description confirms his negative appraisal of Jones and his ilk:

> He is cautious, suspicious, patient and proud of his "quality folks" white friends, who greatly admired him. Through them he can get things done. With Negroes he is hard and revengeful and doesn't like to be crossed by them. He is considered an opportunist, a go-between also, and there is a suggestion of the racketeer in his activities. But he can get

things done, in his way, which is the way of the old school, the not so very old school of plantation days, whose pattern has been refined by but not lost to many modern Negro leaders.

Bunche's negative assessment continued, as he described Jones as "a large, fat, pot-bellied, dark brown-skinned man . . . [who] was considerably knock-kneed."[20]

Jones represents only one of the six leadership types that Bunche identifies and analyzes in his memorandum, but it is helpful to pause here and spend a few more moments thinking through the significance of Bunche's assessment and Jones's position. Although it is unlikely that Bunche was recalling W. E. B. Du Bois's dismissal of Marcus Garvey as "a little, fat black man, ugly, but with intelligent eyes and big head," the similarity in word choice is telling.[21] Just as Du Bois considered Garvey to be a leader on the make, Bunche clearly felt that any power and influence that Jones had was an extension of his proximity to white leaders and a manifestation of his self-interested desire to feather his own nest.

The bulk of the Jones interview revolved around his development and leadership of the county's Negro Fair. As it happened, Bunche and Myrdal arrived the night before the fair was scheduled to open (which was two days after the much larger white County Fair had closed). Jones went on at length about his stewardship of the black fair and how his hard work was unappreciated by local blacks but praised by influential whites, the people in Jones's opinion who mattered most. These were the individuals who financed Jones's ventures and secured his position as a powerbroker in the black community. Jones openly admired these whites, resented other local black leaders such as the head of the city's NAACP chapter, and was equivocal about the local Interracial Commission. According to Bunche, the only thing he and Myrdal could extract from Jones about the commission was his observation that there were some "'fine white people' on it" ("A Brief and Tentative Analysis," 115).

Although Jones worked to deny or dismiss it, other African Americans in the community resented him. They acknowledged his access to powerful whites but disapproved of the terms on which he won it. He was, in their eyes, an "Uncle Tom" and "stool pigeon" who was "against any project unless that project goes through him" (117).

Clearly, the local blacks did not like Jones. And even though he had many fans in the white community, he never really enjoyed full access there either. A white police sergeant who held Jones in high esteem said as much, confirming that Jones could go anywhere in white Seaport—even the restaurants—as long as "he goes in on business" (115). One can see, then, that Jones lived his life between two worlds. Jones understood as much, claiming "I knows how to keep peace between the races" (115). More than playing the role of a peacekeeper, Jones was philosophical about his own marginality, simultaneously pointing out his special privileges in the white world and knowing that his privileges were dependent on his ability to know his place. "Every Negro," Jones observed, "ought to know what he is and what he can do" (114).

One can see that Jones had escaped many of the daily challenges that defined the lives of similarly employed blacks. After all, he had worked at various times on rich whites' kitchen staffs and as the doorman for Seaport's leading white social club. But in observing this, one needs to ask what it was to which Jones escaped. It is in asking this kind of question that one extracts the greatest value in reading the Bunche-Myrdal-Jones interview. Jones's position in Seaport underscores how black authority depended on white approval. It was certainly easy enough for someone to gain power by playing the role of the "political stooge," but that decision came with consequences. One could break free of many of the limited constraints of black possibility, but one could only meet success in both the black and white worlds when one had the support of both worlds. This was impossible for leaders like Jones. In Bunche's eyes, it was damningly easy to become intoxicated by power—an addiction so overwhelming that in Jones's case he sought to keep it all for himself. In this way, Jones was paradigmatic of so many other black leaders who, once in a leadership position, worked hard to preserve their status and always worked against other blacks who sought similar access.

Bunche argued that, much to his dismay, these were some of the most prevalent traits of black leaders. Very near the opening pages of "A Brief and Tentative Analysis," he summarized the mentality that was typical of the self-interested black leader. Bunche observed, "leadership itself is a form of escape—the leader, having attained power and thus escaped above his group, would degrade himself by voluntary descent again to the level of the mass through application of the democratic precepts in his personal relationships" (37). By looking at Jones's situation we can

W. E. B. Du Bois. (Photo by Carl Van Vechten, Carl Van Vechten Papers, Yale Collection of American Literature, Beinecke Rare Book and Manuscripts Library, Yale University)

see that if leadership was a form of escape, fully realized leadership was contingent on having a desirable place to which one could escape.

Bunche makes it clear that Jones was prototypical of a prominent leadership type, but he did not represent all forms of black leadership. And while Bunche devoted more attention to Jones than to any other individual, he made sure to detail other types of leaders, providing examples of them through vignettes, interviews, and scholarly prose.

Including Jones, there were, in Bunche's view, six different types of black leader: (1) those who were dynamic and aggressive, (2) those who were cautious and timid, (3) those who were the stooges and professional politicians like Jones, (4) those who were symbolically important, (5) those who led on the basis of their prestige, and (6) those whom whites designated to lead. It is clear that these categories are sufficiently broad such that one individual can be described as belonging to two or even three of these groups. Bunche admitted as much but did not worry about it, encouraging the reader, in this case Gunnar Myrdal, to draw his own conclusions as to what was of greatest value in this schema. It is also evident that the last category of race leader—those who were placed in their position by powerful whites—is the broadest in terms of its applicability. There is little doubt, for example, that Sam Jones was both a political stooge and an opportunist (type 3) at the same time that he served at the pleasure of influential whites (type 6). Even though this last category is in some ways the most fluid, it may be the most important because it underlines that in the 1940s most black leaders only had a limited range in which they could operate before they ran afoul of powerful social mores, hit barricades of institutional racism, or were simply silenced.

A survey of Bunche's typology reminds us that the freedom prominent blacks may have enjoyed because of their leadership status was constrained. Whites' omnipresence as sponsors, censors, or facilitators guaranteed that black leaders' "escape" was never independent or unconditional. The following excerpts from the respective sections where Bunche describes the six types of black leadership speak to these facts:

Type 1: Aggressive Leaders

A.M.E. preacher of Winston-Salem, North Carolina, who has been in town only two years, but has initiated a local chapter of his Colored

Improvement League and a youth conference. Feels that town organizations have stood too far from the Negroes en masse, and believes that if they are corralled and exposed to organization benefits they will lose their timidity. Is very outspoken, and some say he has been warned to "go easy." (80)

Mrs. Susie Hoover—Beautician, former school teacher and former census taker of illiterate Negroes in Highpoint, North Carolina. Aggressive and very politically minded. Sincere Republican. Energetic in getting out vote. She did say, however, that if Republicans get back in power, she could get work in the city. Might be her motive. (80).

Type 2: Cautious Leaders

A Negro undertaker, and something of a "leader" in a deep southern town, defends the white people, even a peonage farm operator. In speaking of a young Negro woman teacher who was beaten by a white bus driver, this leader said: "I bet it was her own fault. A lot of these old teachers don't know how to stay in their places." His defense of the peonage farm operator is probably influenced by the fact that he turns the funerals of his dead Negro "hands" over to the leader." (89)

An A.M.E. minister in Denver is referred to by both Negroes and whites as the outstanding Negro leader. Seems cautious and suspicious of persons who are too curious and inquiring. Gives the impression of weighing very carefully every word and action. . . . Plenty of ego, and likes to "boss" everything. Proud of his white friends. (90)

Type 3: Liaison Leaders (Stooges and Politicians)

Custodian of County Court House in a Tennessee community. Negro appendage and shrewd political slave of Judge who appointed him. Heads Seventh Ward Club and votes from seven to eight hundred Negroes on request of the machine. Delivers Negro vote for some financial consideration and some personal patronage. . . . "He would like to be an honest guy, but is too deeply obligated to the powers that be." (103)

Type 4: Symbolic Leaders

Negro woman president of a southern college. Accepted by whites as a very influential Negro leader and ideologist of the Negro group. Had done nothing to establish her prestige except run the school and affect a high degree of culture. At the first Southern Conference for Human Welfare, someone referred to her by her first name and she arose majestically and stated "for the sake of the record I am known as Mrs." It is quite possibly true that she is not an Uncle Tom in the true sense of the term, but it is equally true that many Negroes are very skillful in knowing just what to say and how to say it and when to say it to white folks. They appreciate that there is a certain type of "tolerated impudence" which they can get away with in the presence of whites and give the appearance of being courageous [to] naive Negroes. There is probably something in the thought that people take to this personality *because* she symbolizes the possibilities of Negro escape. (137–138)

Type 5: Prestige Leaders

One of America's most famous Negroes (Dr. [Ossian] Sweet, of Sweet Case fame) who figures in the most publicized case involving civil rights for Negroes is said to never take part in any more race fights. He is now the highest exploiter of city funds for his private hospital in one of America's largest cities. (142)

Type 6: Negro Leaders Designated by Whites

Richmond Negroes have received their leaders from their white rulers. The Interracial Commission is busily engaged in selecting, grooming, and promoting Negro leadership. The only obligation the aspiring leader is under is to the "good white folks" who promote his campaign so that he will do everything in his power to frustrate all genuine movements which may take root among the Negro people and that seek to tilt the balance of "racial harmony" away from the status quo toward equal rights. (152)

Although this is the briefest canvassing of the leadership types Bunche identifies, it is important to examine more closely this last category for two reasons. The first reason was mentioned above: white control over black leadership is one of the more important factors to take into consideration when developing an analysis of the actual potential for real leadership in the black community. The other reason speaks to Bunche directly and also allows us to return to the theme of escape that is so useful when thinking about black leadership.

In the second chapter of the memorandum, Bunche offers a general survey of black leadership and devotes several pages to the phenomenon of white patronage. Bunche talks about, among other things, a 1933 meeting sponsored by the NAACP that the association designed to identify and assess the next generation of black leadership. The meeting, called the Second Amenia Conference, was held at the home of NAACP president Joel Spingarn. Thirty-three men and women gathered in August of that year to debate the future role of the NAACP. While the meeting is of some importance to the history of the NAACP and to the Marxist leanings of several young black intellectuals of the 1930s, its present value is found in how Bunche discusses this conference in his memo.[22]

> There is undoubtedly a large grain of truth in the popular assumption among intellectual Negroes, that when an important white man puts an approving finger on a Negro, this automatically elevates him to a position of importance in the Negro world. In similar vein, patronization of Negro individuals is a factor of no little importance. . . . To cite a specific example, when the Spingarns decided to hold a conference of young Negroes under the direction of Dr. Du Bois several years ago, and invited some thirty younger Negroes to the Spingarn estate at Amenia, New York . . . it soon became very evident that many of these young people, who were, by and large, just young Negroes and quite undistinguished, talked and spoke of themselves in terms of Negro "leaders." They had been chosen from the masses and this patronization and condescension, though most certainly not deliberately or consciously offered by the Spingarns, had almost magical effect upon the thinking of these young Negroes. . . . They had been accorded a recognition, which, in their minds, distinguished them from the rest of their group. Such distinction is enough to make a leader of any Negro. (59)

This passage clearly speaks to the ability of white authority and privilege to convey leadership on blacks. Upon closer examination, it also figures into a conversation about escape. If we accept Bunche's version of events, then we can see that these young blacks felt anointed by the Spingarns and were thus prepared to claim leadership status, thereby elevating themselves up from the black masses. However, accepting Bunche's version does violence to history. As it happened, Bunche was one of the roughly thirty younger "quite undistinguished" blacks who attended the conference. Given the fact that Bunche did not hesitate to write himself into the memorandum on other occasions, one must ask why he chose to escape from his own history in this case.

It may very well be that he was now older and wiser and did not want to associate with the strong-headedness of his own relative youth. Or it may be that Bunche wanted to distance himself from this radical past that had been on full display at the August 1933 meeting. Was Bunche's revision a simple quest for respectability? If so, was such a quest a hallmark of a driven leader?

Whatever the reason, Bunche's evasion forces the reader to go back and reassess Bunche's own position vis-à-vis the various black leadership types he critiques so aggressively in the text itself. Perhaps Bunche would have done well to be more self-reflective about the "truths" he identified in the memorandum. Perhaps he should have remained true, for example, to his own observation about the ways that race and racial thinking complicated the ground on which leadership was forged. If he had done this, he would have been better prepared to deal with the unique aspects of black leadership life that made escape so enticing and so damning at the same time. Perhaps he should have paid more careful attention to his own words near the conclusion of the manuscript:

> The Negro minority is in dire need of a strong and clear-headed leadership to steer it through the dangerous rapids of current domestic and international affairs. The very complications of the Negro's racial position make it difficult for him to comprehend clearly the full significance of events as they relate to his interests. Racial thinking is an obstacle to clear thinking, and the Negro is easily and often led astray. No group can be so easily violated ideologically as that which blindly seeks escape. (195–196)

Bunche's agenda for an enlightened race leadership was simple. Responsible blacks who maintained a genuine interest in improving the lives of all black people needed to unite with like-minded whites to make sure that blacks moved "toward an ever-widening horizon of decent, respectable life in America, to immersion in the mainstream of that life, to acceptance in the society as a full, unqualified and respected citizen on a level of absolute equality with all other citizens" (197). This was not escape; this was engagement.

But if fully realized citizenship was the goal and uniting with white leadership was a means to that goal, which type of committed or engaged black leader would be the most effective to facilitate the movement? Would the work of "cautious leaders," for example, be more effective than that of "prestige leaders"? Did "aggressive leaders" make more sense than "symbolic leaders"? Given Bunche's disdain for at least some characteristic in all of the types he identified, one has to wonder how Bunche would have answered the question. Also, in light of the facts that Bunche was undoubtedly a leader in academia, that he interviewed so many of his peers in the study, and that he even inserted the names of his closest Howard colleagues in the survey he gave to college students designed to test leadership recognition, it is fair to ask where Bunche ought to be placed within his own leadership typology.

If this question were posed to Bunche, one might expect that he would hedge, trying to avoid a specific category. Part of this would be the honest result of the fact that the boundaries between these different types are blurry at best. Bunche makes clear throughout his narrative that there is a certain arbitrariness to his typology, that it was developed largely in an effort to categorize the evidence from the field notes his assistants prepared rather than determined in advance of any research findings. That technical qualifier aside, the question deserves an attempt at an answer because even the attempt adds texture to our understanding of Bunche and black leadership in 1940s America.

Given Bunche's deep engagement with class politics of the 1930s, his repeated calls for a class-based interracial workers' movement, and his commitment to grassroots and national political struggles, there is little to challenge the suggestion that in the early years of his career Bunche would have been classified as an "aggressive" leader. The repeated dismissal, even ridicule, in the memo of many black leaders makes it safe to say that much of that 1930s aggression was still present when he drafted "A Brief and Tentative Analysis." But we must remember that built into his analysis of white control over black leadership was the evasion of his own involvement in that process. We should also consider that after

Bunche completed his work for *An American Dilemma,* his public pro-
file as a politically engaged antiracist activist evaporated. By the mid-
1940s, Bunche had lent his expertise to the Office of Strategic Services,
the State Department, and then—and for essentially the rest of his life—
the United Nations. In each of these positions, Bunche kept ever more
careful control over his public image, always trying to walk what he felt
was a fine line between an engagement in domestic politics and a professional commitment as an international public servant. By the mid-
1960s, the new black activists dismissed the value of Bunche's carefully
crafted image of American possibility. To the militants who declared him
an "international Uncle Tom," Bunche was no different than Sam Jones,
the political stooge from Seaport who Bunche and Myrdal mercilessly
derided.[23]

If he looked back on his life when attempting to answer the question
of what kind of leader he was, Bunche probably would have responded
that at one time or another he reflected some aspect or trait found in
each of the leadership categories. While he would have been reluctant to
accept that he ever acted the political stooge, there is no doubting that
many saw him as such. This last fact speaks directly to the utter fluidity
of Bunche's leadership typology. Where one fell in the spectrum of leadership types was dependent on who was passing judgment. In the end,
leadership was constantly contingent on context.

But while the typology is, at best, a crude indicator of leadership types
in the black community, we would be rash to dismiss it out of hand.
Bunche's leadership categories resonate because they reflected a gut-level
sensibility of different types of black leaders. Readers could identify
any number of community, city, state, or national leaders who fit into
Bunche's categories. The slipperiness of the typology is also useful because it underscores the ephemeral nature of leadership itself. Even
within categories, there was no single type of leader. The field notes and
transcribed interviews implicitly say as much when one considers that
they present black leadership cadres filling a spectrum that included
town beauticians and morticians, academics and attorneys who were essentially invisible to the masses, as well as local interracial committee
members and nationally recognized political activists. In this regard, the
index of leaders Bunche provides at the end of the memorandum is
extremely valuable, for it demonstrates the many ways in which leadership could be embodied or articulated in black America. Indeed, the

Myrdal, Gunnar (index)
(praises Bunche's
writing for Myrdal
study — wants him
to publish memoran-
dum on Ideologies
as book)

Mr. Ralph Bunche   May
Coordinator of Information   5th
Washington, D.C.   1942

Dear Ralph:

        I have now completed also my chapter on Leader-
ship and Followship and while working on it, I have been
reading your two memoranda on Ideologies and Leadership.
It just occurred to me that with very slight editing, you
could publish your memorandum on Ideologies as a book of
actuality. You should skim out some good phrases from the
Leadership memorandum and perhaps also some from the Organization memorandum, but on the whole keep to the frame of the
Ideologies manuscript. Probably you would want to add a
short chapter on the Negro morale in the war. I think such
a book would be extremely useful, and I know it wouldn't take
much time to do it. It will not overlap my work at all as
I am building up my chapter in a different way. Couldn't
you get some youngster to help you for a couple of weeks?

        I have had use of your memoranda. Some are bulky
and you didn't have time to organize them, but there is a lot
of stuff in them. I sincerely hope this damned war will end
soon and that you, once more, can take up the bigger tasks in
the proper way. Meanwhile I think you should bring out the
smaller thing. As you know Louis Wirth had the same feeling
when he read it. We both think it is a brilliant writing.

        Well, it is too bad that we never see each other,
but I am taking no time off, only working and working. If
you and Ruth came over some evening, we would celebrate, however. Think it over.

                                    Yours,

GM:rm   Gunnar Myrdal

A letter from Myrdal encouraging Bunche to publish his research findings.
(Ralph J. Bunche Papers, Collection 2051, Department Special Collections,
Charles E. Young Research Library, University of California, Los Angeles)

absolutely mundane nature of this list makes it mesmerizing. Here, leadership appears more democratically distributed than the typical narrative would have us believe, that which speaks almost singularly of great black male leaders of profound moral purity who possess a refined political savoir-faire.

In some ways, it is a pity that Myrdal valued Bunche's insights so much. Myrdal was less fond of the scholarship produced by other contributors to *An American Dilemma* and did not feel compelled to incorporate their contributions in the final product. Myrdal, for example, disagreed with cultural anthropologist Melville Herskovits's contention that African culturalisms survived in American blacks. And although Myrdal invited Herskovits to participate in the study—largely out of professional courtesy—Myrdal essentially ignored Herskovits's contribution. Free in the knowledge that his scholarship would not be duplicated, Herskovits gladly took the opportunity to publish his findings as a stand-alone book. The resultant text, *The Myth of the Negro Past*, remains a major contribution to anthropology, and scholars recognize it today for paving the way for the establishment of Black Studies programs in the 1960s.[24]

But Myrdal admired Bunche and incorporated his ideas, if not his literal words, throughout *An American Dilemma*. Although Bunche, like Herskovits, had the opportunity to publish an independent book out of the more than three thousand pages he submitted to Myrdal, he never followed through. Bunche was, no doubt, distracted from completing his planned project, "Negro Politics and Political Organizations," due to his increasing commitment to war-related work at the Office of Strategic Services and then the State Department. He may also have felt that it would not have been worth the effort required to extricate his thoughts from *An American Dilemma,* to sift through the massive amounts of data he produced, and then to polish what he always considered a "rush job." In any event, we are left to wonder exactly how Bunche would have developed the ideas that we find in "A Brief and Tentative Analysis of Negro Leadership." We are more than a little lucky, then, that we do have the opportunity to hear his rough thoughts on the topic, that we can walk ourselves through a unique ethnography of black leaders, and that we can bear almost first-hand witness to the way that promises of escape and realities of containment simultaneously defined black leadership in the 1940s.

NOTES

1. Most famously, *An American Dilemma* found its way into the Supreme Court's 1954 decision in *Brown v. Board of Education*. Chief Justice Earl Warren called attention to the social science literature that demonstrated the dangers of racial separation. For the court, Warren wrote, "See generally Myrdal, *An American Dilemma*, 5/8/1944."

2. Ralph J. Bunche, *The Political Status of the Negro in the Age of FDR*, ed. Dewey Grantham (Chicago: University of Chicago Press, 1973).

3. Ralph J. Bunche, "A Brief and Tentative Analysis of Negro Leadership," this volume, 31.

4. Harold Gosnell, *Negro Politicians: The Rise of Negro Politics in Chicago* (Chicago: University of Chicago Press, 1935); Charles S. Johnson, *Growing Up in the Black Belt: Negro Youth in the Rural South* (Washington, D.C.: American Council on Education, 1941); E. Franklin Frazier, *Negro Youth at the Crossways: Their Personality Development in the Middle States* (Washington, D.C.: American Council on Education, 1940); John Dollard, *Caste and Class in a Southern Town* (New Haven: Yale University Press, 1937); and Hortense Powdermaker, *After Freedom: A Cultural Study in the Deep South* (New York: Viking Press, 1939).

5. Bunche, "A Brief and Tentative Analysis," 31, 194.

6. As quoted in Charles Henry, *Ralph Bunche: Model Negro or American Other?* (New York: New York University Press, 1999), 107; as quoted in Jonathan Scott Holloway, *Confronting the Veil: Abram Harris Jr., E. Franklin Frazier, and Ralph Bunche, 1919–1941* (Chapel Hill: University of North Carolina Press, 2002), 183.

7. On this issue it is probably worth noting that a year after completing his memoranda for Myrdal, Bunche moved his family into a house that they commissioned architect Hilyard Robinson to build. The Bunches were one of the first black families to move into the Brookland neighborhood in Washington, D.C. Despite this move to an integrating neighborhood, Bunche's children could not go to the school that was around the corner from their new home. Instead, they had to attend the black school three miles away. Sandra Fitzpatrick and Maria Goodwin, *The Guide to Black Washington* (New York: Hippocrene Books, 1990), 80–81.

8. Bunche, "A Brief and Tentative Analysis," 52.

9. Ibid., 63.

10. Holloway, *Confronting the Veil*, 160–61; Henry, *Ralph Bunche*, 11–15.

11. Holloway, *Confronting the Veil*, 161–62.

12. Ibid., 161.

13. In 1933, Weaver and Davis founded the Negro Industrial League, their attempt to represent the needs of black America during the federal government's

hearings on New Deal administrations. Weaver soon joined Franklin Roosevelt's presidential administration and became one of the leading figures of Roosevelt's "Black Cabinet." He later became the first black to serve in a president's official cabinet when Lyndon Johnson named him secretary of Housing and Urban Development. Davis continued in a watchdog role until 1936, when he helped establish the National Negro Congress, a major Popular Front–era activist organization largely dedicated to workers' rights. Hastie went on to teach at Howard University Law School, become the first black federal judge, and become the first black governor of the U.S. Virgin Islands.

14. See, for example, Ralph Bunche, "A Critique of New Deal Planning as It Affects Negroes," *Journal of Negro Education* 5 (January 1936): 59–65; "Education in Black and White," *Journal of Negro Education* 5 (July 1936): 351–58; "The Programs of Organizations Devoted to Improvement of the Status of the American Negro," *Journal of Negro Education* 8 (July 1939): 539–50; *A World View of Race,* Bronze Booklet Series, no. 4 (Washington, D.C.: Associates in Negro Folk Education, 1936).

15. Holloway, *Confronting the Veil,* 50–76.

16. A wide range of social scientists contributed to the project, many of whom were already well-established scholars in their own right. Among them were Melville Herskovits, Charles S. Johnson, E. Franklin Frazier, Otto Klineberg, Louis Wirth, Edward Shils, Guy Johnson, Arthur Raper, T. Arnold Hill, Doxey Wilkerson, Ira DeA. Reid, and St. Clair Drake.

17. Walter A. Jackson, *Gunnar Myrdal and America's Conscience: Social Engineering and Racial Liberalism, 1938–1987* (Chapel Hill: University of North Carolina Press, 1990), 122.

18. As quoted in Henry, *Ralph Bunche,* 94.

19. Bunche declined to provide the real name of the interview subject or the city in which he lived. However, at one point in his interview with "Sam Jones," Bunche tells the reader about "Faber." Bunche seems to have slipped up on this occasion. Brian Urquhart confirms as much in his Bunche biography without addressing the slippage when he also refers to Faber and to "Faber's Fair in Charleston." Charleston, it would seem, is Bunche's "Seaport." Brian Urquhart, *Ralph Bunche: An American Life* (New York: Norton, 1993), 86.

20. Bunche, "A Brief and Tentative Analysis," 107. Hereafter cited in text.

21. As quoted in Lawrence Levine, "Marcus Garvey and the Politics of Revitalization," in *Black Leaders of the Twentieth Century,* ed. John Hope Franklin and August Meier (Urbana: University of Illinois Press, 1982), 133–34.

22. For more on the Second Amenia Conference, see Holloway, *Confronting the Veil,* 1–34.

23. Benjamin Rivlin, "The Legacy of Ralph Bunche," in *Ralph Bunche: The Man and His Times,* ed. Rivlin (New York: Holmes and Meier, 1990), 23.

24. Melville Herskovits, *The Myth of the Negro Past* (New York: Harper,

1941). Several other books grew out of the project: Richard Sterner's *The Negro's Share* (New York: Harper and Brothers, 1943), Charles S. Johnson's *The Shadow of the Plantation* (New York: Harper and Brothers, 1943), and Otto Klineberg's edited volume *Characteristics of the American Negro* (New York: Harper and Brothers, 1944). Jackson, *Gunnar Myrdal,* 110, 165, 316.

A Brief and Tentative Analysis of Negro Leadership

Introduction
Negro Leadership

We are lacking in the data necessary to undertake any comprehensive analysis of Negro leadership. Practically nothing of a scientific nature has been written upon the subject and it has been found impossible to devote any considerable time to the task of sifting out leadership materials from the great mass of publications on the Negro— newspapers, periodicals and books. The field workers, in their hurried journeys here and there, did jot down occasional and casual notes on the Negro leadership encountered in the various communities. We also have 50 specially prepared short life histories, written or dictated at our request, by selected Negro leaders and white inter-racial leaders. On the whole, these scattered and sketchy materials do not lend themselves readily to integration in any scientific analysis of Negro leadership. As a matter of fact, I do not consider myself equipped with the tools essential to any such analysis. For these reasons, this treatment of the subject must be viewed as largely impressionistic, based upon my personal observations and opinions as supplemented by the field and other materials at hand.

An effort will be made to indicate what needs to be done on the subject and to suggest where greatest emphasis ought to be placed. In this particular memorandum, emphasis is directed to the social mechanisms by which Negro leaders are chosen and permitted to exercise influence. In my estimation, it is of prime importance to determine how particular individuals have attained the influence and status of leadership. This is no easy task, however, and the necessary data are not readily available. The very nature of the subject implies an analysis of those social factors which are responsible for the elevation of individual Negroes to positions of prominence and influence among Negro or Negro and white groups. What is the social process involved here? What are the frustrations encountered by the individual in the American social milieu? For, if the subject is to have any meaning at all, it can only be through its interpretation within the framework of the American social process in its entirety. Thus, the primary concern should be a study of Negro leadership in its relationship to the general social milieu, and in its reaction to those social pressures which impinge peculiarly upon the Negro minority. Thus, the analysis must devote itself to the ways in which Negroes of prominence adopt and accommodate themselves to the known social conditions, or resist them. What, if any, peculiarly "Negro" factors enter into the Negro leadership equation, which would not be found in the white leadership equation? It would seem important, also, to include in any such analysis those white individuals who have attained a status of prominence and influence precisely because of the Negro-white problem in the country. Thus, the scope of the analysis would be expanded to include an appraisal of the factors responsible for projecting white interracialists into positions of eminence in the Negro world.

It is often remarked that Americans make a fetish of leadership. It does appear oftimes that Americans do put greater emphasis upon leadership and personality than upon social processes and issues, though this is admittedly a debatable question. In the South, especially, the individual leader and his personality play a vital role in the life of the community. It is not uncommon, in this country, for successes or failures to be credited to "good" or "bad" leadership; yet, it is not very clear just what we mean by "leadership." In this memorandum, for instance, I find myself in the rather embarrassing position of realizing the necessity for defining the term leadership, but, at the same time, forced to admit the impossibility of doing so. For our purposes here a rough definition of leadership as we will use it would refer to a relationship involving the actual or potential influence of one individual over the thought or action of a number of others through means other than physical compulsion. There are certainly different categories of leadership. There are experts who have no following and who exert no great influence. There are ex-officio leaders, who hold positions of prominence because of their offices. Then, there are individuals who actually lead and influence significant numbers of people. How do American leaders, in general, acquire influence? How important is money, affiliation with pressure groups, family name and background, status, class and personality in this process? What is the significance of the assumed passivity of the American masses to the leadership phenomenon? How important is the role of the "symbol" in the process? It would seem clear that the American masses, in general, follow personalities because they are symbols of something—of the common man, of the fighter, of the person who gets things done, of American business, etc. Thus, the broad topic involved is the role of the power and influence of personality in the American society, broadly, and in the Negro society, specifically.

The study of American leadership is the study of the "great American bandwagon." The line "get on board, little children" from the well-known Negro spiritual, has a very apt pertinence to the bandwagon tendencies of the American public. No public is ever more eager than the American, and this includes the Negro American, to get on the "right" side, and to be with the winner. To be done properly, it would seem to me that an analysis of this kind would need to dig deeply to the roots of American cultural history. Though I would not undertake it, I think this can and should be done without recourse to the meticulously rarified and obscurantist terminology of some of the social psychologists. I should think that, as far as possible, it would be well, in an analysis of this kind, to deliberately avoid terms having technical, psychological, and sociological meaning.

With specific regard to Negro leadership, my own impression is that most of the prominence of Negroes is something confined to a very narrow world; that is, largely to the world of the sophisticated Negro intelligentsia. The media for reaching the Negro masses, other than through the church, which is rather rigidly controlled by mainly conservative and selfish ministers, are not well refined. There are certainly no effective leaders of the Negro masses other than Negro ministers in the Negro world of today. This is all the more unusual, in view of the circumscribed range of power and prestige of the Negro leader, due to the subordinate status and segregated social life of the Negro. Were the job to be done thoroughly, serious attention should be devoted to the extent to which urban Negroes and rural Negroes, also, though less importantly, are aware of the existence of Negroes of influence and of those whites of influence active in the field of race relations. Only a mild effort in this direction has been attempted in this survey. A leadership schedule has been drawn up, carrying the names of a fairly large number of Negroes and whites having varying degrees of prominence in the Negro world, and has been submitted to approximately 1,000 Negro college students in several institutions through the South (a copy of this schedule is appended in Appendix I). The tabulation of the results of the attempts to identify these leaders lends support to the view that the masses of

Negroes know very little about those figures which loom large on the Negro upper-class horizon. My own assumption is that Negro leadership should also certainly include those Negro individuals who are perhaps potential leaders, but who have been shelved or blacklisted because of an inability to adapt themselves to the mores of the dominant group. Information on the class background of the individual leader, on his racial experiences and his contacts, and the nature of his contacts with whites, the section of the country from which he comes, his educational background, his income status and his organizational affiliation is also pertinent.

It would be very useful to make a comparison between Negro leadership and that of other minority groups, especially that of the Jew. We might well inquire into the essential motivations behind Jewish or immigrant-group leadership and attempt to determine in what respects, if any, the motivations behind the leadership in such groups differ from those found among Negro leaders. Direct comparisons between the status of, let us say, Jewish and Negro leaders could be profitably made.

As I conceive it, a fair analysis of Negro leadership would include the following: (1) A carefully selected, but extensive list of prominent Negroes in all walks of life, and of prominent whites in the interracial movement. These would be culled from all available sources, including the Negro *Who's Who*, Negro periodicals and the Negro press. (2) A careful selective sampling would be taken from this list, affording a sound occupational cross-section. Representatives from the following groups would be included: doctors, lawyers, school teachers, preachers, educational administrators, businessmen, government employees, leaders of labor unions, leaders of protest organizations, newspaper men and professional politicians. (3) All available data would be obtained, covering the lives of the individuals included in this sampling, with special emphasis upon family background, relative wealth or poverty, education, contacts with sympathetic whites and prominent Negroes, publications, positions held and political and economic philosophies. Data should be collected upon the positions now held by such individuals, which give them prominence and influence in the society, and a special effort should be made to determine just what factors have been chiefly responsible for their elevation to higher status. It is important to obtain the individual's own assessment of the factors leading to his success, though such assessments need obviously not be taken at their face value. The individual's own assessment should be checked with the views of others in the community and with all other materials obtained from other sources relevant to the individual's rise. Emphasis should be devoted to the question of the extent to which fortunate white contacts have been influential in the elevation of the individual Negro leader. An appraisal of the individual's position of eminence should be based upon the achievements of the person, either in the world of scholarship or of practical affairs. Efforts should be made to determine the extent to which the individual leader has relied upon tactics of caution, tact, the spirit of compromises and conciliation as a means of moving up the social and power ladder. It is equally important to determine to what extent such individuals are noted for their courage and their fighting qualities, their unrelenting and uncompromising attitudes in the struggle for Negro equality. Are they assertive and aggressive? Another important factor entering into the equation is the extent to which oratorical and "spell-binding" ability is a factor in the rise of the individual leader. (4) An assessment should be attempted of the nature and extent of the actual influence of the leader. To what extent does the leader actually influence many people in their thinking and their actions? How is this influence exerted through organizations? the Negro press? speeches? or, the pulpit? Can it be said that the individual actually commands a following? (5) The leader's consistency in social thinking and acting should be tested, and a special check should be made upon opportunism. (6) It is of importance, also, to determine how widely the individual leader is known and to determine whether his reputation is confined to the Negro intelligentsia or whether he is known to the Negro in the street. In this connection, it would be well to determine, also, the extent to which the Negro leader commands respect and whether he is generally thought of as honest, devoted to his cause or as purely opportunistic.

It would seem to me that the primary problem in a survey of this nature, once the objectives could be clearly defined, would be that of collecting sufficient data on the lives of selected individuals to make possible scientific and defensible deductions of a general nature. The heaviest attack upon the problem, I should think, would be dynamics, toward the selective mechanism, in the choice of Negro leaders.

The background against which the data on Negro leaders should be significantly compared and contrasted would be an analysis of the subject of leadership in general in the American society. This would be in accordance with the basic assumption that all aspects of the Negro problem are integrated in the total American scene and are not to be considered as isolated phenomena. Another helpful basis for comparison with Negro leadership would be an analysis of leadership among American minorities in general. This should be rather less difficult than the broad analysis of American leadership in view of the fact that there is some useful material available on immigrant and Jewish leadership in the country. It may well be that there are general patterns of leadership typical of all minority groups, and especially racial minorities in the United States, to be found in such analysis. It would be helpful to know the factors responsible for the influence exerted by Jewish, Mexican or European immigrant leaders, the nature and direction of such influence, the means which they employ to attack the social problems confronting their group and the ways in which they accommodate themselves to the social scene.

It needs repeating that there will be many questions raised concerning Negro leadership that cannot be answered in this memorandum. Obviously, for instance, we cannot designate all of the Negro leaders, nor even suggest an estimate as to how many there are. We can suggest certain types however and provide some illustrations of them. We do know also that the horizon within which the Negro leader can function is severely limited by the racial mores of the country. It is beyond the conceptions of both Negroes and whites that, for instance, there should ever be a Negro president in this country. Only a very emancipated few can think in terms of Negro leadership attaining the exalted heights of a position in the cabinet, or on the Supreme Court, or a general in the Army, or even a Senator. The upper limits of Negro leadership are quite rigid and whenever one Negro breaks through it creates quite a sensation. Among other questions which arise in connection with Negro leadership and to which we can here give only partial answers are the following: By what means do Negro leaders rise? How are they recruited? This involves the mechanism of selection and we will devote some attention to it. What traits do Negro leaders prize and which do they avoid and why? Obviously the answer to these questions depends upon the situation, upon the mores of the community and the section of the country in which the particular leader functions. A Negro leader in New York may employ techniques which it would be disastrous for any Negro to attempt in Tuscaloosa, Alabama. What is the extent of the power exerted by the Negro leader? How much influence can he actually wield and just what can he accomplish? Can he lead whites as well as Negroes? What kinds or types of leadership are there and what recognition is there in the community of the existence of such types? Clearly the two types most generally referred to in the Negro community are the "race man"—the intensely race-conscious and racially loyal leader—and the "Uncle Tom" —a much abused and loosely used label which covers a wide range of attitudes. How do Negro leaders differ in different fields of activity, among different classes, in different geographical areas and periods? Has the migration of Negroes northward had any effect on Negro leadership? Are there regional differences affecting leaders with regard to the importance of such factors as family background, color, class, status, etc.? Certainly such factors would weigh more heavily in Charleston and New Orleans than in New York or Chicago, though it would be difficult to gauge these differentials accurately. Is leadership transferable? In some instances, as in the presidencies of some Negro schools, it has been, but by and large Negro leadership seems not to be handed down from father to son. What differences, if any, are there between urban and rural leadership? For the most part rural Negro leadership would be confined to the ministers, and perhaps the school teachers, to a much more limited extent, since they are far less independent. In recent years also there has been felt in the rural areas the influence of the county agents and farm demonstrators, and in a few scattered localities the more or less under-cover influence of the sharecropper and tenant farmer union leaders.

How do Negro leaders differ from white leaders and from other minority-group leaders? Prestige and power are scarce commodities among Negroes, and the attainment of such attributes tends often to "do something" to the Negro leader. For when a value is scarce its possession tends to inflate the possessor. The Negro leader often quickly puffs up when given power. He "struts" and puts up a big front, or puts on "airs," often indulges in exhibitionism. It is often truly said that the Negro leader "can't stand power." Actually, there is a sort of ambivalence which characterizes the attitudes of Negro leaders. The leader will pay lip-service to the concepts of democracy for he understands their significance and appeal to the Negro as a group. But in his personal views and relationships the Negro leader is ordinarily very allergic to democracy—he prefers to play the role of the aristocrat, or the dictator or tyrant. For leadership itself is a form of escape—the leader, having attained power and thus escaped above his group, would degrade himself by voluntary descent again to the level of the mass through application of the democratic precepts in his personal relationships. It follows, too, that since there is so little range and opportunity in the exercise of leadership, the struggle among the leadership aspirants frequently become ruthless. What are the rewards of Negro leadership? There is a limited prestige value, of course, a certain amount of power, but for the most part the pecuniary gains would seem generally to be rather petty. Yet it does not take a great income to elevate one far above the masses in the Negro community, and consequently even the limited dividends of the leadership position, sometimes legitimate and sometimes not, are much sought after. As an example, note the frantic scramble for the Negro bishoprics and the leadership contests within the lodges. How much competition does the Negro leader receive from the white leader? On the whole, probably very little directly, since often the actual white leader works through a Negro "front." The white man arouses great suspicion when he tries to lead Negroes directly. Are Negro leaders encouraged or suspected by whites? The answer is both yes and no, though many Negroes pride themselves on their ability to "pull the wool" over the eyes of the trusting white man, and there can be little doubt that this is often accomplished. The tendency is, perhaps, for the white man to regard the Negro as rather innocent and free from guile, and this plus an attitude of sympathy for the Negro with the lugubrious air makes the uninitiated white man a perfect foil. How stable or continuous are Negro leaders? The Negro following is itself fickle and consequently there is little stability in Negro leadership, except perhaps, in the churches and lodges where the controls are not altogether free. To what extent is Negro leadership reserved for that marginal man—the mulatto? There can be no doubt that there are many circumstances in which any aspirant for Negro leadership would find a light skin a definite handicap, and vice versa. Is the Negro leader isolated? To quite the same extent as his group, of course. Can Negro leadership be bought? There is purely opportunistic and irresponsible Negro leadership and there is some that is of unimpeachable integrity. That which can be bought, however, is usually purchasable for "peanut" money. The scorn for the practice among Negroes, frequently expressed, is often less due to the fact that Negro leaders "sell out" than because they do so so cheaply. Is there a hierarchy of Negro leaders? To what extent have whites risen to leadership because of the Negro-white problem? What are the selective mechanisms in the choice of such whites?

A General Survey of Negro Leadership

This discussion of Negro leadership will confine itself entirely to contemporary leadership. With the exception of those courageous souls who led the slave revolts, the pre-emancipation leadership of the Negro group was largely in the hands of Negro ministers, for then, as now, the Negro minister had closest contact with the people, and the church was the pivot about which Negro social and organizational life revolved. Something of the nature of this earlier leadership, of its attitudes, objectives and tactics, for both the slave and the free Negro, can be gleaned from the two memoranda on ideologies of the Negro question prepared by Dr. Guion Johnson and myself for this Study.[1]

The outstanding figure in the period immediately following emancipation was Frederick Douglass. Douglass, Pinchback and numerous others, were essentially political leaders.[2] They were entranced by the new-born political freedom granted the Negro and, thinking entirely within the framework of civil libertarianism, felt that the future of the Negro would be made secure through the exercise of the franchise. This exercise of the franchise, however, as conceived by them, was entirely within the Republican Party, which they regarded as the savior of the race. There were other lesser-known Negro leaders, such as Wesley, who were very sensibly convinced that political democracy for the Negro would have meaning only insofar as the Negro was able to obtain an economic base for himself in the society.[3] They, therefore, advocated labor unionism as a vital concern to the Negro's future, but they met with little understanding or support on the part of their more illustrious politically-minded contemporaries.

Reconstruction was, indeed, the period of most intense political activity for the Negro in the nation's history. There were a great many important Negro political figures, many of whom sat in the state and

Frederick Douglass. (Yale Collection of American Literature, Beinecke
Rare Book and Manuscripts Library, Yale University)

national legislatures and in the state administrations. By and large, these leaders followed in the Douglass tradition. They looked to politics as the vehicle upon which the Negro would ride to full equality and citizenship. They had great faith in education too, as the means whereby the Negro might prove to the world his ability and his right to citizenship. Yet the Negro was not entirely to raise himself by his own political and educational bootstraps. The Negro had a right to expect aid from the influential white man—political aid from the Republicans; philanthropy for Negro schools from the wealthy whites. Politically and economically, they were bourgeois in their thinking. This was only natural since they were not the products of any marked uprising or of any revolutionary group. They were merely representatives of a group which had been an innocent pawn in an internecine conflict between northern and southern upper-class groups. There was nothing in the background or the experience of the majority of the Negro leaders of this period which would have stimulated them toward the formulation of a progressive economic program to secure the future of the Negro. The masses of Negroes, themselves, were peasant minded and inarticulate. They vaguely wanted land and land reform, but there was no medium through which they might communicate their will to their newly acquired representatives and leaders. Though Du Bois, in his *Black Reconstruction,* might suggest it, there was, in fact, no revolt of the black proletariat at this time.[4] In fact, it can scarcely be said that there was a black proletariat. The newly freed slaves were agrarian and peasant minded, and tied to the land. The Reconstruction governments were little more than rump parliaments created and maintained at the will of the victorious industrial North and supported by the strong military arm of the Federal government.

Following Reconstruction—the Negro's political hey-day—came the dark days of reaction, and the old Negro leadership swiftly went into eclipse. True, a number of the political leaders of the Reconstruction period were able to hang on throughout the period of reaction and to remain in the legislatures of some of the states until the end of the century, but the determination of the South to drive the Negro out of politics and to maintain white supremacy in all walks of southern life, together with the crass desertion of the Negro by the North, dealt a shattering blow to the political idealism of the Negro, and to those leaders who had placed all of the Negro's eggs in the civil-liberties basket. When there was no longer political activity among Negroes the political-minded leadership lost its position and its appeal. Moreover, once slavery had been abolished, the white abolitionist leadership of the Negro became less influential in Negro life. After emancipation, the abolitionist elements exerted their main influence upon Negro life in their capacity as school teachers in the Negro schools of the South. And this was a very important influence—it molded most of the Negro leadership until very recent years. Clearly, a new leadership, with a new philosophy, was demanded, and in the 1890's, Booker T. Washington, the Negro conciliator, stepped into the breach.[5] Booker T. hammered out for the Negro a philosophy that could fit itself into the philosophy of the dominant white population. His was a pragmatic doctrine of "getting along" and of making the best of things as they are. These were hard times for the Negro, for his political dream world had come tumbling down about his ears. Booker T. tried to yank his head below the clouds and have him put his feet solidly on the ground once again. At least, it can be said for Booker T. that he properly interpreted the spirit of the times, and recognized the complete lack of realism shown by the politically-minded Negro leaders of the earlier period, who had been unwilling to give thought to the Negro's economic future. Booker T. proceeded to develop an economic program for the Negro and to sell it both to the Negro, and to that part of the white population which counted; i.e., that part of the white population which would be inclined to subsidize it.

But Booker T.'s policy of appeasement, of "casting down your bucket where you are," of thrift and skill and industry, did not mollify all elements in the Negro population. There were a good many Negroes at the turn of the century who were unwilling to surrender their dreams of political equality and equal rights for the Negro. They were determined to fight on relentlessly toward the goal of full citizenship for black and white within the nation. This group soon found a willing, vigorous, and inspired leader in W. E. B. Du Bois, who refined and reformulated the civil-liberties creed and, for thirty years, led an unceasing assault against the bastions of Negro disability and discrimination.

There seems to be no other course but to be rather arbitrary in my definition of leadership as it is employed in this memorandum. The term "leadership," itself, is perhaps ill-chosen and should be used cautiously. Many individuals, who might, for our purposes, be considered leaders, would vigorously resent being referred to as such. This is in part due to the opprobrium connected with many Negroes who have projected themselves into the public eye by fair means or foul and who are styled "self-appointed leaders." For our purposes here, it seems to me that the

Booker T. Washington. (Prints and Photographs Division, Library of Congress)

criteria of selection are much more important than the designation it-self; that is to say, the selection of individuals considered as leaders would be directed toward those individuals who, by one means or an-other, actually hold positions of prominence and influence in any Negro community either because of the respect paid them by Negroes or the confidence placed in them by responsible whites, or both. Thus, for all practical purposes, the Negro or interracial leader would be any person having a degree of prominence and influence in the Negro community for whatever reason.

Probably most of the "respectable" Negro leadership comes from the ranks of the Negro intelligentsia; from the doctors, lawyers, ministers, professors, and business men. A good deal of the political leadership, especially the political bosses, lieutenants and ward heelers, however, is recruited from the ranks of the Negro sportsmen and racketeers. Yet no hard and fast distinction can be made at this point. There are, certainly, "respectable" Negro politicians, and quite as surely, some of the Negro leadership which is accepted in "respectable" Negro circles is recruited from ranks other than the intelligentsia. But such leadership is not as readily accepted among Negroes as it is among whites, perhaps. It may well be that it is a greater asset for a white than for a Negro leader to be able to boast that he comes "from the people." I am not at all certain that it would pay dividends for an aspiring Negro leader to be able to say that he comes "fresh" from the cotton fields. Certainly it would have no appeal to the Negro elite, who are always trying to forget the cotton fields, and it might arouse more ridicule than admiration among the Negro lower classes. On the other hand, there is something to be said for the ability to speak the language of "the people" among Negroes. Negro Baptist preachers—even some of the best educated among them—are expert at this. They often affect their "dis" and "dat" and use the figures of the cotton field and the corn patch. But these are merely stage props.

There is one type of Negro leadership that might be called the "glamour" type and embraces those individuals who acquire a glittering prestige because of the acclaim accorded them by the population. The glamour and prestige is, in fact, largely measured by the extent to which the acclaim comes from the white population. Within such category would fall personalities like Bill "Bojangles" Robinson, the king of taps, who is practically illiterate. He is catered to by large elements in the Negro upper class, however, because of the glamour attached to him from his Hollywood and vaudeville exploits. I have heard "Bojangles" address, by special invitation, a very swanky Negro breakfast club group at its Sunday morning meeting in an open-air pavilion in California, on the subject of "My Philosophy of Race Relations." In a strange admixture of mellow Uncle Tomism and Falstaffian bravado, "Bojangles" un-

Bill "Bojangles" Robinson. (Photo by Carl Van Vechten, Carl Van Vechten Papers, Yale Collection of American Literature, Beinecke Rare Book and Manuscripts Library, Yale University)

grammatically thrilled his audience. His philosophy consisted essentially of "kowtowing" to the big white man who holds the money-bags and "slugging" the little white men who can do nothing for you. In this same category would fall Jesse Owens who, because of his remarkable exploits at the 1936 Olympics in Berlin, at which he established himself as the world's fastest human and one of the greatest track athletes in history, came back to the United States and was employed by the Republican Party as a campaign feature to attract the Negro vote. Not long after the campaign was over (after Jesse had run a few races against race horses at country fairs), a leading whiskey distiller decided to capitalize upon his prestige in the Negro race and put him on the payroll as a sort of good-will-salesman-at-large for the company's product.

This sort of "glamour" is a form of prestige, of course, a prestige deriving from a specialized activity. The same reaction can be found among whites, but is not so readily generalized. When a Negro wins wide acclaim in the white world it is the *sine qua non* of "having arrived," and this is indispensable to generalized leadership in the Negro world. The Negro reaction is simple: "If the white folks say so, he *must* be good."

The analysis of Negro leadership must, of course, be made in terms of the milieu in which the Negro leader operates. It is not necessary here to undertake any description of this milieu, for this will be gleaned readily enough from the materials gathered in other sections of the Study.[6] It must be clear that we cannot treat the Negro leader realistically unless we picture adequately the field in which he works. Particular emphasis must be directed to the social pressures operating in various communities against the Negro group. Other factors, which must be weighed carefully, are the vested interests which white people may have in the inferior status of the Negro, the various manifestations of white interests in Negro leadership as, for example, the active interest shown by white business men and politicians in the heads of Negro schools, or the relationship between white leaders of a political machine and Negro go-betweens or lieutenants, or the relationship between white interracial leaders and their Negro associates in the community. More specifically, what are the stakes in the Negro situation that are held by white bankers, merchants and landowners in a given community and to what extent do they actually exert or attempt to exert influence in the selection of Negro leadership? What effective demands do they make upon such leadership and how tractable must it be in order to be successful? To what extent does the social situation permit really independent Negro leadership? In other words, in any appraisal, it is necessary to take into consideration the social controls operating against the Negroes in their special application to Negro leadership.

Quite as great a problem as that of defining leadership itself is the problem of working out a rational system of categories or classifications covering the various types of Negro leadership. It would be possible to work out an unlimited number of systems of classification and the one selected would depend largely upon the goals aimed at. One system might revolve about ideologies and broadly devote itself to the social attitudes and the conduct of the leaders; the specific classification of the particular leader depending upon the nature of his social philosophy, whether to the left, the right or in the middle. On such basis Negro leaders might be divided into three broad categories: (1) those who openly and deliberately seek a fundamental change in the political, economic and social order; (2) those who believe in struggling entirely within the existing framework of the society; and, (3) those who are quite willing to accept things as they are. Another classification might be based broadly upon the techniques employed by the leaders to obtain and maintain a position of eminence. Here we could work out as many and [as] detailed refinements of classifications as we would wish, since, if we deal in details, there are an almost unlimited number of ways of obtaining prominence and influence in any community. Still another classification might be worked out on the basis of the classes of the Negro population to which the leaders make appeal. Some appeals are to the upper class only, to the intelligentsia. Some appeals are to the working class. Some appeals are to all Negroes on the basis of color chauvinism. Some appeals are to dark Negroes. Some to light Negroes. Some to native-born Negroes. Some to foreign Negroes, etc. It should be noted here that really only two appeals have ever been pitched on a level to reach the Negro-American masses, and these have been at the two extremes. One of these was the Garvey movement, which took the position that there is no hope here, in this white man's country, for the Negro, and the other is the Communist position, which holds that the only hope is from the ultimate revolution.[7] It seems doubtful to me that Booker T. Washington's appeal was an appeal to the Negro masses. I should say rather that his was an appeal to the responsible whites of the North and South and to the non-educated Negro middle classes, the small Negro farmers and the Negro skilled workers. His was essentially a philosophy of conciliation rather than a movement with those dynamic qualities likely to stir the inert masses. In essence it was a retreat, and it is difficult to get a people to rally around a retreat. Moreover, the very nature of the audiences to which Booker T. habitually spoke, the circles in which he moved, were such as to suggest that his appeals were not made to the

Marcus Garvey. (Prints and Photographs Division, Library of Congress)

Negro masses. That the Negro masses respected him was due less, I think, to the appeal of his philosophy than to the fact that he was so widely acclaimed by whites. Negroes who had no idea of what Booker T. stood for did know that he had been invited to the White House for dinner. Dr. Washington's appeal, however, was certainly on behalf of the Negro masses, and to a great extent the achievement of his objectives depended upon the full cooperation of the Negro masses. But Washington devoted little if any attention to the Negro peasants, the sharecroppers and tenant farmers. Nor did Dr. Du Bois appeal to the Negro masses. His appeal was to the sophisticated Negro intellectuals. But it is not correct to distinguish between Washington and Du Bois by claiming that one appealed to the "masses" and the other to the "classes."

Simply in order to make possible the employment of our materials in some organized form so as to suggest their essential meaning, I propose to employ a more or less arbitrary classification in order to isolate the various leadership types. In the realization, however, that such classification identifications should be utilized very carefully, purely for purposes of convenience, I propose to employ the following broad types of Negro leadership as categories: (1) The dynamic and aggressive, which bases its appeal on the fighting attitude, on boldness, on the uncompromising stand. It is true that this is often merely bombast and rabble-rousing, but in many communities, it provides a sure basis for the following. It runs the gamut from leaders in the radical organizations to the intellectual "young Turks." (2) The cautious, timid type, which is often "pussy-footing" and which frequently exerts its influence because of the favor which it wins with influential whites. Negroes in governmental positions of responsibility, both local and national, sometimes fall into this category; not entirely by choice, but by the desire to hold on to their jobs. Other Negroes adopt such attitudes as a means of winning the favor of influential whites. It is part and parcel of the "Uncle Tom" psychology inherited from slavery. Such types are found in profusion among the Negro intellectuals, the churchmen and the leaders of Negro reform organizations. They do not always carry black bumbershoots, but they are always willing to pursue a policy of appeasement. (3) The "undercover" agent, who performs the role of stooge for responsible whites and who, because of the favors he is permitted to distribute among Negroes, assumes a position of considerable, but *sub rosa* influence in the community. A former intermediary for a big utility magnate in the middle west, who was often in position to distribute largesse among favored Negroes, is an example of this type; professional politicians often employ Negro intermediaries as public-relations or good-will ambassadors to their Negro constituents. Negro numbers bankers and other "big shot" Negro racketeers would be included in this classification. (4) The "symbolic headship" type, which exerts its influence because of the position it holds. For example, it has been traditional, due to the confidence won by

Booker T. Washington, that the principal of Tuskegee Institute should be an influential Negro leader, and should be employed by white officials as a spokesman on all vital problems affecting the Negro. Thus, the office is symbolic of influence and when Booker T. Washington's successor inherited the position, despite the fact that he was a man of decidedly insignificant stature and ability, he proceeded to play the role of Negro leader and spokesman by white election. The present incumbent of the position is so lacking in qualifications of leadership and intellect that this traditional reliance upon the principal of Tuskegee fortunately promises to be broken.[8] In many southern communities, the head of the Negro school, irrespective of his merits, and even though he may not be respected by the Negroes of the community, is accepted as *the* Negro leader and spokesman for his people. (5) The "prestige personality," who attains leadership because of the prestige connected with his name. Great singers like Roland Hayes, Marian Anderson, and Paul Robeson attain prominence and exert influence over Negroes because of the reputations they have made as artists. Similarly, entertainers, who have attained varying degrees of notoriety, such as Bill "Bojangles" Robinson, "the mayor of Harlem," and Ethel Waters, are figures of appreciable prominence and influence.[9] Joe Louis, had he any desire to do so and enough intelligence to express it, could exert tremendous influence over Negroes merely because of his fighting ability. Other individuals possess influence because of the prestige of their organizations. Those who are responsibly connected with organizations such as the N.A.A.C.P. and the Urban League automatically assume the mantle of local leadership and influence because of the prestige which their organizations exert among certain groups of Negroes.

It sometimes happens that Negro figures from the underworld—the world of the numbers rackets and other forms of vice—because of their affluence and their "success" become influential personalities in the Negro community. They often exert important political leadership and are frequently more generous in their support of a contribution to Negro enterprises than are the more respectable Negro business men. They are looked up to by many Negroes because they can give evidence of so many attributes of having "arrived"—big cars, fine homes, elaborate wardrobes and "fat" bankrolls. When their world crashes because the law catches up with them, as it usually does, they can always claim to be martyrs and cry that they are "taking the rap" for racial prejudice.

Right here, perhaps, it should be mentioned that it would be highly

Ethel Waters. (Photo by Carl Van Vechten, Carl Van Vechten Papers, Yale Collection of American Literature, Beinecke Rare Book and Manuscripts Library, Yale University)

desirable to draw a line of distinction between Negroes of prominence and those who might actually be regarded as leaders in the sense of commanding a definite following. This is, however, an extremely difficult thing to do, for, among Negroes, any prominent Negro is a potential, if not actual, leader, especially if this prominence is due to acclaim by white people. A Negro of prominence has among Negroes, perhaps, a symbolic significance not attached to the white man of prominence among whites. Whites never have to react to white achievement on the same basis as Negroes do to the attainments of Negroes—they never have to gloat over the fact that "one of our boys made the grade"—for the Negro has to have a special set of achievement values—the racial barriers make it imperative, since Negro life is an attempt to break through them.

This is related to the fact that inevitably Negro computations are on the basis of escape from lower status or improvement in status. To the degree that any Negro has attained prominence, to that degree he has thrown off some of the stigma attached to identification with the group labeled as inferior and subordinate. The Negro individual, therefore, who attains prominence symbolizes the hope of every member of the group for escape from the shackles of the racial curse.

The actual fact is, of course, that there are no Negro leaders today who can command national followings among the Negro. That is, there are now no national Negro leaders who can lead large groups of Negroes as Negroes—as Garvey did. A. Philip Randolph can lead Negro Pullman porters nationally, but has little following otherwise. There are leaders of Negro Baptists or Methodists, leaders of organization members and sympathizers, but there are no truly national movements among Negroes, and no leaders to initiate and lead them. If we except Father Divine and his heterogeneous flock, there is no single Negro leader in the country who even makes a pretense of commanding a national following, nor has there been any since Garvey.[10] Each Negro preacher has his congregation. The Negro politician has his local political supporters. The heads of the important Negro organizations have virtually no personal following. There simply are no "big" Negro leaders, no "race" leaders. There are Negroes cast in the molds of demagogues, but they are petty demagogues and play only for grubstakes in their local communities. A Marian Anderson, or a Paul Robeson, or Joe Louis, or Henry Armstrong, or Duke Ellington, or Louis "Satchmo'" Armstrong, or "Cab" Calloway can pull more Negroes into a meeting than any Negro leader, by technical definition, that can be named. It would be purely pedantic, therefore, to attempt to distinguish between the Negro leader and the Negro of prominence to try to determine, for

Paul Robeson. (Photo by Carl Van Vechten, Carl Van Vechten Papers, Yale Collection of American Literature, Beinecke Rare Book and Manuscripts Library, Yale University)

Marian Andersen. (Photo by Carl Van Vechten, Carl Van Vechten Papers, Yale Collection of American Literature, Beinecke Rare Book and Manuscripts Library, Yale University)

instance, whether Professor Carver of Tuskegee is a Negro leader or just a Negro of prominence.[11]

For many of the same reasons, it would be useless to attempt to distinguish between the "big" or national leaders and the local Negro community leadership. This, also, would be a hollow distinction for the reason that the so-called "big" Negro leaders are known only to the very limited Negro intelligentsia and a relative handful of liberal and informed whites, who come in contact with this group of Negroes. Thus, a Du Bois or a Walter White, or a Eugene Kinckle Jones is little more known to the black masses than to the white.[12] There is no reason that they should be known to the black masses for the organizations they

Father Divine. (Scurlock Studio Collection, Archives Center, National Museum of American History)

have led reach into only the upper crust of the Negro society. Their appeals, their house organs have been pitched on a level to reach only the Negro intelligentsia class. The only Negro leaders anywhere, in fact, who actually come in contact with the Negro masses are the Negro ministers who reach the church-going masses, the lodge leaders who reach a fairly large segment of the black population, a very few Negro labor organizers and a very few old-time politicians who have never been able to crash into the ranks of the Negro upper crust.

In addition to the major types of Negro leadership mentioned above, there are a number of sub or secondary type categories, which may be employed. These include the following: (1) Leaders designated and approved by whites. These may be either an outstanding individual or just a "faithful servant." (2) Professional Negroes, all of whom have a certain degree of eminence in any Negro community. These would include lawyers, doctors, ministers, professors and teachers. (3) Sheer opportunists: that is, cheap, selfish racketeers of one kind or another. In this category, too, would fall a number of the Negro "war-horses" who are pulled out of storage on ceremonial occasions to make personal appearances and rabble-rousing speeches. They are usually masters of old-fashioned oratory and have a certain amount of hoary glamour. They believe in no principles and have little to say, but they can make it sound pretty. They are a breed of professional political prostitutes of a high order and the political parties often purchase their services. (4) The self-appointed Negro leaders who push themselves to the front at every opportunity and who revel in the spotlight, though endowed with no other qualities of leadership. An effort will be made to give some examples of these several types.

To a considerable degree (how considerable it is difficult to say and the degree surely varies from locality), leadership among Negroes depends upon white acceptance. Thus, when a Negro received general recognition or acclaim among whites, for whatever reason, the mantle of leadership and influence is automatically bestowed upon him. Jesse Owens was a great athlete, not yet out of college, but because of the acclaim accorded him in the white press, Owens was considered a valuable asset for political campaign purposes by the Republican Party and was elevated to the position of political expert on the Negro problem. On the white side, it is still largely true that all Negroes look alike to many whites and that whenever one, by whatever means, projects himself into the public eyes, he is regarded as an outstanding individual by whites and thereby assumes a position of unwarranted importance in Negro affairs. There seems to be no necessary correlation between the Negro's ability, intellect or qualities of leadership and his position of influence and prominence in the Negro community. It may well be that there is no universal correlation between ability and prominence in the white society either, but if this be true, the reasons are certainly different, for in many Negro communities the finger of approval from a responsible white citizen is all that is necessary to give that Negro a degree of leadership authority in the community. Nor is there any essential correlation between the respect in which Negro leaders are held by Negroes and their acceptance as Negro leaders and spokesmen by whites. For example, Perry Howard, member of the Republican National Committee from Mississippi, is widely scorned by Negroes, but, due to his shrewdness, his humility in the presence of whites and his tractability among whites, he is fully accepted as a Negro leader by leading white Republicans. The fact that great numbers of Negroes regard him as a mountebank and a "white man's nigger" is of relative unimportance—to the white Republican leaders. His rise to prominence was along the easy road of Republican party politics in Mississippi, where there are only a handful of Republicans and all of those are seeking Republican patronage. The test of fitness in that game is one's ability to play shrewd politics and at that, certainly, Attorney Howard is an expert. Once on top, he has remained there by playing his political cards well, "staying in" with the white folks as he well knows how to—it is often said of him that he is a better "lily-white" than a white Republican of Mississippi would be—and by a robust, all-out, Lincoln-freed-the-slaves-the-Democrats-be-damned brand of Republican soap-boxing.

What are the essential conditioning factors in Negro leadership? To determine this, it is necessary to scrutinize carefully the essential social factors operative in the selection of Negro leaders or in the elevation of Negroes to positions of prominence and influence in the Negro community. It is not necessary to make any anticipatory assumptions in order to do this and the most effective presentation is in the form of a simple picture of the functioning of the Negro group in the American society and the role of the Negro leader in the social process.

The primary factor is that of the minority status of the Negro group and the psychological, social, economic and political implications incident thereto. It must always be kept in mind that the Negro leader is not just a leader, but a minority-group leader who operates in a microcosm. Minority-group status manufactures both Negro leaders and white leaders on the Negro problem. In every case, it is important to direct attention toward the determination and the extent to which the Negro leader or the white leader on the Negro question leans upon this minority problem as the prime basis for his leadership. To put it bluntly, such leaders are often expertly able to exploit the racial situation.

The perspectives and attitudes of the individual leader are also matters of concern. Does the horizon of their thoughts extend beyond the narrow view of race or minority status? It is important boldly to appraise their worth, their realism or lack of it, and their sincerity. Do they give value for value received in terms of effective good to the group they claim to serve? To what extent do they profit personally from this convenient racial situation? Certainly there is room for the suspicion that many minority leaders, both white and black, find a profitable hunting ground in the minority situation and thereby develop vested interests of a personal nature in the problem. In this sense, it may well be that many of them will have relatively little sincerity in their presentations on behalf of the Negro group, but a strong personal interest in the organizational approaches to the problem. Much of such approach is certainly pure humbug and the individuals who participate in these activities for a price are merely tilting with windmills and know it. On the other hand, there is unquestionably a great amount of sincere effort, even though often misguided or short-sighted or opportunistic. The extent to which the minority problem obscures an individual's broad social perception and his understanding of wider social issues is also of vital significance to any such analysis. With the Negro, for example, it is clear that race is the basis of all the social thinking done by many leaders. All interpretations and attitudes are subject to control by this concept.

It is further of importance to inquire into the basis of leadership appeal. On the surface, at least, it appears that any Negro leadership or aspiring leadership can make a far more effective appeal to the masses of Negroes on purely racialistic grounds. Black demagogues use it, as do leaders of reform organizations, churchmen, lodgemen and intellectuals. There are, in the Negro universities, a good many "academic Garveyites." It is unfortunately true that the evidence seems to point to the conclusion that race is the common denominator in the success equation for Negro leadership.

It is important, too, to attempt to discover to what extent such factors, coincident with minority status, as isolation, segregation, restricted access to the greater resources of the majority world, self-imposed psychological inhibitions and complexes, affect Negro leadership and white leadership in the Negro world. To what extent do such leaders fence themselves within the minority problem or, to put it differently, to what extent does the minority problem, itself, fence them in? That is to say, is there a definite pattern of social and intellectual introversion that typifies Negro leadership and nurtures its peculiar growth and form? My own opinion is that this is definitely so and that it is extremely unfortunate that the typical Negro leader, for this reason, usually has a peculiarly warped view of the world in which he lives, and especially of that larger world of which it is a part. This warped view he transmits to his followers. Thus, the Negro too frequently has not merely a provincial attitude toward the world, but a distorted picture of it and of his relationship to it.

It can be repeated again here that white groups have vested interests in the inferior status of the Negro and exert varying degrees of influence in the selection of those who hold positions of prominence and influence among Negroes. Such vested white interests exert their influence in many ways and a very careful study of this part of the social process needs to be made. There is undoubtedly a large grain of truth in the popular assumption among intellectual Negroes, that when an important white man puts an approving finger on a Negro, this automatically elevates him to a position of importance in the Negro world. In similar vein, patronization of Negro individuals is a factor of no little importance. Patronization remains a very real force in the world of Negro-white relationship and, it might be said, especially in the relations between black and white intelligentsia. To cite a specific example, when the Spingarns decided to hold a conference of young Negroes under the direction of Dr. Du Bois several years ago, and invited some thirty younger Negroes to the Spingarn estate at Amenia, New York, to discuss the young Negro's attitude toward the problem of the Negro, it soon became very evident that many of these young people, who were, by and large, just young Negroes and quite undistinguished, talked and spoke of themselves in terms of Negro "leaders." They had been chosen from the masses and this patronization and condescension, though most certainly not deliberately or consciously offered by the Spingarns, had almost magical effect upon the thinking of these young Negroes. The logical process in the thinking of these delegates was simple. The Spingarns are important and prominent and wealthy white people. From the great mass of lowly Negroes, this handful of young Negroes had been selected. This automatically gave to them a status which they had theretofore not had. They had been accorded a recognition, which, in their minds, distinguished them from the rest of their group. Such distinction is enough to make a leader of any Negro. It should be noted, also, that leadership, as a concept in the thinking of Negroes, is often simply the attainment of that higher status which will make it possible for the individual to look down upon the great mass of Negroes below him.

It is difficult to say just what are the criteria used by these whites who are in a position to designate or influence the selection of Negro leadership. It would always depend upon the particular circumstances and the nature of the function to be performed, I presume. By and large the criteria would be within the broad framework of "sanity," "soberness," "safeness," and "temperateness in utterance." Ordinarily whites do not approve of a Negro leader who does too much violence to the prevailing racial patterns unless they are quite radical whites, and then the more reckless and bombastic the Negro is, the better. But it is quite well demonstrated that a Negro leader who wants to "get along" needs to trim his sails in order not to offend the sensibilities of the whites to whom he is responsible. The "place" of the Negro has degrees of humility, and even Negroes working in positions of responsibility with prominent whites have often discovered that it is expected that they too will respect established boundaries of conduct.

The application by whites of the double standard to Negroes, the frequently misplaced sympathy for Negroes by whites or the lack of information on, understanding of, or indifference to Negro ways and affairs, sometimes leads to a situation in which a very responsible white man will give to a very inconsequential or even disreputable Negro the sort of recognition upon which he can trade as a leader. For instance, just last year I was button-holed for a donation by one of the Washington religious demagogues, one "Prophet" Battle, who conducts an evangelical racket in the nation's capital. The prophet, an illiterate but shrewd young Negro, was soliciting funds for his "movement" in a Washington attorney's office. There was some skepticism expressed concerning his "movement" and the "prophet" immediately pulled out of his pocket the *coup de grace*—a worn letter from Secretary of State Hull, guardedly endorsing his "movement." With his eyes shining, the "prophet" rebutted our skepticism with this statement: "If the great white man, Secretary of State Hull can recognize me, then every 'nigger' has to." And, there can be no doubt that this letter from Secretary of State Hull would be the source of no little credibility for this man among Negroes.

Not infrequently, Negroes are shoved into positions of leadership by white leaders for purely strategic reasons. It is a common practice in numerous organizations and movements today, especially those of the liberal variety, to say "we must have a Negro on this." This attitude has even found reflection in the purely academic and scholarly organizations where it has been deemed necessary to project a Negro now and then into some position of prominence in order to demonstrate the liberality and tolerance of the group.

Other Negroes have been elevated to positions of power and prestige due to the activities of the philanthropic foundations in the Negro field. In such instances, however, the Negro often has a valid liaison function to perform. It is, in fact, often quite difficult to distinguish between the Negro who is elevated because of merit, or because he has a definite function to perform, and the Negro who is selected merely for "window-dressing" purposes.

A thorough study of Negro leadership would need to assemble enough data covering a large number of individual cases to determine the pattern, if such there be, in the selective mechanism for the choice of Negro leaders. In any such study, there will be found to exist significant differentials between individuals and these should be carefully noted and analyzed. However, it would seem that less emphasis should be put upon the individual and as much as possible upon the social process involved. That is to say, there should be less interest in the compilation of a series of biographies than in working out the details in the general mechanism of Negro leadership selection. The biographical data obtained, therefore, would be only a means toward this end. For example, there would be vast difference, perhaps, between Mary McLeod Bethune and Father Divine as to backgrounds, attitudes, nature of influence exerted, personality, and the nature of the appeal employed.[13] Yet, it must be true that each of these individuals has undergone a process of adaptation and adjustment within the social milieu. Serious efforts should be made to read out of the life histories of such individuals precisely those factors which may be primarily responsible for the unusual status they now enjoy.

It will also be important to determine, wherever possible, the significance which such factors as class status, occupation, education and background have to the selective mechanism in the choice of Negro leaders. I doubt very much, however, that it would ever be possible to give any accurate rating to these factors or any others involved in this process, but it may be possible to make some general conclusions concerning such factors. It would be desirable to know what effect, if any, class and social status within the group would have upon selection for leadership. It would be of similar importance to know the significance of family background, the extent to which Negro leaders have been identified with the common working-class Negro, whether such matters as culture, a fine education and scholarship are aids or handicaps in the attainment of leadership status. We would want to know, also, the extent to which some leaders may be accepted by one class or stratum of the Negro society, and not by others, as well as the extent to which resentment may be expressed by lower-class Negroes against the upper-class or "dicty" Negroes.[14] To again use Mrs. Bethune as an example, it is not at all irrelevant to inquire as to the extent to which her broad "A," her affected "culture," her walking stick, her general appearance, and even her color have been assets in her climb to leadership. In a given case, color may be a factor of tremendous importance, depending upon the locality and the mores of the local population, both black and white.

A very important, albeit difficult, part of a thorough-going leadership investigation would have to concern itself with what might be designated the "manipulative adeptness" of the Negro leader. This is largely a matter of his personal relationships, his ability to influence the "right" people, to rub the white "boss" the right way, to flatter, beguile, and outwit. Unquestionably, many Negro leaders have accommodated themselves to the social situation in much the same way that the Pullman porter flatters his white charges in order to get a larger tip. The Negro leader, in his relationship with his white sponsor, is usually, though not always, more subtle than the Pullman porter, but the pattern is the same. Such materials, however, are obviously difficult to harvest. It is hardly likely that many of the individuals themselves would relate these more revealing episodes in their life histories other than to their closest friends. Nevertheless, most Negroes are acquainted with a goodly store of such stories, certainly enough to conclude that this is a widespread device. There is a good deal of folklore and legend in circulation concerning such affairs, much of which reduces itself to the level of gossip. It may be subject to question as to how reliable a source of information for a study of this kind unverified gossip can be. On the other hand, there are often elements of truth, subject to verification, in the daily chit-chat among intellectual Negroes who are often on the inside of things.

There would seem to be little doubt, also, that a great many Negro leaders have a dual standard of behavior. That is, one for Negro and one for white consumption. They play two roles and must wear two fronts. This is a feature of the problem which should certainly be carefully checked upon, yet it is admittedly difficult to obtain the materials with which to check it. The stories of the demeanor of Negro college presidents and the administrators of other Negro institutions, when they appear before white legislators, governors, educational officials of the state and philanthropic foundations, are legion, and these would be extremely revealing sources of information on how the Negro leader can "go into an act" when he wants something from responsible white men, [and this would also be found] in the demeanor of Negro Republican political leaders in their contests for recognition as the official delegates from their states before the Republican National Committee. Just recently a prominent Negro Republican politician demonstrated to the Committee how Negroes can "strut" as a means of winning their favor—and he got it. The strategic personal adjustments to the attitudes of the dominant group made by individual Negro leaders afford a wide vista and a very challenging subject for research. The adjustments and adaptations of the Negro leader are apt to be more pronounced and in bolder relief than those of the common Negro for the reason that the Negro leader clearly has much more to lose. He has two worlds to please and to seek his status in.

Another important aspect of the problem concerns these devices employed by Negro leaders to attain their status of leadership, to maintain it and to exert their influence over Negroes. Any such analysis necessarily would involve an examination of the extent to which the Negro and white press are employed, as well as political, fraternal and religious organizations. It is also to be noted that "front" is an important factor in such status. "Front" is a valuable asset to any aspiring leader dealing with a group which is ambitious and covetous of the better things in life, but which has so long been denied them. In this way, the leader who puts up the front symbolizes the aspirations of the deprived individuals whom he leads or aspires to lead. In a sense, he becomes a symbol of escape or a means of vicarious release, since Negroes can get a "life" out of seeing "one of the group" perform at the top of the tent.

Leadership rivalry is often keen in the Negro community. Most frequently, the clash is a clash between personalities rather than issues. Bitterness, vitriol, and character assassination frequently characterize the rivalries between Negro leaders. The struggle for leadership is itself a form of political activity in most Negro organizations and groups, but this internal leadership politics is a feeble substitute for that legitimate political activity so widely denied the Negro.

* 2 *

Illustrations of
Negro Leadership Types

It may be useful to present some specific examples illustrative of the several types of Negro leadership outlined in the preceding chapter. The illustrations presented in the pages following are based upon interview materials gleaned from the field notes. The interviews were on the basis of a purely random selection. It must be emphasized here that the classification of these types has absolutely no reference to personality. The basis for classification is solely the expressed (or exposed) attitude or the conduct of the individual leader. This is considered, for our purpose, of greater importance than the individual himself.

There is an almost universal tendency among Negroes to declare that Negro leadership is "bad." It is common practice to ascribe many of the ills of the race to the lack of competent leadership. That leadership is often condemned as incompetent, selfish, dishonest, venal, treacherous and corrupt. Hope for the future is often predicated upon the possibility of developing a "new and better leadership." This is not a Negro trait, however, for it is common in America to relate social problems to the quality of leadership. It is not unusual for liberals in the South today, for example, to place the burden for the major share of the South's distress upon the incompetence and corruptness of its political leadership. Presidential campaigns are fought out often on the American slogan concerning the danger of "changing horses in the middle of the stream." Despite the fact that Negro leaders are legion, the Negro race, in this country, lacks any real leadership, in the sense of an ability to influence the thinking or conduct of large numbers of Negroes. There are no real ideological leaders. There are no effective organizational leaders. This despite the fact that Dr. Du Bois has for years preached his own brand of ideology, as have men like Randolph. But their audience has been limited and there has been no movement behind them. They have operated only

A. Philip Randolph. (Prints and Photographs
Division, Library of Congress)

within a very narrow Negro world. There was more promise of a real
ideological leadership in the days of the *Messenger* radicalism of the
early twenties, when Randolph and Chandler Owen were actively contacting the Negro people, than there has ever been since. It may well be
that the racial situation, itself, creates a condition in which leadership is
difficult for the reason that leadership is postulated upon respect. The
racial mores in America are such that all Negroes are lumped together. A
Negro is a Negro and deserves no more respect than another Negro.
Thus, it is much more difficult for a Negro leader to command the respect from his following than the same following would extend to a
white man, even granting the truth that the white leadership would quite
probably be looked upon with suspicion.

Negro leadership in America has been frequently condemned for its
lack of philosophy and its extreme opportunism and emotionalism.
Some point to the fact that since the Negro group, itself, is dependent

economically, it is impossible for Negro leadership to be independent. There have been few effective Negro organizers and little cooperative leadership. Negro leadership is factional and competitive leadership. This "cut throat" individualistic quality even extends into the usually more placid fields of research and science. Many Negroes look longingly to the past and regret that the contemporary Negro has produced no outstanding leaders with the stature of a Frederick Douglass or Booker T. Washington. While there is widespread criticism and indictment of the leadership qualities of the Negro minister, the belief is very general that the church still affords the most effective medium for reaching the masses of Negroes.

The following opinions on Negro leadership have been expressed by a representative group of prominent Negroes resident in Washington, D.C. (1) Negro leadership, at the moment, is a failure. It has no philosophy and is definitely opportunistic. To make matters worse, the Negro has not been a good follower. However, the outlook is bright. It seems likely that we will turn from the agitator, who works through sheer emotion, to those who will combine the intellect with the emotion and grip the imagination of the people. Such development will bring a greater moral substance into the race. (Ambrose Caliver, Specialist in Negro Education, United States Department of the Interior) (2) The church has made the greatest appeal to the Negro, but even here as in other fields, the leadership is selfish. Indeed, it is not a real leadership. No Negro has been able to chart a course which large numbers could follow. There is no combination of leadership whose general course is the same. The great trouble with the Negro is economic and because of this dependence, the leadership is also not independent. (James A. Cobb, former Municipal Court Judge, Washington, D.C.) (3) Negro leadership is split and competitive. By and large, Negro leaders have failed to be good organizers although ideologically they may function well. Trade unions are now offering us a new kind of leader: one who is both ideologically and organizationally sound. (John P. Davis, Secretary of the National Negro Congress) (4) Negro leadership today doesn't mean much. It is not very strong and is scarcely recognized as being real leadership. (John R. Hawkins, recently deceased Financial Secretary of the A.M.E. Zion Church) (5) There is no real Negro leadership. This is because the Negro hasn't had time to produce any. We must consider that the American Negroes are not a homogeneous lot. They came from different African tribes, originally, and their mixture is even more heterogeneous in Amer-

Charles H. Houston. (Scurlock Studio Collection, Archives
Center, National Museum of American History)

ica. Those who were captured and brought here as slaves were of the
humble and meek type. Further, it takes all races a considerable time to
develop a real leadership. For example, it took the English 800 years.
(Lafayette M. Hershaw, retired government employee) (6) A strong
Negro leadership has not been developed yet, but it is developing. We
have no one or few great leaders, but we do have a number of small
ones. Many of them are doing a good job without a great deal of publicity. The presence of a number of small leaders is a healthy sign. It indicates a general development of the race and is to be preferred to one or
two great leaders, who lead at their own caprice. (Charles H. Houston,
legal counsel for N.A.A.C.P.) (7) There is, today, a lack of moral and
spiritual leadership. There has not been a single leader since Booker T.

Kelly Miller. (Scurlock Studio Collection, Archives Center,
National Museum of American History)

Washington. Du Bois promised, but failed, Walter White is, today, the
most aggressive of prominent Negroes, but he is merely carrying out an
organization. The white people who went into Negro schools in the past
were able to lead the Negroes and did a good job, but now that Negroes
have taken over themselves, Negro leaders are not leading. (The late
Kelly Miller, retired educator) (8) The term leader is a misnomer. Frequently, if a Negro is prominent in one field, he is called a leader and his
influence extends to even unfamiliar fields. We have had influential men,
such as Douglass and Washington, but no real leadership. The most
prominent Negroes have only influenced a limited number of the masses.
Leadership must be delimited to particular spheres for it is impossible
for one to grasp all realms. The quality of the leadership we have is

marred by its general confusion. Here again, it must be pointed out that there is still much bewilderment concerning our objectives. (James K. Nabrit, Jr., Secretary of Howard University) (9) Leadership, today, is going through its most crucial period, due to misdirection of efforts and lack of preparedness that one must possess when moments of crisis arise. This is especially evident in the bewilderment of Negro business leaders and the collapse of Negro insurance. Out of this will come the new Negro inbred with new traditions. Negroes have, in the past, followed their old traditions blindly. For example, their clinging to the Republican Party was purely an unthinking attitude. (William J. Thompkins, Recorder of Deeds for the District of Columbia and prominent Negro Democrat) (10) There have been no leaders since Washington and Douglass. Instead of leaders, we now have professional agitators. The so-called leaders of today are more radical than in the past, but are not constructive. (Perry W. Howard, Republican National Committeeman from Mississippi) (11) "Leaders" and "leadership" are rather mystical terms, but in the sense commonly used, Booker T. Washington closely approximated a leader, but since him, there have been no others. There are no Negro leaders. There is no Negro leadership. (Carter G. Woodson, author and editor) (12) There is not one leader, but many leaders, most of whom receive little publicity. Of all great Negroes, Douglass ranks first and Washington second, as leaders. The leadership of Washington was antagonized by W. E. B. Du Bois and those in the Niagara Movement, but Du Bois did not remain firm and soon abandoned his attitude of non-compromise as is evidenced in his articles in the *Crisis*.[15] Some of the best and most militant Negro leadership after Washington was typified by Abbott in Chicago and John Mitchell in Richmond as well as by some lesser-known, but equally capable Negroes in Texas.[16] The Negro is an emotional and agitative race, and a great number of divergent views among its leadership is to be expected (Emmett J. Scott, prominent Republican).

No one of these twelve prominent Negroes was entirely satisfied with Negro leadership as it is found today. However, one of them expressed the belief that it is not as bad as generally pictured and that, in reality, there are some very capable leaders, though they have not received much attention. One of them voiced the opinion that too much stock is taken in leaders and leadership and that frequently when one becomes prominent in one line of endeavor, he is called a Negro leader, and many come to think of him as an oracle of wisdom, even in fields with which he is

Carter G. Woodson. (Scurlock Studio Collection, Archives
Center, National Museum of American History)

unfamiliar. It was rather generally agreed that the American Negroes are
extremely disunited and that they will have to pull themselves together
and head towards a common objective to attain much further progress.
Some were extremely pessimistic with regard to the hope for the future,
while others were quite as optimistic.

With many Negroes, Booker T. Washington remains the one ideal
among Negroes. It is perhaps true that Booker T. Washington assumed a
status after his death that he never attained during his lifetime. It may be
that the only great Negro leaders must be dead ones. One prominent elderly Negro, who formerly held high office in the Federal Government,
recently told me, "Don't let anyone abuse B.T. in your presence. If he

Robert Abbott. (Langston Hughes Papers, Yale Collection of
American Literature, Beinecke Rare Book and Manuscripts
Library, Yale University)

was living, Mr. Carnegie would have consulted him before employing
you for this study."

Another criticism of Negro leadership commonly heard is that there
are too many leaders and that they are all fighting each other. No one
seems to be very clear on whether it is the leaders who create the cliques
and the factions or whether it is the cliques and the factions which create the leaders, but the net result is the same—a tremendous expenditure
of energy on petty inter- and intra-group rivalries.

One prominent Negro organizational leader of Atlanta, Georgia, has
worked out a five-point gauge of leadership which he holds is essential
to any effective leadership among Negroes. The criteria, as he outlines

them, are as follows: (1) A leader must first have a vision and understanding of mass psychology; (2) he must have a dynamic personality in order to inspire his people; (3) he must know how to organize; (4) he must possess scholarship, not degrees, but the kind that Lincoln had acquired; (5) he must be genuinely unselfish like Mahatma Gandhi and Jesus Christ.

The materials set forth below are classified under the type categories discussed in Chapter 1. It is readily admitted that it is not possible to apply any absolute definitions or classifications. There is unavoidable overlapping and it is unfortunate but true that many Negro leaders have not so shaped their conduct and expressed attitudes that they fit nicely into our artificial molds. The best we can do is to try to hit as near the marks as possible. Let me re-emphasize that we are not attempting to classify personality types here or to give individuals type labels. The type categories are employed merely to afford a convenient means of classifying field materials covering the attitudes and actions of some Negro leaders. In this way it is hoped only to help clarify the picture as to the status and characteristics of Negro leadership in general. It would clearly be ridiculous to try to "type" Dr. Du Bois, for example, either within the classification system here employed or any other. Du Bois is a great Negro character and in his long life of prominence and leadership among Negroes has made utterances and committed acts which might conceivably use up all or most of the categories in any system of classification. To illustrate with my own system, Du Bois has certainly been a "dynamic and aggressive" leader, but he has often been conciliatory and tactful too—every effective leader must be so at sometime or other. As editor of the *Crisis* for many years, he was a "symbolic" leader. His voluminous writings and his very appearance warrant his inclusion as a "prestige" personality, etc.

The categories employed are not designed to give an exact description. For example, the dynamic and aggressive type necessarily covers many sub-types. In general, Negro radical leaders would fall within this category. You have to put them under different categories when looked at from different angles. But there are a number of kinds of radicals among Negroes. There are what, for want of a better name, are designated as "racial radicals"—that is individuals who though outspoken and courageous, confine their thinking and action strictly within the narrow limits of race. To again use Du Bois as an example, though an unquestioned leader of courage and aggression, his thinking has often been extremely chauvinistic. To cite an extreme example, Du Bois recently wrote: "No white sage has sense enough to see the Color Bar as the basic cause of world wars." ("As the Crow Flies," *Amsterdam News* [New York], March 25, 1940). Other Negro radicals have had a much broader perspective and have seen racial problems only as offshoots of more fundamental disorders in the world. Then there are others—"Aggressive" Negro leaders who are merely bombastic, and who have no understanding of the problems of their group—they simply feel the pinch of racial oppression and just yelp about it like a dog whose tail is stepped on. Yet all such "types" would be lumped together as "Aggressive." We could refine the system of classification to a much greater degree, but I am afraid we would end up with a separate category for each individual leader.

The following are examples of Types, the dynamic and aggressive, fighting and uncompromising leadership. (The classification of these illustrations under the various type headings has been done very hurriedly and without opportunity for too careful analysis. It may well be that some of them would, on more careful study, be placed under a different category than the one in which they are now found).

Aggressiveness generally has it limits and, among Negroes, these limits are often very narrow. The Negro is dependent and, therefore, extremely vulnerable. Aggression, among Negroes, is usually undertaken at a risk—loss of a job or position, loss of the good will of the dominant population, loss of the possibilities for a secure economic future in the community. The following is an example in point:

A Negro politician and city job holder in Denver states that he wrote a column in a Negro weekly which pointed out that before the present mayor of that city got in office he was favorable to a proposal to provide playgrounds for Negro children, but that after he was elected, largely on account of the Negro vote, he seemed to have forgotten all about it. The politician charges that the mayor told his superior on the job that if he (the Negro) did not stop writing such statements, he would have to be dismissed. He states: "I stopped."

The aggressive Negro leader also often runs into difficulties with the members of his own race when his aggressive attitudes come in conflict with the established mores of the Negro community, as in the following cases:

The editor of a Charleston Negro newspaper is a bit militant. When head of the N.A.A.C.P. in 1935, he went to police headquarters to protest against the killing of eleven Negroes by the police. Nothing came of his visit, but it in itself was an act of militancy in a place like Charleston. He made attacks on local discrimination and the Republican party in his editorials. However, the dreaded name "radical" has been tacked onto him, and as a result, he is not accepted enough by the community to actually offer much actual leadership, although most of the Negroes read his paper.

The aggressive Negro leader, in a southern community, soon becomes labeled as a radical and, in the majority of cases, from that time on, even Negroes shun him.

Father Hughes pastored a swanky Negro church in Charleston, South Carolina, which had been traditionally attended only by "light" Negroes. Coming from the rectory one day soon after his arrival in Charleston, he asked a black man where to find the nearest mail box. He then asked the man if he had a church home, and when he said "no" Hughes cordially invited him to come to St. Marks to worship. But the man said apprehensively, "Oh no Sir, no Sir, that's for high yellers."[17] Hughes assured the man that this policy would be abolished under his leadership and attempted to do so. Hughes has become "fed-up" with the Charleston situation and has gone to Boston.

Active participation in organizations such as the N.A.A.C.P. in southern communities is regarded as "radical" activity by many white people, and the individual, particularly if this individual holds public employment, is regarded as daring. The following example is cited from Tampa, Florida:

A young Negro woman, a school teacher in Tampa, dares to act as the secretary for both the N.A.A.C.P. and the Voters League. Succeeded in getting almost 100% membership of teachers in N.A.A.C.P. Making great effort to establish close cooperation between the N.A.A.C.P., Voters League and Community Improvement League.

* * * *

A young woman school teacher in Miami. Alert, plain spoken. Has brought more Negroes into the local civic league than any other person. Clear on issues and is very outspoken about the plight of Negro school teachers in Miami. Had stirred up more interest in politics among Negro women than any other person.

* * * *

Widow of Dr. Green, who was last Negro Alderman in Knoxville, Tennessee. He had been elected from Fifth Ward for a term about 25 years ago. Wealthy and owned a large section of real estate in the slum area. She is strong Negro rights champion and a voluntary school worker.

It should be noted that Negro women occupy roles of active organizational leadership in many Negro communities.

A Negro who defies the Ku Klux Klan is indeed an aggressive Negro in the South. A spectacular example of this kind of leadership occurred last year in Miami, Florida:

Sam Solomon of Miami, Florida, is a young Negro undertaker who made national headlines last year by leading the Negroes in their defiance of the K.K.K. ultimatum—"niggers, you better not vote." Quiet and soft spoken with a lot of determination. Was a delegate to the Republican National Convention.

Negro labor leaders in the nature of the case must be classified as aggressive and courageous, especially those who work in the South. Even among Negroes, the union organizer is looked upon as something of a radical and a person who is not quite respectable. The Negro labor organizer is seldom accepted as a social equal by the members of the "Negro elite."

Henry Thornton, Negro leader of Knoxville, Tennessee, capable, and militant. Could be very influential community leader, but for the lack of strength labor has in this anti-union town in which union leaders have no caste.

Unfortunately, many of the aggressive Negro leaders lack the background and the knowledge for an understanding of the Negro problem, and the basis for a broad vision. They are active, but not intelligently so.

The Negro leader who becomes undesirable in the community may be the victim of a frame-up. Moreover, the white community in the South has many ways of warning over-zealous Negro leaders to "slow down." Since so much of the Negro leadership comes from the Negro professional class, it is strictly "part-time" leadership. The Negro professional man in most places has to devote the greater part of his time to the struggle of making a living. It should be noted also that though many Negro leaders have gotten their reputation in the Negro community for their bluntness and outspoken criticism, they are much more severe in their criticism of Negro institutions and organizations than they are of white abuses and those whites who are responsible for them.

Among many Negroes, there is a strong prejudice against Negro leaders who have "too much" education. The Negro Ph.D. is often referred to as "useless" as a leader.

It may often be found that a Negro leader is aggressive and progressive on many issues, but completely reactionary toward such important movements as labor organizations. Uneducated Negro leaders who "don't belong," often find it difficult to obtain cooperation from the Negro upper classes. A great many Negro leaders are strict individualists, and through their refusal to cooperate with others and to work with organizations their qualities of aggressiveness and independence are wasted. With many Negroes the test of a leader's quality is his ability to get them jobs—which usually can be achieved only by working cooperatively with whites.

Some other examples of militant, aggressive Negro leadership in the South are the following (It will be noted that some of this leadership is from the church. There is no evidence to indicate that this sort of militant leadership is at all typical of the church, however.):

Snow Grigsby, President of the Detroit Civic Rights League. Has been the active spirit in the organization for several years. He is as courageous as he is ungrammatical. Works in Post Office. Had been chairman of the Civic Rights League for some time, but last year the postmaster of Detroit called him in and told him that he would have to give up his responsibilities as chairman of the League or resign from the post office, on the ground that the Hatch law would not permit him to continue to be active in politics. Grigsby denied that he was active in politics in a partisan sense, but admitted that if efforts to get justice for Negroes is politics up to his neck, and would continue to remain in politics. [sic] However, the postmaster insisted that Grigsby give up his chairmanship, and Grigsby, who has a family of four to support, did resign, but he still guides the organization.

* * * *

An A.M.E. Minister in Virginia—tall, fair, flashy, imposing type. Has reputation as fighting, independent leader and both knows and likes it. Deplores lack of intelligent, honest leadership, and believes people have lost confidence in their leaders. Says that intense jealousies and factionalism among local leaders nullifies their efforts. Thinks the Negro Ph.D.s offer next to nothing in leadership. Believes only real improvement that could come to Virginia now would be through importation of about ten all-trained, intelligent, aggressive and coura-geous Negro pastors, who would give needed leadership. After making continual reference to "Negroids" and "Negroid types" and "traits," he finally said that after traveling in Europe, Africa, and Asia, he had concluded that the "Negroid" was just not yet ready to assume responsible leadership, and would not be for several generations yet. Claims to say what he thinks, firmly and clearly, but not radically. Made it clear that radicalism and craziness are synonymous to him. Deplored the fact that so few Negroes take philosophical view of things, as he does, and they seldom develop a logical system of thought, since "so few" have read and traveled extensively. It was being said in the community that this leader was a candidate for the bishopric; and that members of his congregation were being assessed $10.00 to defray his "campaign expenditures." He is known as an aggressive Negro leader, however, and an unflinching champion of Negro rights. Often, the courage to "speak up" boldly and frankly to white people, as this man unquestionably does, is enough to satisfy Negroes that the individual is a mili-tant, aggressive, fearless leader.

* * * *

Dr. Sweeney. Louisville, Kentucky. President of local N.A.A.C.P., dentist. Ran for school board in 1938, and was defeated largely because of the Negro voters, who, some say, did not know how to use the ballot to best advantage. Well thought of by whites and Negroes. Militant, honest, sincerely interested in race affairs.

He says,

> The most able and best element of Negroes don't go into politics and this leaves the field open for the less scrupulous individuals to represent the Negro's inter-ests politically. . . . However, the trend is definitely upward.

* * * *

"In 1933, the newly elected Democratic administration started out with the in-tent of holding the Negro and enlarging their support. Therefore, they dished out a few Negro jobs. . . . All of these job holders are, of course, key men in the machine set-up, and could force the administration to make many needed im-provements in city services to benefit the Negroes as a whole, but rather than use their advantageous position for the general welfare, they have followed the nar-row line of self interest, entrenched themselves in their own self enrichment, thereby compromising their social effectiveness and limiting their ability to rep-resent the best interest of the Negro people as a whole. As politicians, we have shamelessly missed the opportunity to do something really effective for the Negro citizen as a whole." (Mr. John Walker, Deputy in Tax Commissioner's office, Louisville, Ky.—J. Jackson's interview)[18]

* * * *

Wm Worley, editor of Louisville, Kentucky, weekly. Helped form independent party organization in 1929 as a reaction on the part of the Negro Republicans of Louisville to the rule of the lily whites who had come into power in 1917. Group put up a full Negro ticket and conducted hot campaign. Has met with violence on the part of Negro Republicans and at the hands of the white police who were tools of the lily whites. His printing press was smashed, and he was beaten, along with several others. Ran for State Legislature in 1919 from the 58th District.

* * * *

The editor of the Houston *Defender* is spoken of as the most outstanding leader Negroes have ever had. Since his death, according to many of the citizens, no single individual has emerged to supply group leadership on a city-wide scale. The most prominent Negro leader of Houston today is R. R. Grovey of *Grovey vs. Townsend* fame.[19] He is described as a militant, progressive, old-line Republican leader. He is head of the most vital civic organization in the city: the Third Ward Civic League. Closely associated with Grovey in the N.A.A.C.P. and the Third Ward Civic League is Carter Wesley, who is described as the most socially conscious and progressive Negro in Houston, Texas.

* * * *

A young Negro school teacher of Augusta, Georgia, has been labeled as a "radical" probably because he organized a forum about three years ago. It was a discussion group which aimed at airing the entire history behind disabilities from which Augusta Negroes suffered. They helped secure a Community Library for Negroes. Negro citizens tried to have this young man made principal of the new elementary school, but because of his "radical" tendencies—one of which was his refusal to pose on the school's steps with a Negro racketeer and big-shot politician who is a stooge for the local machine—he did not get the job.

* * * *

Reverend O. H. Whitfield, of Missouri sharecropper fame, is honest, sincere and a fighter. Practically no formal education, but a seeming wealth of "horse sense." Attracted nation-wide attention when he led Negro and white sharecroppers out onto the Missouri highways in protest against their plight. Recently made a vice-president of the National Negro Congress. He says that he has been preaching the Bible to the people, but now he realizes that they must have bread. Hopes that oppression will bring all the people together—white and black alike.

* * * *

Dr. Mance, A physician who is very aggressive and rather outspoken on the Negro problems in Columbia. Though sincerely interested in its solution, he does not participate in any organization to express this interest because he is disgusted with "compromise" organization. Together with the Negro principal of a high school there, he anticipates problems, attacks them through letters and the like and gets the largely paper organization's heads to sign them. Dr. Mance and a Negro school principal are called "radical" because of their direct attacks upon problems. For instance, they opposed a former Governor of the State (Johnson) when he tried to get a federal judgeship on the grounds that while Governor he [vetoed] a free-books bill because "the darkies would get as much as whites of South Carolina." They drafted a telegram, got many signatures thereto, and sent it to Washington. The school principal is labeled radical too, because his executive committee of the teachers club is engaged in "equal salaries" talk with the school board.

* * * *

A Professor Bailey of the high school is also labeled as radical because he has applied for admission to the University of South Carolina's Law School.

* * * *

Retired school principal of Knoxville, Tennessee. Family tradition of education and leadership since Civil War period. Of old freed man and independent stock. "Don't-trespass-on-me" type. Honest and independent.

* * * *

Zack Alexander, Charlotte, North Carolina, Native of the town; a mortician. Outspoken and rabid individualist who is fed up with Negro authorities "who have no time," and who is ardently racialistic. Resents most whites because they're "just crackers, that's all." Tired of incessant factionalism among Charlotte political groups. Embarked upon a one-man job to help lead Negroes in right political paths. No white man in the town can stomach him, but Negroes respect him highly. One man said, "White folks tell you 'that Alexander nigger, he always rubs me the wrong way.'" He can afford to, however, because he makes his living off Negroes.

* * * *

Methodist Preacher of Baton Rouge, Louisiana, is a militant independent about 45 years old and a mail carrier. Served on Baton Rouge Grand Jury and is listened to and respected by the white politicians. His major concern is the recreational needs of Negro youth, and was instrumental in getting a small playground. A sincere participant in all civic [modes] on the part of the Negro in Baton Rouge.

* * * *

Attorney Valentine. Petersburg, Virginia. Young lawyer, operates successful service station, financially independent. When not occupied with commercialism is a smooth-mannered, sagacious, and vigorous young militant. Lacks broad vision.

* * * *

Pastor of a Dallas, Texas, Baptist Church. Most of his activity has been centered around his church. Common slogan in community is that if you join his church he will get you a job. Dynamic, young and efficient. Represents best in the newer leadership.

* * * *

William Anderson, Greenville, South Carolina. Head of N.A.A.C.P. Youth Council. Victim of recent frame-ups of robbery and attempted rape. Militant but imprudent. When told by head of local K.K.K. that he could be given thirty years, he retorted, "I know as much about the U.S. Constitution as you do."

* * * *

A.M.E. preacher of Winston-Salem, North Carolina, who has been in town only two years, but has initiated a local chapter of his Colored Improvement League and a youth conference. Feels that town organizations have stood too far from the Negroes en masse, and believes that if they are corralled and exposed to organization benefits they will lose their timidity. Is very outspoken, and some say he has been warned to "go easy."

* * * *

T. V. Smith, of Highpoint, North Carolina. High school teacher. Pres. of local N.A.A.C.P. Outspoken. One citizen says of Smith, "too busy to do much." Democrat.

* * * *

Mrs. Susie Hoover, Beautician, former school teacher and former census taker of illiterate Negroes in Highpoint, North Carolina. Aggressive and very politically minded. Sincere Republican. Energetic in getting out vote. She did say, however, that if Republicans get back in power, she could get work in the city. Might be her motive.

* * * *

Rev. Dr. —— of Knoxville, Tennessee, ran for school board in November 1937 and lost by narrow margin. Represents modern swing to labor-progressive-New Deal leadership. Has large following. Militant, social view. Respected and listened to by white officials. Heads interdenominational Ministerial Alliance. Believes in and has initiated joint activities between Negroes and whites.

* * * *

Dr. Martin, of Highpoint, North Carolina. President of Voters Club. Devoutly Republican, but many call him radical because of his blunt, outspoken criticisms of Democratic Party methods. Wields large influence. Thinks of Abraham Lincoln and Republican Party as one, and can't see anything Democratic.

* * * *

L. E. Austin, Editor of *Carolina Times,* only Negro weekly in Durham, North Carolina. Called radical by most people, yet admired by them for his vitriolic editorials against policies of the powers that be. Somewhat chauvinistic. Fights for better conditions and insists that the Committee take firm stand on jury service, schools, etc. Many Negroes call him "traitor," however, because he went through Reynolds factory by special permission, then wrote about how much better conditions were in the Winston-Salem plant (the one he inspected) than they were in the two Durham plants where large majorities of workers are organized. Not trusted to any extent.

* * * *

J. C. Allen, Newport News, Virginia. Stevedore and civic leader for many years—ex-president of town's oldest Citizens Voters League. Active in labor, political and religious organizations and highly respected. Head chosen [*sic*] deacon in church. He, too, is immediately named as a leader by those interviewed.

* * * *

Ione Diggs, Norfolk, Virginia. A young Negro woman who is head of the Women's Auxiliary of the Independent Democratic League. Dynamic, honest. Has been called radical on account of activities in C.I.O. unions. Vigorous N.A.A.C.P. worker.

* * * *

Jerry O. Gilliam, Norfolk, Virginia. Among Negro "anti-Administration" forces. A Railway mail clerk, who is head of the local N.A.A.C.P., exalted ruler of local Elks and past president of the National Alliance of Postal Employees (Negro). Is forceful, dynamic and highly regarded by most of Norfolk's Negroes. Admired for his open break with the "old heads" in 1936 when he helped form the Independent Democratic League—the anti-administration group among Negroes.

* * * *

Ernest Cooke, Norfolk, Virginia. Negro realtor, active in Independent Democratic League. Bitter against Negro machine stooges. Bluntly honest.

* * * *

P. B. Young used his *Journal and Guide* as a publicity medium in the Norfolk teacher salary fight cases, and was criticized by whites.

* * * *

A retired Navy Yard worker, Portsmouth, Virginia, is a ward leader. Described as blunt, honest to a point, lacks ingenuity, keen on leaders' faults, narrow in perspective. He feels main job is to stick to local elections now, get needed community improvements and then move up. Is liked because of his honesty.

* * * *

The pastor of the biggest A.M.E. Church is one of the town's outstanding leaders. He is dynamic, forceful, shrewd, well educated. Only been in town three years, but has gained respect and admiration. It is said Negroes will follow him "at the drop of a hat." Claims disinterest in politics—but is running for Bishop. He is described as Portsmouth's nearest approach to a clean, forceful, dependable leadership.

* * * *

A Negro barber from Dallas, Texas, testified before the Senate sub-committee on the proposed anti-lynching bill in February, 1940. There is no available data on his activity in Dallas, but in the hearings he was militant and courageous enough, defying all efforts of Senator Tom Connally to embarrass him. In fact, he turned the tables on Connally more than once during his testimony, and when the audience laughed quite audibly at the Senator's discomfiture, he demanded that the chairman restore order.

* * * *

A young Negro attorney of Birmingham has waged an unrelenting fight against police brutality and for registration of Negro voters. On more than one occasion Negro stooges have come to him with offers of the whites to make things pleasant for him if he will "lay off" his activities. He has been adamant, and finally the whites tried unsuccessfully to "frame him."

* * * *

Tuscaloosa, Alabama, had an undiplomatic, fighting leader, who asked for no favors. He said what he pleased and wrote articles to the editor of the local white times. When he sought protection from city officials they did not flatly refuse him, but indicated that he could expect little by suggesting that he leave town. He owned a drug store, shoe repair shop and a house, but had to leave all. He went to Columbia, Ohio, and entered business. Some of the "better-class whites" say it was a pity that such a smart Negro had not confined his smartness to his businesses.

* * * *

Father Hughes is regarded by Charleston, S.C., whites as a "radical." Negroes looked upon him with hope at first, but now take a passive attitude toward him; fear that he is too hot-headed and out-spoken, and will get them into trouble. They say that even a radical should be diplomatic.

* * * *

Roscoe Dungee, editor of the *Black Dispatch* in Oklahoma City, is described as the ideological leader of Oklahoma Negroes. There is no outstanding Republican leader, but the Negro leadership supports either one Democrat or another. The situation has been such that if one Negro leader supports one candidate, it is certain that another leader will support his rival. For example, the *Black Dispatch* supported one candidate for governor in the 1938 elections, while the Tulsa *Eagle* (Ed. Goodwin, editor) supported another. Goodwin's support of his candidate was based solely on the fact that Dungee had supported the other man, and to him, his candidate was the anti-Dungee choice. The Negro vote would have been decisive in this election had the spokesmen for the Negro people lined up solidly in support of a single candidate. Three thousand votes were the margin of victory for Dungee's candidate. Dungee has done a lot for the progressive forces generally. A marked individualist, his progressive contribution is solely in terms of an individual leadership which centers on himself. If he is not the key figure in any movement, he won't support it. Because of this insistence upon dominating all organizational efforts among the Negroes, he handicaps the development of a collective Negro leadership, and "contributes to the perpetuation of the factionalism which at present reduces the potency of the Negro minority group pressure." Though an outstanding progressive on questions of civil liberties and labor, politically he is a pure opportunist.

Roscoe Dungee has this to say of himself:

Nationally, I am a member of the Association for the Study of Negro Life and History, serving on its Executive Council. I am a member of the National Negro Business League and a National Director of the N.A.A.C.P. I was one of the organizers of the Oklahoma Commission for Interracial Cooperation and served as its secretary for five years. I was regional director of the Elks's oratorical contest for two years, and in 1922 organized the Oklahoma State Negro Business League, remaining president for five years. I am also chairman of the Conference of State Branches of the N.A.A.C.P. During the World War, I was elected chairman of the Oklahoma County Council of Defense (Negro Division) and served through the period of the conflict. . . . I was given the Merit Award for distinguished service among Negroes in 1935 in the St. Louis Municipal Auditorium for the N.A.A.C.P. before an audience of 5,000 people. For the past ten years I have spent a great deal of my time lecturing before interracial groups in white churches and colleges. I broadcast over the radio on one occasion from the station at the University of Oklahoma.

In speaking of using his vote in the House, former Congressman DePriest had this to say:

My vote may be the balance of power in the next Congress, and I'll use it the best way I can. The Republicans may not be able to elect a speaker without me, and they will have to see me. If I can make conditions better,

I'll drive the bargain, if I never go back to Congress. . . . I was called on by one of Hoover's right-hand men and he said he'd heard I was going to vote for a Democratic speaker. I'm going to use my vote to advance my people, and I may vote for Oscar DePriest, so I can vote for somebody they can't tell what to do. Perry Howard of Miss., came to me and asked me not to accept any White House bids, but I am going there at the first opportunity, because I have a right to go there. I stand on my rights. When Mrs. DePriest went to the White House, it was a case of official recognition and not a social one. She is the wife of a Congressman.[20]

With reference to "social equality," DePriest said on one occasion: "The federal census shows an increase by thousands of mulattoes mostly in the South. They have Jim Crow theater laws; and they have Jim Crow street-car laws; but what they need most is Jim Crow bedroom laws."

In answer to threats warning him to stay out of the South, DePriest said: "I am going to continue my tours. I am going to try to teach the colored people their rights." (As a step in this direction, DePriest sent out 10,000 copies of the Declaration of Independence and the U.S. Constitution to Negro leaders.)

The proprietor of a barber shop heads a County Civic League in Hampton, Virginia. Recently his organization has waged a fight on the political front, and has stirred up great interest. He says that he succeeded a lawyer as head of the League, and that most of the professional folks give little or no support now, because they object to him as head because he is uneducated. He is opposed to labor unions, and says . . . "I don't believe that a union ought to tell me how to run my business."

Foreign Negroes, that is, West Indian Negroes, even if competent, have their difficulties in their attempts to act as leaders in Negro communities. For example,

Dr. ——— represents the best Baton Rouge, Louisiana, has in the way of Negro leadership. Very intelligent, sincere and unselfish in his attempts to aid the people. Yet, because he is a West Indian and his wife is an "aristocrat" (a Dumas girl) (Dumas—a prominent Negro family in Baton Rouge), he is the constant object of petty attacks. All that has been accomplished toward the organization of the Negro in activity for his needs in the past several years has been directly initiated or inspired by either him or his wife. Until recently was chairman of Executive

Oscar DePriest. (Yale Collection of American Literature, Beinecke Rare Book and Manuscripts Library, Yale University)

Committee of N.A.A.C.P. Until he took over leadership of that organization, it had never attempted to do anything and was merely a closed sect. Through his efforts it came to the fore as a real representative of the people and conducted some struggles; its membership growing with influence. Under his leadership the N.A.A.C.P. fought several court fights in efforts to eliminate discrimination and injustices in the courts. In all these fights he gave freely of his time and money. He quit the N.A.A.C.P. over the equalization of teachers' salaries case. The N.A.A.C.P. sent a brief to the school board presenting its argument for equal salaries for Negro teachers, and stated that if no reply were received within ten days the N.A.A.C.P. would consider the claim rejected and would file suit. The school board secured a group of hand-picked Negroes under the leadership of the Negro high school principal to memorialize the N.A.A.C.P. to refrain from such action for one year. Included within this group were: the president of a Negro college in the city, a prominent Negro doctor who hoped to get his daughters in the school system, and a Baptist preacher. In addition, the president of Southern University warned his faculty to steer clear of this contest. Over the angry objection of Dr. Huggins, the Executive Committee accepted this stall. Huggins called the members of the Committee "vermin," and quit. In 1931, he and his wife fought for relief appropriations for Negroes, and his wife organized a barter exchange whereby the unemployed could get clothes and food. He also led delegations of unemployed to the relief headquarters and demanded relief for them. The old leaders stood on the side lines and did not turn a finger to help him. He organized the Boy Scouts among Negroes and insisted that they be allowed to wear the regulation uniform, and sent a scout to a camp in New Jersey at his own expense. He is extremely bitter against the old leaders and feels that work with the youth will be more productive than attempting to maneuver the old conservative Negroes into a progressive position. His idea is to take them at "school age," following the line of the Catholics, and inculcate the principles of militancy and sacrifice in them under the guise of scouting. Already has some 300 Boy Scouts organized and is their Executive Chairman. He contributes to the Farmers' Union and feeds their organizers when they come to town. Has put forth efforts to have Negroes join labor unions and urges Negroes to fight from the inside of the unions for equality. May be termed somewhat of an anarchist because he believes that whenever there is a change, or even confusion, the progressive nucleus has a chance.

The "race man" type of leader is the intense racial chauvinist, whose appeal is to the racial emotions, the racial pride and loyalty of Negroes, the racial sensibilities of the group. His interpretations are in terms of race, as were Garvey's. He makes exaggerated claims as to the cultured background and heritage of Negroes. Negro history is painted in beautiful shades of black and synthetic Negro geniuses and immortals are manufactured by the bushel. The racial chauvinist knows no modesty. The true story is related of how at a New York Garvey street meeting in the twenties, a speaker proceeded to extol the greatness of Garvey, the black leader, by favorable comparisons with other great but white leaders in history. He employed rhetorical questions to drive home his points: "Is he a greater man than Abraham Lincoln?" he cried, and went on to explain his affirmative response. He ran the gamut of great men of history in this way—George Washington, Napoleon, Cromwell and Julius Caesar were all tolled off. Finally a little fellow in the audience raised his voice and inquired timidly: "Is Marcus Garvey a greater man than Jesus Christ?" This checked the speaker, but only momentarily, and he quickly replied: "Ah, that I cannot say just now. But Marcus Garvey is a *young* man yet!"

The severe racialist interprets all events within the narrow racial framework. For example, just last year at the —— University, two of my colleagues criticized me for deviating from my previous pacifist attitude after Munich. Their argument was that there was no reason for the American Negro to get excited about the violation of Czecho-Slovakia, since the same countries, rising to the defense of Czecho-Slovakia, sat by complacently while Ethiopia was being raped. Their argument ran that there was little difference between Germany and the way in which the American Negro is treated here. The fact that they had made their reputations in even this semi-democratic country by fighting for the rights of their group—something that they as members of the non-Aryan population could not do in Germany and Italy, seemed to make no impression upon them. Yet this is the very same sort of racial nationalism which impels these same individuals during a time of war to advise Negroes not to stay out of war, but to demand for Negroes an equal chance to fight in the front lines with whites, i.e., they would argue against restricting Negro troops to labor battalions, to exclusion of Negroes from the air corps, the marines, etc.

Among the racial militants even the Negro children are supposed to know well the catechism of racialism. One of my acquaintances, who is a medical doctor, has a small daughter, 9 years old. Riding in the car one day with his daughter, she began to tell him of the visit she had made to a small friend of hers who had not recovered very quickly and was having many complications. My doctor friend said that he couldn't understand why this should be since it was merely a simple fracture, a girl of that age should have healed up very quickly, and that there must have been something wrong with her doctor. The small daughter said, "Oh no! That couldn't be possible because she had a *white specialist.*" My doctor friend severely berated his daughter for making such a remark, warned her never to express a thought of that kind again, and accused her of having gotten it from her mother, and lectured her to the effect that "A specialist is a specialist," that Negro specialists "are as good as white specialists," and that on the whole it had been a very *terrible* thing for her to say.

The racialist leaders are usually very militant and are often extremely bitter. They sometimes like to shock innocent white people with extremist remarks and delight in making it clear that they have no love for palefaces. There are no lengths to which their imaginations will not carry them in their racial diagnoses of events. I recall one instance in which a racially-minded academician delivered an important address in which he read an international significance into the fact that Joe Louis, the Negro, fought Primo Carnera, the Italian, in Harlem during the Italo-Ethiopian war! He rated a box on the front page of the *New York Times* for his unusual perspicacity.

Type 2: Cautious and Timid Leadership

There are a great many degrees of shading among the "cautious" or "reserved" or "timid" type of Negroes. They run the entire gamut from sane, sober restraint to downright and deliberate "kowtowing," "pussy footing," and "Uncle-Tomming." There are many honestly conservative Negro leaders who are convinced that within the existing racial situation the Negro can make best progress by slow, patient but determined plodding along, by a restrained approach to the problems of the group, so designed as to avoid stirring up any more racial feeling than already exists. They take what to them is a realistic view and conclude that since the white population is dominant and at the same time reluctant to see the Negro move across the traditional racial lines too rapidly, it is folly for the Negro to presume that he is able to demand anything or to assume an attitude of militancy. They believe that the Negro can be assured of making slow but steady progress toward ultimate equality if he does not agitate the always restless waters of racial hostility. There are other Negro leaders who strike the same attitudinal pose, but for other than honest and sincere reasons. They are personally ambitious and have figured it out that this is the best tactic for the Negro leader who wishes to rise in the scale, for it is best calculated to please the white man in the driver's seat. The extreme of this attitude is the fawning, "handkerchief head," "hat-in-hand" Uncle Tom, who adheres closely to the pattern of slave days, and for reasons of personal ingratiation, deliberately puts himself in the role of the slave and the white "boss" in the role of the "massa." There are some few authentic Uncle Tom types left as survivals from the days of bondage. There has been no sophisticated rationalization in the shaping of their attitudes—it was a pattern well established and accepted in slavery. But the modern Uncle Tom, sometimes crudely direct, sometimes subtly sophisticated, has thoroughly refined the art and understands fully the nature, implications and objectives of his self-determined role. A certain amount of conservatism in conduct is instilled in Negro leaders, especially in the South, through sheer fear of the consequences of offending white people.

Many Negro leaders who religiously keep to their "place" in their contacts with white people are very severe in their attitude toward members of their own racial group. They can be suave Uncle Toms with whites and harsh tyrants among Negroes. They are often given to berating Negroes and are apt apologists for the white attitudes toward Negroes. They frequently employ the white man's stereotypes with regard to Negroes.

A Negro undertaker, and something of a "leader," in a deep southern town defends the white people, even a peonage farm operator. In speaking of a young Negro woman teacher who was beaten by a white bus driver, this leader said: "I bet it was her own fault. A lot of those old teachers don't know how to stay in their places." His defense of the peonage farm operator is probably influenced by the fact that he turns the funerals of his dead Negro "hands" over to the "leader."

* * * *

A Negro leader of Raleigh, N.C., says,

> Negroes are lazy and don't want to do anything to help themselves. You can't feed everybody out of the same spoon, and the Negro has not got sense enough to know it. Whites don't treat a chauffeur like they treat the Governor, but Negroes want to treat everybody the same, especially when you give one authority.

* * * *

The head of the Negro University, about 68 years old, is often described as a "misleader" of the people. He is the most influential Negro in the school affairs of the southern state. With his disapproval no Negro could get a job as a teacher in the school system. In the eyes of official whites, he is the chief representative of the Negroes on all matters. Has always put the building of the school ahead of the general welfare of the race. Arrogant and aristocratic. Two years ago Negroes sought to get a Negro Postmaster in a little all-Negro community a mile or so out from the campus, but the University president intervened to squash the effort in the name of "preserving the good relations now existing between the races in our community." He has been a teacher all his life, and although a Negro teacher's salary in the State is notoriously low, this man has amassed a young fortune. Owns several city blocks of property and in his private garage there are four cars: two 1940 Buicks and a 1939 Ford and Chevrolet.

* * * *

An A.M.E. minister in Denver is referred to by both Negroes and whites as the outstanding Negro leader. Seems cautious and suspicious of persons who are too curious and inquiring; gives the impression of weighing very carefully every work and action. . . . Plenty of ego, and likes to "boss" everything. Proud of his white friends.

* * * *

Active member of one of the national organizations, does good work in the border-state community and makes good "front" man if accompanied by group that will hold him to the issue. Usually too ready to give in. At a conference with some influential people of both races who were considering a move for a city orphanage for Negro children, this man was present. A young white woman, who took a position in the discussion of the plans which was a compromise of the Negro demands, seated herself next to this race leader, patted his knee and all the opposition in him vanished. In fact, he endorsed her proposal 100%. He is said to be susceptible to the flattery of the whites, especially the pretty women who might pat him on the knee.

Fear plays a vital role in shaping the attitudes and conduct of Negro leaders, especially in the South. The Negro leader, like the Negro generally, has so little economic security that he dares not take any risk of losing it. Fear is, of course, an essential element in the southern racial pattern, and it finds vivid reflection in the attitudes of Negro leaders and their followers, too. The Negro is well aware of the many forms of reprisal which may be demanded of the Negro by whites when a Negro is accused of having gotten out of line. Often the innocent as well as the guilty may be made to pay the penalty.

One Negro excuses the timidity of Negro leadership on an economic basis. He says, "A Negro with a job, or a white man's mortgage on his house, isn't going to stick his neck out. Then, the educated man separates himself from the masses."

* * * *

The Birmingham N.A.A.C.P. had wanted to undertake the fight for teachers' salaries, but not a single Negro teacher was a member of the N.A.A.C.P. and none had asked the organization to make the fight.

* * * *

About a year and a half ago a Negro leader went to a southern school board with a recommendation for improved Negro school facilities and couldn't get any co-operation from Negro principals and teachers who were afraid to be identified with it. But a short time before, they had scoured the county at the request of the superintendent to sign up freeholders on a petition for a bond issue for improvement of a white school.

* * * *

In Durham the judges permit white attorneys to refer to Negroes in a court as "niggers." The Negro attorneys don't object for fear it would prejudice their client's case.

* * * *

Certain Negro preachers in a southern community claim that some white people at the city hall advised them to stay out of the N.A.A.C.P. Most of the Negro churches are mortgaged to whites, and the preachers are afraid, because most of their congregations work for whites, too.

* * * *

The chief obstacle in the way of Negro organization in Savannah, according to a prominent Negro informant, is that the Negro middle class is pussy-footing and they regard any affiliation with a progressive organization as a red label in the eyes of local whites.

* * * *

In 1938, a policeman in Macon, GA, slapped a young Negro school girl for skating on the sidewalk. Nothing was done to the policeman, but the girl was arrested for skating on the walk. When no law could be found against this the 16-year-old girl was charged with disorderly conduct. The Negro leaders organized a fight against the case and employed lawyers for the girl. The girl was convicted, but the sentence was suspended. The "good white folks" advised that for the good of race relations it would be better not to follow up the case, and the "good Negroes" agreed.

* * * *

The head of an important Negro organization in Atlanta purchased a Pullman ticket for a trip to Oklahoma, and to his surprise discovered that his seat was located in the middle of the car. Some of his friends told him that there must have been some mistake, and that he knew he did not belong there. Out of sheer fear he returned the ticket and was given an end seat after the ticket collector scolded him for even having accepted a ticket in the middle of the car.

* * * *

A prominent Negro citizen of Tuscaloosa states:

> Some fellows came here in August to organize a N.A.A.C.P. . . . they called a meeting but hardly anybody was there—none of the doctors came. They went about it wrong. The best way to get an organization like that started here is to go talk to the white man first. The effort failed.

* * * *

Prominent Negroes in an Alabama town now refer to a Negro business man who was run out of town in these terms: "He was a smart man and plenty courageous, but he talked up to the white man too much."

There are many Negro leaders who are merely anxious to "get along" in the community, while working on in their own way for the betterment of the group. Often, perhaps, they have trimmed the sails of their conduct without being aware that they have done so. They are cautious and conservative, but they do not believe in playing the role of the Uncle Tom. Often the vested interest which they have in their position is enough to counsel them to "go slowly." They believe that the spirit of compromise is an important instrument in Negro advancement. They take the South for what it is worth and point out with resigned realism that there are just simply things that cannot be done in the South.

In Richmond many Negro leaders become irked whenever anyone criticizes whites publicly . . . e.g., one of the Negro members of the board of an important Negro organization rebuked white members of the board for their inactivity—and other Negro members rebuked him for "criticizing our friends in their presence." White board members (interracial) turn over rapidly, but the Negro members stick. Consider it an honor. Negro members never speak "out of turn."

* * * *

A Negro leader in Durham constantly alludes to the fact that "Durham is the South" and that "We know it is Mississippi dressed up in frills," but yet Negroes have some power there. He admits implicitly that whatever is done there must be done within the southern framework and seems to accept the implied limitations.

* * * *

A Negro undertaker is one of the race leaders in Miami, Florida. Highly respected by both Negroes and whites and was president of local civic league among Negroes for years. Easy going and always careful not to do anything which might disrupt the existing "favorable race relations."

* * * *

Dean of Men at a southern Negro college—cautious, mildly progressive. Involved in all sorts of group activity ranging from Community Chest chairmanship to executive committee of the Student Worker Council. Has fear that he will be dragged into front organization for Communist Party. He is respected by most of the people though some are touchy about his close relationship to the "interests." Feels his way very carefully.

* * * *

Editor of a Negro paper in the South is characterized as cautious, quiet spoken with all the earmarks of a good compromiser. Townspeople suspicious of him and believe him to be unusually susceptible to any proposition which means pecuniary gain for himself. Negroes claim that he carefully edits his public-letter column in order to avoid offending anyone—especially among the whites. Whites have much respect for him.

* * * *

President of N.A.A.C.P. branch in South Carolina and district manager for Negro insurance company. Believes in Negroes developing their own businesses. . . . Believes in aggressive actions, to some extent, but a little afraid of too much of it, lest repressions occur.

* * * *

In commenting on the fact that a Negro was a member of the Chicago school board, a resident of that city says that although the Negroes are happy over this, what they wanted most was a more aggressive Negro on the board. The present member is characterized as "Successful for too long a time. He does not care enough about the poor people. He doesn't identify himself with the masses. He is just a sophisticated 'Uncle Tom.'"

* * * *

The president of a Negro university in the southwest is a "leader by virtue of his position only." Well educated and has several degrees. He states: "I feel that the biggest hope for the solution of the Race Problem will come about as the representatives of the talented and intelligent section of our people go forth to establish contact with the white youth. Also a pressing need is for a type of inter-racial education for both groups." Also expresses the opinion that Negro's economic emancipation depends upon his getting into the trade unions.

He further states,

It is my observation that too often the Negro leaders have been selfish and opportunistic. I used to express myself stronger on this point, but since I have been here. . . . I have had occasion to experience the tremendous pressure that is brought to bear on Negroes in positions of influence, and who command some patronage. Finally, I believe if every Negro would get at least two white people and concentrate on winning their respect and getting them to understand the Negro people as human beings, I believe a great step forward will have been achieved in this state as you probably already know that this school has been the political football for many years and the tenure of all connected with the institution is most uncertain and compromised and conditioned by whims and fancies of the politicians, rather than the several abilities of the individual educators.

The Negro preacher as a leader comes in for his share of criticism. In general he is described as extremely conservative, cautious and timid, if indeed he is not labeled as an outright "Uncle Tom!" More is expected of the Negro preacher as a leader because of his relative independence. One of Savannah's leaders says,

> Large numbers of Negroes could register but don't—this is in large part due to the Negro ministry. Out of 100 active preachers and another 100 "jacklegs" only about six are registered.[21] They won't encourage Negroes to register. They feel that is too worldly for them to touch. One issue was that of betterment of our juvenile-delinquency system, but one preacher refused to join our delegation to the authorities, counselling that we must not do anything to offend the whites, they'll look after us. In the early twenties the leaders didn't want too many Negroes registered for fear they couldn't control them.

There are ninety Negro churches in Savannah. One Negro preacher says, "All we preachers is supposed to do is to preach the Lord and Saviour Jesus Christ and Him Crucified, and that's all." According to some people in one Virginia town, the Negro preachers as a whole do not urge their congregations to vote. In fact some ban civic meetings from their churches.

* * * *

The Negro preachers in Memphis as a whole have avoided social questions and remained silent about the economic and political exploitation of Negroes.

* * * *

It is charged that Negro political leaders in Portsmouth, VA, tend to confuse rather than help the Negro. According to one citizen "they are selfish and refuse to pool their guiding interests behind one man, because they are for the most part paid and, therefore, fail in making the race's fate felt in Portsmouth." Political apathy on the part of the local preachers is one reason for the Negro's backwardness in the city. Another citizen of Portsmouth says, "yes sir, that's our main trouble, these preachers. They are the only ones whose hands aren't tied. If they would only insist on their membership getting qualified to vote. They talk too much about heaven and too little about down here." On the whole the town's leaders do not have the respect of the townspeople. Most of them are allegedly weak, spineless and prone to deceive. They are easily controlled by party machines.

* * * *

Physician in Tennessee school system. Has mixed practice. Very religious. Advises best moral course. Cynical about race progress. Holds his tongue and job. Honest, but has nothing to recommend him for leadership.

* * * *

Physician, in a Tennessee community. Successful practice. Ran for Alderman in 1938. Talked vaguely about recreation, Negro policemen, teachers' pay, etc. Did not prosecute campaign with any energy, but used campaign for self-aggrandizement. Race appeaser.

With a good many Negro leaders the submissive humility of the Uncle Tom in their contacts with whites is a definite means to an end. It is their means of rising to and staying on top of the heap, and if it is necessary to fawn and bow to do so, they will do it—deliberately and with eclat.

One southern Negro "leader" outlines the most effective technique to use when approaching influential white people when the Negroes want something, i.e., "Don't emphasize the Negro's 'right' . . . don't *press* for anything . . . make him feel he's a big man, get to other white men to make him want to avoid seeming small, and you can make him jump through the barrel. You can make him a friend or a rattlesnake, depending on your approach."

One influential leader in New Orleans says:

> I'm a respectable citizen, but when I try to get my rights I do so in a way that will not be obnoxious, and not in a radical way. I don't believe in radicalism. We *ask* for things, but never *demand*. When I'm in Rome, I burn Roman candles . . . but I don't "Uncle Tom"; never did, my father was white and my mother a Moor; I was born in Cuba, and my father owned slaves. I know nothing about inferiority feelings.

This same man is a staunch Republican, but in spite of this, says that the Negro is 100% better off since Roosevelt. But he will be compelled to vote for Wilkie, because he couldn't keep his self-respect if he voted Democratic in New Orleans. Although Negroes cannot vote in the Democratic primary, he claims that he can get more done through local Democrats than through the Republicans. He distrusts labor unions, though admitting them as a necessary protection for workers. Thinks labor is too hard on capital.

* * * *

A Negro preacher in Tuscaloosa readily admitted that the preachers are held responsible for holding the Negro masses "in check." He said, however, that all

Negroes are not under the control of the church, and that therefore the church cannot be held responsible for those Negroes who "don't belong and go out drinking and carousing at night and stirring up trouble between the races." He was proud that he had been invited to speak in white churches in Birmingham and Tuscaloosa. He obviously had no respect for what he termed the "lower-class Negroes."

* * * *

The editor of a weekly paper in Birmingham, 41 years old, says he is a "tired radical—tired of raising hell." He wants some money to do some of the things he wants to do, *now*. He says, "If a Negro goes so far as to make an enemy of the white man who has the power he is foolish. You can't hit a man in the mouth and expect him to loan you money. By all means keep in with the man who hires and pays you. A man wouldn't be head of a big concern if he weren't a smart man, and a smart man will always react to facts. My approach is to the fellow on top because he is going to have to take care of me and I must work with him—he has the stick."

* * * *

Negro attorney, manager of Housing Project—"White man's nigger." Rated highly by white politicians in this southern community because he observes all the southern etiquette when in their presence, e.g. riding freight elevators, hat in hand, "yassa boss." Claims large Negro organization, but his political influence is based not on the size and effectiveness of his organization, but on his personal contacts with the several politicians. Gets any lucrative job possible for himself. As resident manager of the Housing Project he has formed a committee to corral the votes of the residents for support of the mayor's candidates.

* * * *

A Negro Episcopal minister. Has headed several fact-finding committees on Negro affairs and believes that their work has been helpful in getting nearly everything Negroes have in Miami. Very critical of Solomon and his cohorts (who lead the registration campaign) and expresses the opinion that the relations between Negroes and whites in the city before the Solomon affair last year were much more congenial than they are now. Member of interracial committee and is smugly self-satisfied with the type of theoretical "coloring" of race problems such groups specialize in. Opposes Solomon vigorously and allegedly is doing his bit to sabotage his plans.

* * * *

Among the old liners in Tampa there is the editor of Florida's largest Negro weekly. For years has been front man for the Negroes to the whites in power. Strictly "hat in hand." Since Negroes have organized and registered to the point where they can demand more and beg less, this "leader" has jumped on the progressive side. But the Negroes are suspicious of his motives, and believe he is riding the band-wagon for what *he* can get out of it.

* * * *

A Negro in Savannah states that there is no forum there for the discussion of Negro problems. He says, "When we need something some of us just get together and go to the proper authorities—all of us are leaders." This man referred to a particular Negro as having most influence with whites. It is obvious why, because he is modern, timid Uncle Tom. Negro leaders in Savannah lament the fact that they're losing some of their most sympathetic white friends, e.g. an old white judge who died recently was referred to as "not a better man in Georgia—a high-toned Christian gentleman, he believed in the right thing."

* * * *

The problem of crowded schools could have been properly solved in Charleston, S.C., but some Negroes gave the whites an alibi by representing that double sessions would be an adequate solution, and so through this selling out they now have double sessions. A Negro principal received an additional salary for the afternoon sessions—$600 per year.

* * * *

College professor in a Virginia school which recognizes no right of academic freedom. Most concerned with entrenching self in job. Community civic activity is more for purpose of enlisting community promotion to improve his position in eyes of college administration. Seems to be conscious policy of the State College to dispatch its faculty members to capture leadership of all community moves of the people. This is insurance against these movements taking a militant course and wins favor for the vassal college head from the masters of the state.

* * * *

A Negro labor leader in New Orleans who is vice-president of one of the internationals, is well-to-do, has fine house, elaborate combination radio-bar, owns two large barber shops for Negroes, has worked 21 years as longshoreman. Says he has been able to keep out of strikes by being "broadminded enough to sit around the table with steamship company representatives." He runs his union with a tyrant's hand, is brutal to all Negro opposition. But is meek in his dealings with employees and his "Union" is virtually a company union.

* * * *

A Negro citizen of Beaumont, Texas, after listing the needs of the Negro community, complains that the community is thwarted in its efforts to organize for its own protection by such Uncle Toms and "misleaders" as the editor of the

Negro weekly, the Negro supervisor of colored schools, and a Negro notary public and self-styled go-between for Negroes in their relations with the city administration. These men have consistently refused to support moves for paved streets, adequate street lighting, cemetery, playgrounds, library and other improvements for the Negroes of the city.

* * * *

R. R. Grovey, of *Grovey vs Townsend*, in Houston, Texas, says that the Third Ward Civic League achieved certain reforms in the school set-up, i.e., having the probationary period fixed at a maximum of two years. He states that the principles [*sic*] and most of the teachers were opposed to his interference in their sphere. The teachers tried to incur favor with the superintendent by criticizing or attempting to break up any effective Negro struggle for improvement in local conditions. The idea was that they had to be "Uncle Toms" to hold their jobs. When a Negro ran for the school board, another Negro wrote a letter to the *Houston Post* opposing the election of Negroes to the board, and declaring that Negroes were perfectly satisfied with the school board as it was then constituted.

* * * *

An important Negro leader of Birmingham declares: "There aren't any political leaders here, Negro or white." He referred to an incident in which a Negro church was closed on a mass meeting protesting the police shooting of a young Negro steel employee as an example of the way in which Negro leaders work. Negro leaders, he charged, have concurred with white politicians in closing the church. "There aren't any leaders—they're nothing but a half-baked, half-educated, corrupt bunch." Continuing on the incident, he said, "The doors should have been broken down, and the meeting held anyway."

There are a number of ways in which Negro leaders can win the respect of the white community, or at least the responsible section of it, and not all of them require deep humility.

R. R. Church, Sr. of Memphis, Tennessee, started as a cabin boy on a steamboat on the Mississippi River. Worked up to steward on the boat then settled in Memphis. Went into saloon business and dabbled in real estate in what was then Memphis's famed "red light" district. Built fortune estimated at a million dollars when he died in 1912. In 1901, the Confederate reunion was held in Memphis, and the city made elaborate preparations for the reception. Eighty thousand dollars was contributed for the purpose and one of the most conspicuous contributions was a check for $1,000 from Church, who was an ex-slave. This indicates that though Church was financially the most important Negro Memphis has produced, he had to buy the good will of his white fellow citizens. This donation assured him, in the minds of the whites, of his place as one of "high merit and refined feeling." After securing his economic security, Church insured his social status by the best means of girdling race antagonism—the use of money in a strategic cause.

* * * *

The City Manager of Beaufort, South Carolina, referred to Mr. H. G. Fisher, Negro undertaker and recognized by local whites as a Negro leader, as "no ordinary nigra," and one that should be approached "like a man."

* * * *

A Negro business man and political figure in Raleigh, N.C., wails,

> We got 10 or 12 doctors, 3 or 4 lawyers, and a lot of college graduates, and they don't do nothing but figure out how to beat the common Negro—they rob the poor Negro worse than the white man. Between the white man and the college Negro, the latter is the poor Negro's worst enemy. If the educated Negroes would get together and organize an organization to help the common Negro they would do more for the progress of the race. But first they have to establish confidence between the common Negro and themselves. They've mistrusted and lost confidence in the educated Negro so that all of us suffer. The educated Negro has been willing to be the white man's tool.

This same man states that Negroes elected a Negro magistrate twice since 1930, but that in neither case did college Negroes help. He says that the white politicians hired a Negro preacher four years ago for $100 to go to the polls and challenge Negro voters . . . he would challenge the dark Negroes and let the light ones go by. He says that the whites encourage all of the different Negro churches in order to keep the Negro in his place. This keeps Negroes divided. He points out that the same tactic was used on the plantation. The Negroes on one plantation were told that they were better than those on another, etc. He calls the various churches "white folks nigger churches." He says, "we got plenty of modern Uncle Toms now. We go in to talk with the white man about what we want, and he comes out and quotes what some other Negro has said against us, and we know someone's been slipping in the back door."

The rank and file of Negro leaders are reluctant to be identified with radical movements because it usually entails the loss of jobs and their social standing with their own group. They have the idea that it's bad enough being black without being black and red. The Negro thinks in terms of solving his problems within his own group. He keeps his nose in his own "black yard" [*sic*].

The Negro schools in the South do not do much to encourage a bold Negro leadership. The schools, run by extremely cautious and often frightened Negro presidents, tend to produce a leadership of resignation and acceptance of the established patterns. For instance at one well-known southern Negro institution students are taught that they should return to their own communities, where they will become local leaders. They are anti-union. A student leader was not long ago suspended from the school for writing an editorial in the student paper criticizing the administration for its support of a segregated hospital.

Type 3: Liason Leadership

In this category are embraced that brand of leadership which runs the gamut from more or less respectable politicians to out and out stooges and those who would willingly sell out their entire group for a paltry sum. There are undercover agents who perform various types of missions in the Negro community for their white bosses. Sometimes they reap all of the petty rewards for themselves while in some instances they distribute some largesse on behalf of their employers to Negroes in the community. There are in many communities well-known Negro liaison agents between white politicians or other prominent white citizens and the Negro group. They are intermediaries, propagandists, good-will ambassadors, who reflect in the Negro community the power of their white retainers. These "go betweens" who do, in the Negro community, what their white bosses are unable to do for themselves, are occasionally in position to hand out some valuable favors in the form of jobs, fees and donations—sometimes in return for cash, other times in return for services. There are many varieties of such agents. They are usually crudely opportunistic and without principle or honor. They are insecure, since their income depends on pleasing their not too reputable white masters by delivering the goods. They are generally leading apologists for white attitudes toward Negroes.

In addition to such prostitutes, we have included in this category some examples of "big shot" politicians. While most of such Negro political leaders are also responsible to some white benefactor or political boss, they operate with more dignity and are able to exert more influence and to maintain more independence. They too have their Negro lackeys who carry out their bidding. Beneath the big Negro politician are found the Negro ward-heelers, whose job it is to line up and get out the vote. They are political flunkies and are often little tyrants toward Negroes in their local districts. There are included, too, the old-line politicians who are "Republican born, Republican till I die" in their blind allegiance to the party of Lincoln.

The game of politics breeds some degenerate types of local leaders for both races. There are innumerable Negro hirelings of the political bosses, black and white, who will attempt most anything for a hand-out. There are very many stool pigeons, some professional and some voluntary and amateurish. There are Negro leaders who, either to curry favor with whites or to blast away at a rival leader, freely betray each other and their group. There are all sorts of racketeers who exert one or another kind of influence, and who are, when "in the money," sometimes quite liberal in their support of and donations to worthy Negro causes.

Above all such leadership—above all Negro leadership, for that matter—is the constant threat that the Negro leader will barter away his honor and his group for a job.

Negro leadership in Portsmouth is said to be "poor." There are so many self-styled leaders that every fifty voters among Negroes can appropriate one. On the whole this leadership lacks ingenuity, is not dynamic, sells out, and is split by factionalism. When asked who their leaders were most of the townspeople said "we don't have any," but on further questioning named a few. One of those few is a lawyer, active in Portsmouth politics since 1915. Has not much personality, never had strong political organization, pre–New Deal, has handled several discrimination cases.

* * * *

A leading Negro citizen in a Tennessee city declares:

> Negroes lost their position in local politics, not so much from outside pressures, but through internal organizational disintegration brought on by the machinations of corrupted, self-seeking, traitorous Negroes who had wormed their way into the leadership, splitting the solidarity of the Negro vote and betraying the confidence of the Negro voters for their own selfish promotional interests.

* * * *

One prominent white official has expressed regret that Negro leaders are "such slaves of their organizations that they have to put most emphasis upon the more sensational fights, i.e., relatively unimportant matters like seating arrangements, rather than the more significant economic problems of the Negroes."

* * * *

Negro café owner in North Carolina; former head of Negro bank for about ten years. Plain, unlettered, makes plenty from café which feeds four or five hundred a day at very low prices. In the pay-off. Bondsman for Negroes. Knows thousands of Negroes. Disgusted with the professional leadership and isolation from the masses. Eager to have *one* Negro leader.

* * * *

A Chicago preacher of the Father Divine type is described as the liaison man between the politicians and gangsters on the one hand, and the Negro masses on the other. This preacher has in his power the appeal to the ignorant masses, and he keeps these masses for his employers. The employers pay this minister very well. At election time this same man of God is kept very busy, since he is one of the instruments in keeping the Negro masses in line. (Dr. Myrdal's interview with H. Cayton, Jan. 1940)[22]

* * * *

In Beaufort, South Carolina, there are said to be a few Negro leaders to whom the whites in town look as liaison agents. One of those recently died. He was a lawyer, a leader of the local Republicans who had been a prominent office-holder back in the old days. He was allowed, by the county's lawyers, to practice at the bar with them on equal terms. The leading Negro intermediary now is H. G. Fisher, the Negro undertaker. (Stoney's interview with Mr. Belson, City Manager of Beaufort, Beaufort County, South Carolina, June 1940)[23]

The Negro liaison agent or go-between is often in a difficult position, for he must please the white boss, and at the same time must often incur the displeasure of the Negro community which is aware that he is "on order," and because he frequently must undertake missions toward which Negroes in the community are unfriendly, if not hostile.

A white official in the local government of Savannah, in speaking of the Negro concession owner at the Negro Recreation Center, said that men like him are required to carry a too heavy burden of responsibility for their group. He said they are constantly on the spot between the whites and their own people. Men like —— are "feudal lords," he admitted. They are regarded as semi-official spokesmen for their whole group.

Many Negro political leaders are really only ward-heelers in their outlook and function. They engage in political barge trading on the basis of the pitiful little handful of votes they can deliver or claim to deliver.

Custodian of County Court House in a Tennessee community. Negro appendage and shrewd political slave of Judge who appointed him. Heads Seventh Ward Club and votes from seven to eight hundred Negroes on request of the machine. Delivers Negro vote for some financial consideration and some personal patronage.

This same man is described by a neighbor as "the smoothest, most versatile" Negro in the state in contacting whites. He knows just what strings to pull. He is considered by the white people in authority as the best-versed Negro on the Negro situation. He dispenses relief to Negroes and whites, and makes sure that Negroes get their share. "He would like to be an honest guy, but is too deeply obligated to the powers that be."

The Negro agent who has a powerful white boss knows well how to play the role of tyrant. He can demand more obedience and loyalty than a feudal lord, though he is himself only a sub-retainer. Sometimes Negro teachers are responsible for their jobs to such irresponsible racketeers.

One of "big-shot" political leaders, chairman of Fourth Ward organization in a Tennessee town. Delivers about 1,000 votes. Until his patron Commissioner of Education was defeated in 1935, he had final word on all appointments to the school system among Negroes. Also alleged that he sold teacher and janitor jobs to the highest bidders, and commanded complete political obeisance from all of his appointees.

One of the important techniques for rising to power within this category is to "pick a good white horse and ride him hard"—i.e., work into the good graces of a powerful white citizen and let him push you along.

A Negro leader in a Tennessee community is regarded as a self-made man. Reared in orphan home. Little formal education, but got early reputation for being "smart boy" and one who could drive a hard bargain. Entered politics as Republican. Became fixture around courts and City Hall, ingratiating himself with powers that be. When "lily-white" Republicans swept southern Negro politicians into political waste basket, he attached himself to an ambitious Democratic politico. When this politician was elected Mayor [the Negro leader was] appointed health inspector, as he could devote full time to mobilizing the Negro vote. He purchases poll taxes and keeps them in his safe. On election day he passes them out like rain checks and collects them again as the "voter" comes out of the polling booth. Machine furnishes his money to buy poll taxes. His club is made up of poor working people who live in constant fear of the police, conviction, eviction, loss of jobs, etc. If one of voters protests against being ordered how to vote, he threatens them with anything, including jail for some old minor offenses. He gets results.

* * * *

Oily tool of Mayor in a Tennessee town, who appointed him twelve years ago. Controls Twelfth Ward and delivers from eight hundred to one thousand for the machine. All he wants is "a little gold and a little personal patronage."

* * * *

An elderly man and one of the cohorts (of a Negro ward boss in North Carolina) is a stooge. Still "can't vote Democratic" in a national election for President. Though not benefitting much materially from his position, he revels in the so-called prestige. He escorted interviewer to City Hall for election figures, and literally beamed when the tax collector said, "Tom, you show her the Mayor's office and where to get these figures."

Some of these "leaders," though keeping a weather eye peeled for the patronage spoils, try to maintain some dignity and respectability.

A dentist in a Virginia city has been politically active for fifteen years or more. He is energetic, talkative and informed, and has personal files of clippings from newspapers, etc. This leader has been in the thick of all of the recent fights against inequitable treatment of Negroes in his town. Most of the Negroes distrust him, however, because they feel he is personally rewarded by his alliance with the incumbent machine and is merely a tool. Uses compromise tactics, and has been heard to say "those in power have felt constrained to award a few faithfuls."

* * * *

A Negro preacher in a southern city does not come out openly in politics, but works on his congregation to do his bidding at the polls. Contact man with the whites. Vice-Chairman of local Interracial Commission and his position is a mixture of race interest and personal aggrandizement. Good front man, but [not] on the whole progressive.

The small-time Negro leader who tries to be independent is usually at the mercy of the white machine boss—and knows it. Consequently, he is usually "practical" and sells out to the white boss.

Negro insurance executive and head of National Negro Business League of Memphis. In 1936, headed Negro Shelby County campaign committee for Roosevelt. Chairman of Negro Democratic Club. In attempting to gain bargaining power within the local Crump machine, by organizing Negroes who vote in the primary. Crump has all the organization he wants and lets this Negro alone, since his efforts are superfluous. If he ever reaches the point where he threatens Crump's personal dictates to the Negro voters, he will be "busted" by Crump. He realizes this and proceeds only with Crump's approval.

The numbers kings play the political game as a means of getting policy protection for their more lucrative racket.

A Negro "numbers" racketeer (in a large Georgia city) with all white partners, is closely connected with "Ring" politics—has to be for protection. Turns out a good number of votes now and then for the machine. Behind-the-scenes maneuvers of Negro participation in city's politics.

* * * *

The head of the local branch of one of the national organizations, in a northern city, is characterized as the Negro go-between for the whites and Negroes. When a Negro teacher is to be appointed he is consulted. He is the "fixer." Recently received new car as a present from the president of one of the country's largest motor plants, as a result of his sympathetic attitude "during a strike period." Urges Negroes to join unions *individually,* but certainly not publicly. Most of the Negro ministers of the city are reactionary. They frequently advise their congregation members not to join the unions. This, of course, is due to the fact that their church members are employed by the industrialists, and when they are unemployed the contributions become very slim.

Some of the Negro "educators" make tough political leaders and are quite as unprincipled and tyrannical as the less literate bosses.

The most unscrupulous leader in a Louisiana town is the high school principal and supervisor of Negro city schools. Has the ear of the Parish Superintendent of Education and the Commissioner of Finances. Wields almost absolute authority over appointments in the Parish and in the city school systems in harmony with the president of the University. Has sizeable bank accounts in more than one bank and owns quite a bit of real estate. Personally operates the school cafeteria and requires the teacher to raise funds or give programs for the purpose of raising funds for school equipment. He is sole administrator of this fund. He will not allow his teachers to join the Teachers Association or any protest movement, and they acquiesced in order to protect their $40 a month jobs.

* * * *

A Negro woman leader in a North Carolina town who recently died was employee in cotton-knitting mill. When silk stockings came in, the mills cut off many workers. Mill owners "looked out" for those fruitful four who had been instrumental in keeping other workers in line. This woman was such a worker. Although illiterate she was given a job teaching knitting in the Public High School of the city. In gratitude for this beneficence shown her by the former owner of the mill who is now Mayor, she began her political activity. Stooge. Had Negro teachers vote as she was told to have them do. Two hundred teachers voted as told in effort to make jobs more secure. During her last illness a sign was posted directly in front of her house which read, "Quiet, Sick Zone."

Getting jobs for Negroes is one very important function of many Negro leaders and is a sure way to get a following.

Head of a Negro college. Says, "I'm not political man." Yet, due to his assumed influence, the whites lend car to him and he calls up and confers with the Mayor. Gets his men on jobs of one kind or another.

* * * *

A Houston Negro heads a Worker's Aid Club, and puts out Bulletin "labor" paper. Both are "phonies" and he is nothing more than a stooge for the employers. Has been active as a strike-breaker in every labor struggle in Houston in recent years. Has been on the payroll of the Hughes Tool Company, Southern Pacific Railway Company, Southern Steamship Company and the City Laundries. Maintains a running contact with the civic organizations and churches, he is even a member of the N.A.A.C.P.'s Executive Board. Justifies his position by pointing to the continued discrimination policy of the A.F. of L. He is also chairman of the N.A.A.C.P. Labor Committee.

The following excerpts from a field interview undertaken by Dr. Myrdal and myself are presented at rather great length, because the Negro leader interviewed in this Southern seaport provides so excellent an illustration of the attitudes and techniques of a type of leader whom most modern Negroes, even cautious ones, would immediately brand as an "Uncle Tom." We will call him Sam Jones of Seaport, a town along the southeast coast—not that Jones would feel any self-consciousness at

seeing himself identified with the sentiments he expressed. He is cautious, suspicious, patient and proud of his "quality folks" white friends,
who greatly admire him. Through them he can get things done. With
Negroes he is hard and revengeful and doesn't like to be crossed by
them. He is considerable of an opportunist [*sic*], a go-between also, and
there is a suggestion of the racketeer in his activities. But he can get
things done, in his way, which is the way of the old school, the not so
very old school of plantation days, whose pattern has been refined by
but not lost to many modern Negro leaders.

Dr. Myrdal and I went to visit Sam Jones about 10:30 on the evening
of October 29, 1939. We stopped the car and I suggested that I go in first
to see if he was at home and to allay any fears or suspicions that he
might have if he should see a white man coming to his door. After some
delay, Mr. Jones, a large, fat, pot-bellied, dark brown-skinned man of
considerable age came to the door. He was considerably knock-kneed.
He was quite surprised when he saw me and he stood talking to me at
the door without showing any inclination to admit me at first. I told him
briefly that I was engaged in a study of the problems affecting the Negro,
and that I had been told by several of the people whom I had contacted
to date that no man in town could tell me more about the local situation
than Samuel Jones. He brightened up a bit at this and gave a somewhat
sly smile, but immediately tried to evade me or put me off by suggesting
that I come to visit him with Dr. Myrdal at the Negro County Fair which
was to open the next night. At this point Dr. Myrdal entered upon the
scene and asked if it would be possible for us to have ten or fifteen min-
utes of his time right then. Dr. Myrdal added that several people to
whom he had spoken, that is white people, had also suggested that he
see Mr. Jones. Somewhat reluctantly then and rather sheepishly, Mr.
Jones asked us to come in but before permitting us to do so he himself
went in and rather cleared the way.

As soon as we got in and started to talk with him, Jones continued his
policy of evasion by jumping up and waddling out of the room with his
knock-knees at every opportunity. On one or two occasions he remained
out of the room for a considerable period. The first contribution he had
to make to us was his scrapbook which he got in order and had his wife
dust off before bringing it to us. While he was out on one of his periodical excursions, I glanced through the scrapbook and discovered one article which told of how in 1924 the Negro community had failed to
support Jones's Fair. This was in a letter of apology written by Jones to

the local white press, in which he apologized profusely to the white community for the failure of Negroes to support this worthy enterprise. Jones is a completely illiterate Negro and uses the language of the plantation. The letter written to the white paper, however, was in very polished English, very sophisticated, and was clearly written by some of his white friends. Jones is the doorman at Society Hall, one of the most swanky places in white Seaport. Very soon he showed us, with great pride, an article in the New York *World Telegram* of two years ago, which covered the famous Ball held at Society Hall on January 14, 1937. In the article reference was made to Samuel Jones, doorman, "the dignified Negro with top hat who has been doorman for many years and who knows who should and who should not be admitted, officiated again this year." This, of course, is the source of Jones's contact with the white world. He made it clear that he knows very well all of the leading big whites in the State, and that they are his friends. Among them is Mr. —— who is a former mayor of Seaport and the present governor of this state. Jones showed us a number of letters, some of which were written to him by —— when he was Mayor, which were addressed as follows: "Jones, you know that I have set aside money in a contingency fund for the erection of a building for the Negro agricultural exhibit." Or words to that effect.

Jones was continually fumbling about in his pockets pulling out dirty, torn, worn letters from various officials having to do with the activities of the Negro on which he is engaged, most of them concerning the Negro Fair. On another of his excursions out of the room he came back proudly bearing a large, framed certificate of incorporation of the Negro Agricultural Fair, dated 1923. This was printed on a large document in the usual legal terminology and stated the names of the specific individuals connected with the enterprise. Jones explained to us that most of these individuals are now dead or removed and that he, and he alone, remained the power and the influence of this activity. He intimated very clearly that he had picked himself new members on the board of management and that the new president was a man who would be able to help him build up the Fair under his, Jones's, direction. Much of Faber's commitments were by innuendo.[24] His eyes wandered from each of us constantly and he was obviously doing his very best to size us up. He is unquestionably a pseudo-psychoanalyst. This probably has been responsible for a good deal of his success in handling whites and getting them to do for him and his group the things that he wants done. He is very susceptible to flattery though protesting his own "dumbness," his own lack of education and the fact that he has no power. However, whenever we "laid it on him" with sugary thickness he reacted very favorably. After some little time he began to warm up and deliver sermons to us which gave us a very clear insight into his philosophy and also into the sort of tactics which he employs in his dealings with the local whites.

Jones told us that his daughter had been appointed as a supervisor of Negro education in a county of the state. He said that people asked him how it happened that she got the position and he stated that he replied, "She just got it." In doing so, however, and in repeating this statement for our edification Jones made it very clear that she had gotten it as a result of his standing with the "people who count."

Jones at first talked to us exclusively about the Fair. He showed a very strong streak of revengefulness towards those who he indicated had in the early years of the Fair tried to steal it from him or obstruct its operation. He indicated that those were the smart, educated group of Negroes who resented his initiative in getting the Fair started.

In handing me the numerous letters, Jones handed over one that he did not intend for us to see and was rather chagrined later on in the interview when he referred to a letter and admitted that he wouldn't show us that letter, stating as he stated on several occasions that it was necessary to "skip over some of the road because a man does not tell all that he knows." The letter in question was a letter written to Mr. —— a copy of which was sent by the mayor to Jones. This letter apparently had to do with a request that had been submitted asking for a floor to be put in the Negro Fair building, toilet facilities, and heat. The letter promised that a floor would be given. It stated, however, that toilet facilities were available at some distance from the building and could be used conveniently enough and flatly rejected the request for heat. I asked Jones if the floor had been obtained as promised. He said no it had not been and seemed somewhat at a loss to explain why, and somewhat childishly indicated that the whites this time had "let him down."

Jones stated that the Negro Fair Building is a barn (as described to us today by a Negro) while the whites have a luxurious building for their Fair. It appears that the background for this entire situation is found in the fact that as Jones himself told us, the whites decided that they no longer wanted Negroes to attend the white Fair. This Jones explained, or apologized for the whites for, by stating first that it was troublesome for Negroes and whites to mingle together at this Fair and somewhat dangerous; and secondly that there was not sufficient room on the grounds for the great crowds that would result from Negroes and whites being present. The white Fair closed the night the interview took place and the Negro Fair opened two days later. Jones invited us to visit his Negro Fair the next night and told us that when we come out there we will wonder where all of these "niggers" came from. He repeatedly referred to Negroes either as colored people or as "niggers." He never said "Negroes."

The Fair project started in 1934 and my deduction is that it may not have been Jones's original idea but that he was being used by whites who had already indicated that Negroes were no longer wanted at the white Fair. Jones made it clear throughout that he is the "manager" of the Fair and that the manager runs it entirely, the other officials are just stooges for him. At the end of our interview he wanted to show us the permit that had been issued to him for the Fair opening tomorrow. After a lengthy search he found it folded up in one of his pockets and displayed it to us stating, "You see it is not transferrable; nobody can use it but *me*."

We asked Jones why he put forth all of this effort for Negroes who fought him and did not appreciate it without getting anything out of it himself. He said at first that some Negroes do appreciate it and secondly that though the manager of the white Fair gets a finer turn for himself because the white Fair draws large crowds and charges an admission fee of thirty-five cents, the Negro fair [manager] gets no returns because the admission is free and the only source of income is that from the concessions. He never did flatly state, however, that he gets no return from the operation of the Fair. He proceeded to outline for us, in a rather vague way, the large number of petty expenditures which would be involved in the conduct of the Fair. He always came back to the statement made early in the interview, however, that he had white friends who stood behind him on these ventures and that he didn't have to worry. He told about how when the Fair in 1934 failed to draw Negroes (this was the Fair about which he wrote the apologetic letter to the white press) a loss of $500.00 was incurred and that "white friends" of his stood by him and saw to it that he did not have to "take the rap." This 1934 Fair was not a separate Negro Fair. Negroes had not been admitted to the white fair. Jones prevailed upon the white manager to continue the Fair after the date of closing so that Negroes might come, assuring the white manager that large numbers of Negroes would come. However, instead of this, just a few Negroes struggled out, most of whom just stood around.

Most of those, said Jones, were children, and he condemned the Negro group for not coming out and taking the children in, especially in view of the fact that "white people had gone to all this trouble" to make it possible for Negroes to attend the Fair. Jones definitely had it in for the local, educated Negroes, who he said were trying to put something over on him, and who would not stand behind him on it. He constantly stated, however, that he would not give up, that he knew that he could put it over on them and that the Fair would go on. In one instance he told of how he would walk down the street after this initial fiasco greeting these very people who had let him down very cordially but keeping it in mind that "I had a six gun and I only shot one bullet." He explained to us that this meant that if they wanted to shoot it out with him on this issue he was more than willing to do so and that he knew that if the colored press would freeze him out on it he could always depend upon the white press and his white friends to carry him through.

Jones referred to the fact the he was making an effort to get recreational facilities for Negroes but that as usual the educated Negroes had crossed him up. As Jones put it, if other Negroes had not crossed him up on the recreation building, "I would have had it. The white folks had promised it to me but they fell out with it when so many Negroes wrote them letters. I know I could have gotten it, however, but when they all interfered I let it drop." He said also that some of the Negroes who crossed him up were putting in a demand that new facilities for schools be provided first. He said they didn't understand that there were two boards, one handling school matters and another handling recreational matters. He said he could not make requests for both of these things at once. He knew he could get the recreation building and thought that ought to be gotten before they went on to tackle the school question.

Jones told us of how he had visited Washington, not to work, but with his expenses paid. He said that he went into the Capitol and walked into the office of his Congressman who came out and shook his hand and sat down and talked with him. He said that also the man who is the reception officer for dignitaries in Washington, as Jones put it, "the man who received the King and Queen," met him and asked him to have a drink with him while he was in Washington. Of all of this he was extremely proud.

He handed us a heavy green card with the name "Mr. Samuel Jones" printed in large black-face type and under it "Manager Colored Agricultural Industrial Educational Fair Association of Seaport County" with his address on it. Said when he presented this card the Congressman came out, met him cordially and shook his hand. (My own conviction is that Mr. Jones never presents that card to his "good white friends.")

It was when we began to question Jones about what he thought of the N.A.A.C.P. that he really came out with his philosophy for the Negro. He never called any names directly but made it clear to whom he was referring. He entered into a series of sermons each of which had a definite point. One of them, for example, took as its theme that you've got to know how to approach these men. He started out by saying that the law of Washington is different from the law of his State, that Alabama has a different law, Georgia has a different law, Maryland has a different law. Then he pointed out that if a ship goes to sea it has got to have a pilot who knows how to steer it through the channels and keep it off the rocks. His point was, as he stated, that a man might be a good doctor and know all about his profession and still not be a good leader. He was clearly referring to Dr. —— who is the head of the local N.A.A.C.P. He made a similar reference to a preacher who was referring to Rev. —— who is active in the N.A.A.C.P. and spoke for it in the mass meeting this afternoon. He never did wholly commit himself on the N.A.A.C.P. except to say that he had paid his dollar, though he admitted that he seldom got to meetings of it. He stated that he thought (and used the past tense) that N.A.A.C.P. was a good organization and that it ought to be supported, but stated it in such a way and with intimated qualifications as to indicate that there were many doubts in his mind about it. His philosophy is definitely a power philosophy and he indicates that it was his feeling that the people who are leading the N.A.A.C.P. today have no power or, as Dr. Myrdal says, have no sense for power.

His economic philosophy operates entirely within the framework of the highest bracket of a capitalist structure. He thinks only in terms of big railroads, industries, large factories, big land-holdings, big banks, etc., and thinks that the Negro should emulate the white man in those things. He stated, for example, that since the white man has all of these things the Negro is compelled to deal with him on the white man's terms. The way he put it was this: he asked a question, a rhetorical question. He said, if you are anxious to eat a meal with a man you don't come out and criticize him bitterly, denounce him, and then expect to eat with him. Nor, he said, if you are going to ask a man for a job you don't go around telling everybody how bad a man he is, how vicious, and how unkind and still expect to get the job. Summed up, apparently what

Jones meant to say was that one should take the ideas of the man whose bread one is eating.

Jones gave a very dynamic description of his concept of society and the Negro's relation to it. This revolved about a vivid description of the "turning of the wheel" or the man who turns the wheel. It was dynamic industry, big industry all the way through. The man turns the wheel, he said, the farmer turns the wheel, the banker turns the wheel and so on, and in this respect he pointed out that the Negro is today much less needed in the turning of this industrial wheel than formerly. He pointed out that the Negro today must depend upon the whites for his living and that whites have no longer the same need for Negro workers as formerly. He described how whites now occupy jobs that were formerly held only by Negroes, such as waiters, bellhops, and elevator operators. When questioned on this, however, he did admit that whites employed Negroes because Negroes could often be employed more cheaply and then added, very significantly, that really the rich white man fears the poor white because, said Jones, the poor white worker will strike, and the presence of the Negro worker in the South does protect the white rich man or employer against the threat of the white man's strike. The Negro and the poor white, said Jones, will never come together. The only chance for the Negro is if he sticks with the employer. The poor white, said Jones, hates the Negro even more than does the rich white. Jones explained how foolish it is for the Negroes to be criticizing the whites because they keep them on a lower social level. He took the Society of Society Hall as an example and stated how these people came with their diamonds and dresses that cost $500 or $1,000 and that there wasn't a Negro in Seaport who could afford to go to such an affair. This, he said, should be left as a dead issue and the Negro should strive to make the most of his situation.

Jones on more than one occasion indicated the sort of special privilege that he has. He boasted of the fact that he could take Myrdal and me into the white fair and that had we been here or had he known we were here he would have taken us into the fair. When I asked him if I could get into the fair if I went there alone, he just laughed and said "well you ought to know what you can do." When I asked him if other Negroes can go to the white fair he gave a similar answer. He also boasted of the fact that he has gone and has taken friends of his into the —— theatre (which is the Federal Art Project that was leased by the city to a local art group and from which Negroes are excluded). When I asked him if other Negroes can go he said "every Negro ought to know what he is and what he can do" and, he said, "maybe I don't know what I am." He said, "I think I am a colored man but maybe I don't know what I am" and he chuckled vigorously. The whole thing was very humorous to him.

He said that there is so much prejudice between Negroes themselves that the white man can come in with his prejudice and wipe the Negro out. He did say, however, that the local color-caste situation was no longer serious and that he dealt with all groups.

When we got ready to leave, Jones was much concerned to determine what we thought of him and asked us point-blank questions as to just what we did think of him, and especially who had sent us to him and when Myrdal told him that ——, the white editor of a local paper, had sent him to him, then Jones wanted to know what —— thought of him. As Myrdal describes it, Jones's question was put with a sort of dramatic, tragic, seriousness, an almost indescribable questioning in his eyes and a tremendous amount of self-consciousness. Jones's entire philosophical exposition was confused and rambling but we think that this mixture of confusion and emotion was much more deliberate, much more an expression of his technique of evasion and innuendo and indirection than of actual intellectual confusion in his own mind. He was constantly self-possessed, extremely conscious of the fact of his power and happy that he carried on this confusion and was able to make these clever evasions.

Jones raised the question as to whether we know why the Negro banks had failed when Myrdal tried to make a defense of the Negro banks and to explain that they might loan money to churches, schools, etc. Jones pointed out how unsound a basis this would be and gave a vivid description of banks in terms of huge credit, large money turnovers and so on. Then when Myrdal facetiously stated "well perhaps then it would be best for the Negro banks to loan the Negroes' money to the white banks which would have opportunities for these huge investments" Jones showed his first really vigorous happiness by jumping up and childishly, gleefully pointing his pudgy finger at Myrdal, and saying "see, see, you ended up right with me. You've come to my point at last."

Jones said he was very sorry that we couldn't see the white fair and then go and see the Negro fair because in the white fair we would see all the wonderful exhibits and in the Negro fair we would see much less. But, he pointed out, this was especially unfortunate in view of the fact that the white people don't make all of these things they exhibit in their fair but the colored people make them for them, and if they can make them for the white people they ought to be able to make them for themselves.

Jones is a member of the local Interracial Commission but was non-committal on it in general. About all we could get out of him concerning it was that there are some "fine white people" on it. It was often very difficult to understand Jones because of his dialect which was very thick. He made the usual errors of "I has," etc., but the lack of endings on his words, the use of "d's" for "th's" and so on was very noticeable. Jones really employed two levels of speech. One was for ordinary discussion in a very quiet and somewhat reticent way and the other was when he put on what we called the "rousements" and assumed the role of a typical rabble-rousing Baptist preacher. In these moments he became much more lucid and lighted up all over in his attempts to convince us. He did not lose control of himself in this speaking, however, because in his statements he always dealt with generalities which could not be used against him. He did not react at all when Myrdal asked if the Negroes couldn't revolt and kill off all the whites.

Myrdal and I went out to the Negro County Fair Grounds the next evening. There was a large crowd of Negroes on hand and we soon discovered that the so-called Fair is almost entirely devoted to white concessions. It is a typical carnival. Soon after entering the grounds (there was no admission fee), we ran into Jones himself. He proceeded to escort us about. As we walked along he resumed preaching to us where he had left off the night before. He said, "I knows how to keep peace between the races."

Just in front of the Negro agricultural building we ran into a white police sergeant to whom Jones introduced us. The officer was asked by Myrdal, "What are you going to do in order to control the Negroes and keep them in their place after the old men like Jones have gone." The officer was not able to reply before Jones interposed by stating that he was sure that there would be a successor to him who would be even better at keeping peace between the races than he is. But the police officer denied this by saying that Jones is "indispensable." He said, "I don't know what we will do when Jones is gone. There will be nobody left to help us with the Negroes then." The officer proudly explained that Jones can go anywhere he pleases in Seaport: to the white Fair, to the Theatre, etc., and then when Myrdal asked if that would include restaurants, the officer said, "Yes he can go into restaurants, too, if he goes in on business."

Jones took us into the Negro Fair building, and we discovered that there was practically nothing at all in the barn-like structure with a sawdust floor. Jones apologized for the situation by explaining that the Negro farmers had not yet had time to get their exhibits in. While talking to us in this building Jones exhibited a very vicious streak. He stated to me that he let a question go by that I asked him last night but that he wanted to answer it now. The question was why he continued to work with this project after the Negroes had rebuffed him. He said to me, "haven't you ever entered a campaign and lost and then come back knowing that you had the necessary support to win? That's how I feel about this." He then got *hard* and said "I told the Negroes they had better line hands with me because if you don't I'm going to make things hard for you." I remarked that this is quite the same thing that Hitler told Czecho-Slovakia and when Myrdal explained to Jones what I meant by that, Jones chuckled with glee and exclaimed "Yah, that's right."

Jones said that the country Negroes were satisfied with the sawdust floor in the Negro building but that the city Negroes protested about it.

Jones wouldn't have his picture taken at the concession photographers because "I am head of all this. I brought all this here and I don't want to be seen having my picture taken."

Myrdal asked Jones what he would do if one of the white concessionaires got mad, insulted him, etc. Jones replied, "I would tell him to go." Then we asked, "well suppose he is still insulting and refuses to go?" Jones said, "in that case I would call on my lawyer Mr. —— of 'Blank, Blank & Blank' and he'll go all right. When I say go!" he said, "they go." Power was exuding from him as he said it and he was talking in power terms.

Myrdal went in to see the fat white lady on display in one of the concessions. Before Myrdal went in Jones had been boasting to us again about how he "headed up all this." When Myrdal came out he feigned shock to Jones and stated that it seemed to him a very dangerous thing to have a white lady on display half nude before these gaping Negroes. "What will the white population think about this," said Myrdal. Jones, who had been talking to me about using my influence to get Myrdal to obtain money for Jones from the Carnegie Corporation for the building of a floor in the agricultural exhibit, became greatly disturbed. He immediately assumed an extremely worried expression. He got down off of his high horse and began to tell us, "I'm not the head of this show, the Chief of Police looks after this. The Chief of Police and the Sergeant have been looking out for this," he said. Then he entered into a bitter tirade against the poor white man who was responsible for the display of the white fat lady; assuring us that this white man ought to be punished because he was "destroying his race." Myrdal led him on by assuring him that he is only friendly to him and would want only to protect him against any possibility of mis-understanding by local whites. Myrdal explained that some whites might get hold of this and put it in the local press; that Jones was running a show out at the Fair grounds in which a nude white woman was on display before the Negroes. We suggested that maybe we ought to speak to the Police about it, and finally Jones almost childishly agreed and asked Myrdal if he couldn't go and find the Sergeant and tell him about it. These races must be kept apart, said Jones. We found the sergeant and Myrdal told him the situation. The sergeant explained that the woman was not nude otherwise they would have stopped it. She had on enough, he said. Then Myrdal explained and said, well, he feared that his friend Jones might be misunderstood and that the matter might get into the white press. "No fear of that," said the sergeant. "That sort of thing would never get into the papers. We would stop that because we look out for Jones." This relieved and pleased Jones mightily and he agreed with us that it was very profitable to have "friends at the top."

Preen, a Negro social worker of Seaport, says that Jones is considered as an "Uncle Tom" by the Negro population of the city. He said further that it is well-known that Jones plays the role of stool pigeon on Negro meetings, that is, whatever happens at the meetings, Jones takes back to his boss. He states further that Jones is against any project unless that project goes through him. He said it was for this reason that Jones stopped the playground which Preen was making an effort to get but that Jones offered him $75 per month if he would work for him on the playground project. Preen says, however, that the Negroes have to recognize that they must use Jones because of the value of his contact with the rich, responsible whites in the community. Jones knows them from his role in the kitchen and is able to reach them when other Negroes cannot do so. He cited one instance in connection with the group, the administrative authorities in charge of recreational facilities. He said Negroes had been attempting to reach these individuals for a long time but could not do so. But Jones was able to reach them immediately. Preen added further that Jones actually tells the teachers what they must do and threatens them with the loss of their jobs if they do not do so.

An official of the local Interracial Commission spoke of Jones as a great fellow and tells how he comes to the Commission's meetings and keeps them entertained. She spoke of him as the savior of an important white family for which he had worked for years. She said the family suffered great misfortune and it was Jones who kept it together.

Dr. McFall, Sr. says that this carnival racket in connection with alleged "county fairs" is purely and simply a racket since it is not necessary for carnivals to take out State licenses if they are connected with what are called "county fairs." He says that Compton, who runs the white fair, has a number of these subsidiary fairs from which he levies tributes due to the return gotten from the concessions. He says that Compton really runs this Negro fair and that he simply pays off Jones in small amounts. The Police got paid off also he states. McFall admitted, however, that Jones had done one or two good things in the community, mentioning his getting the Negro farmers admitted to the Atlantic-Distributors Company, a wholesale market, as one such incident. McFall states that Negroes have never been admitted to the white fair.

The big Negro political leader is more often than not the self-made, not too well educated man who has pushed his way up from the ranks. He has usually had to pull a good many strings to reach the top and is constantly subject to sniping by his aspiring rivals who themselves often have white support. In most cases the big Negro politician has some white backer, some influential white person who has one motive or another in keeping check on Negroes—most frequently it is to control the Negro's voting. He plays the game of politics for all it is worth, and because of the strategic importance of the Negro vote, the Negro political leader who is at all known can easily make the white political bosses stand up and take notice. But these leaders can seldom be independent—there are too many ways in which the white political bosses can snuff out the influence of any Negro politician who refuses to "play ball" with the real powers that be.

Robert R. "Bob" Church is the most important individual to emerge on the Negro side of the Memphis political situation. Educated at Oberlin. Entered politics in 1912 when he successfully campaigned for membership on the Tennessee Republican delegation to the National Convention. Since 1912 he has continued as a delegate to conventions and has steadily grown in political stature, so that today he is an outstanding national Negro politician in the Republican party. Has kept up a running fight to maintain his position against the attacks of the "lily-white" movement. This in itself is an index to his political shrewdness. He is one of the rare Negro politicians who understands the importance of keeping quiet, remaining outside the limelight, of accepting no personal political jobs as pay for political aid and of pulling political strings from the shadows of the side lines. Has never bought political office, but has been content to remain a representative of the Republican State Committee and a delegate to the national conventions. Has exercised far more influence on national politics than on the political situation of the home town. This is due to the fact that during the twenties there were Republican national administrations, while the Tennessee senators were Democrats. Thus, the patronage was placed in the hands of Church, leader of the Republican forces. Boss Crump had the local Memphis situation under lock and key. His power in national politics was greatest after Harding's election, when Church was placed in charge of all Negro parentage. His power has waned since that time, but he managed to hold to the federal patronage dispensation in the state until the Democratic victory in 1932. As patronage boss for Tennessee he was able to pick the Postmasters of Memphis and, of course, held great sway over them. Thus, he was able not only to appoint numerous Negroes as special delivery boys, but also to protect the jobs of a large number of Negro mail carriers. He could combat discrimination in appointments, and though he was unable to have Negroes appointed as clerks, he did his job well as protector of Negro mail carriers. This was his chief local accomplishment. Since 1932 he has lost his strategic position, and Negro postal employees have felt the loss keenly. Locally he has been quite unimportant politically. Extent of power has been the squashing of traffic tickets and a few appointments of school teachers. In 1938 he opposed Crump's choice for Governor on the quiet, because of increased brutality of Memphis police toward Negroes. As a result, Crump had city officials push Church for overdue taxes, which he was unable to pay. Much of his real estate was sold at tax sale, and with it went his last bit of local power.

* * * *

Negro politician and Republican State Central Committee Chairman. Born in Mississippi. Thirteen years old before he could read and write. Walked fourteen miles a day to and from school, two months a year for seven years. Attended Rust College, getting A.B. in 1892. Graduated from Illinois Medical College in 1897 and practiced medicine for fifteen years. Then went to Illinois Law School, graduating in 1914. Post-graduate work at Michigan. Then entered practice in 1916. During legal practice has had several outstanding cases. Shrewd Republican politician who has fought the lily-whites in Mississippi with appreciable success.

* * * *

An aide of "Bob" Church's in Memphis who exercises the most political power among Negroes in Memphis. Achieved his position mostly through a glib tongue and the ability to straddle many political fences at one time. Although a great admirer of Church, he has held on to dubious friendship of Crump, even during Crump's political assault on Church. Has been able to get city to build a wooden football stadium for Negroes, to build two swimming pools and to erect Randy's Park. He says:

> For the long-term view I believe that the Negro problem will be served by the growth of class consciousness among the southern white masses. This will remove the necessity of demanding rights on the basis of race or color and will place our struggle on the plane of class interest.

So far he has done none of this proposed propagandizing himself.

* * * *

A Negro professional bondswoman is described as the real Negro political leader in a western city who tells all the Negro leaders and would-be leaders when and where to jump. She has power over those on the legitimate and illegitimate side, including a great A.M.E. minister. Also runs Father Divine's local Mission. Unassuming, almost anonymous worker. Even the Mayor considers her as of the utmost value to him. Not educated, but really sincere. With the lower classes and very well thought of. Wields a part of the Mexican as well as the Negro vote. The old heads in the city are accused of sabotaging the work of the youngsters, particularly out-of-town youngsters, i.e., those not born in the town. The bondswoman (already discussed) makes certain demands of a candidate before she supports him. Usually this is what she considers a just portion of the city's patronage for her following. As a rule she supports the Democratic party, but this is not a binding allegiance. She is practical, however, and charges 5% on her bonds, with a minimum of $11.00 from whites and $6 from Negroes. She gets a pay-off if she secures a job for anybody. She insists that she is neither a "fixer" nor a "stool pigeon."

* * * *

Barber—in Tennessee City. Born in very poor circumstances, but early developed a remarkable facility for oratory. Worked as barber and was one of the first Negroes in A.F. of L. local. One time organizer for A.F. of L. Quite a figure in the fraternal world. Much sought after by local Negro and white political heelers. Ambitious. Has many "big shot" enemies. Waged campaign against a rival political leader taking more than his share of the spoils. When Republicans adopted "lily-white" policy and put their affairs in the hands of whites, he saw the "handwriting on the wall," and launched a county Democratic League, and proceeded to negotiate for the admittance of Negroes to the Democratic primaries. Staunch supporter of C.I.O. He is the patron of the younger group of "liberal" leaders who are in the making and considers himself a sort of senior statesman to the young idealists and radicals. One informant says of him:

> He was too far ahead and too smart to be a leader in the old school of political ward heelers: he is a little too old and not quite smart enough to be knighted with the "leadership of the youthful group of socially conscious activists."

It is doubtless of unusual significance that a Negro political leader in Texas can draw on the war chest of the Democratic Party, as claimed by the Texas Negro who was Chairman of the Garner-for-President Campaign among Negroes. He says:

> I was born in 1899 in Houston, Texas. I graduated from Booker Washington High School in 1917. I worked as a filler on the Southern Pacific Railroad until 1928. From 1928 to 1932 I worked as advertising man on the *Houston Defender.* I entered politics as a professional in 1932 and organized a local branch of the Young Negro Civic Club. I am General Chairman of that organization. Our Harris Young Negro Civic Club has the charter from William J. Thompkins, director of the National Colored Democratic Association. I was campaign manager for Roosevelt in 1932 and 1938 among Negroes for the State of Texas.
>
> I was appointed Goodwill Ambassador for the State of Texas during the Texas Centennial Exposition.
>
> At the present time I am the National Negro Campaign Manager of the Garner-for-President movement.
>
> In all my political activities I have received funds from the regular party slush fund just like the white political workers have.

It is generally true in Kansas City, Missouri, that the Negro politicians place an undue amount of stress on national politics every four years, but are most apathetic and uninformed on local issues, i.e., on ward, city and county politics. Also, the old-line political leaders are opportunistic and selfish, with an abhorrence for collective work. This is substantiated by what happened in the February 1940 city elections. An amendment to the city charter offered a fine opportunity for Negroes to improve their political status by voting for a one-chamber aldermanic form of government in lieu of the present bureaucratic eight-member council. This would have given an opportunity for Negroes to have representation in city government. But the Negro political leadership was asleep, and the amendment was defeated with a very small total vote being cast.

Physician. "Bronze Mayor" of an important city in Tennessee. Got title through poll conducted by a Negro paper. The intention was to select a Negro spokesman and race representative for Negroes of town. Reputed that he bought this election because he has been the editor's chief sponsor. Very unsavory record. Called dishonest, crooked, demagogic, seeker of white patronage for own advancement, betrayer of Negro's confidence. Though a member of N.A.A.C.P., when that organization campaigned to get Negroes admitted to University of Tennessee, he came out with open letter to President of University, representing that "the better class [of] thinking Negroes" are opposed to the fight and proposed that a graduate extension be added to the Negro Knoxville College as a substitute. A white professor at University of Tennessee characterized him as a "reactionary opportunist." Weapon of influence is wealth which he has accumulated by exploiting the poor-class Negroes. Has little influence or following among Negroes, but has extensive personal relations with white politicians and office holders who accept him as the Negro leader. Strict opportunist, pledging Negro votes to highest bidder.

* * * *

Houston has a "Bronze Mayor" who does nothing for the people. Some Negroes have awakened to the fact that "this Bronze Mayor business is nothing but a racket."

The *Atlanta World* of October 5, 1932, reports that Carter Woodson, eminent Negro historian, exposed a recent interview with a representative of the Republican machine. He was told that the Republican machine had been trying to get rid of its Negro politicians by sending them to jail for selling Federal positions, because they (the colored politicians) were more expensive than the lily-whites. The Negroes, according to Woodson's informer, do not always stay bought after their initial payment. They must be followed up with "persuasive gifts"—up through the convention. This position is explained by the fact that whereas the white politicians are in on the payoff from year to year—as officeholders; the Negro's chance comes once in a four-year period—naturally the Negro attempts to make hay while the sun shines.

Woodson is unstinting in his vitriolic attack upon the Negro politicians, and admonishes the Negro public that instead of "wining and

dining them, we should exile them." This type of politician is characterized by Woodson as an "imbecile," and "spineless, job-seeking, empty-
honor hunting, bread-and-butter politicians who have disgraced us in
the United States."

"And There Stood the One Hundred," an article in the *Pittsburgh Courier* of October 8, 1932, constitutes an unusually scathing indictment of a group of Negro Republican leaders. Robert L. Vann, owner and editor of the paper, gives vent to his
utter disgust at the spectacle of some 150 Negroes (so-called leaders) who visited
Hoover at the White House and repledged their loyalty to the G.O.P. Vann characterized the incident as the "Black Saturday of the Century," and openly labeled Emmett J. Scott, J. Finley Wilson, John R. Hawkins, et al., as the most
spineless individuals he has ever had the displeasure of knowing. Vann even
went to the extent of declaring that those "leaders" represented no one but
themselves and their individual pocket-books. Since then, editor Vann has been
a Roosevelt supporter, a New Deal office holder, switched back to the Republican fold and is now in support of Wilkie.

Some of the Negro leadership is either of the "stool pigeon" variety,
readily, almost eagerly "sells out" Negro causes for a price, or for reasons of currying white favor or carrying on a personal vendetta wilfully
sabotages Negro organizations and betterment activities.

More than a few Negroes in southern communities complain of the
many Negro "stools" who tell the whites of the Negro organization
plans as soon as they learn of them.

Close to the Negro editor of a Negro weekly in Florida is an insurance executive
who writes a column in the weekly. Oily-tongued diplomat who tried to sell out
the Negro vote of Tampa for $1500. Heartily disliked by most of the town's Ne-
groes. At nearly every organization meeting he is denounced.

Yet, for the leader, among Negroes as among whites, critical comment
in the press is better than none at all, for no leader is so forlorn than the
one whom the followers have forgotten even to condemn.

Attorney. Editor of a Negro weekly in Tennessee. Talks and looks like a "con"
man. Bitterly opposed to N.A.A.C.P. investigation of discrimination in T.V.A.
Consistently scuttled and slandered all attempts at elevating an honest Negro
leadership or effective organization among Negroes. Makes living as lawyer and

through donations for political intrigues. Completely degenerate and immoral character.

* * * *

One young Negro grocer of a Virginia town, who is a ward leader, claims that he was offered a completely financed course in a graduate school, plus a new wardrobe, if he would deliver 200 votes. He claims that he refused. He did not reveal what was offered by the other side which he supported.

* * * *

A local dentist is the same town's N.A.A.C.P. head and treasurer of local Elk's lodge. Good personality, but has reputation for having "sold out" more than a few times. Accused of going to front on race issues only when his organization has chance to profit thereby.

* * * *

There is in same community a Negro probation officer who is somewhat of a leader. His job makes him more feared than respected. Most people think he has "sold out" on more than one occasion.

* * * *

One of the Negro members of an active civic group in a Georgia coastal town was placed in charge of skilled Negro workers in a C.W.A. project and within 30 days he got over 100 men [to] work at $1.00 per hour. He, himself an electrical contractor, was offered a job (as a bribe) which he refused. However the leaders of this Committee were getting jobs as plums. The group demanded a recreational center, and the city gave one. One of the foremost members of the committee was made director of the Recreational Center—he runs concessions, dances, etc. and gets a rake-off. After he got this break he quieted down on the Negro question.

* * * *

In an election of a board of assessors a few years ago—10 men to be elected—a primary was not held. At that time about 600 Negro votes could be used, and would have meant election of men receiving the Negro vote. A group of Negro leaders representing this vote held a census and selected a slate, extending a complimentary vote to the men selected. Three men prominent in the Democratic party were to be given unqualified, complimentary support. Others were to be questioned as to attitude toward assessment of Negro property. There ha[ve] been some abuses in the assessment of Negro properties. One of the members of this Negro caucus decided to support a slate other than the one selected by the caucus, for $25 from a white group.

* * * *

A Negro minister in a North Carolina town corrals the votes of his race for small land cuts.

* * * *

Another minister in the same town respects the things influential whites have done for the Negroes, like building them hospitals, Y.M.C.A., etc., emphasizes the "rational" handling of things. Chairman of local interracial committee who likes to refer to his "friends," who are white. Awed by financial strength of these "friends." One citizen says of this minister "Rev. —— is no good; he'll sell us all out for a pat on the back from the white man."

The Negro leader, as all leaders, finds it difficult to differentiate between serving his personal interests and those of his group.

Negro bondsman and insurance man of Tenn. urban community with valuable real estate holdings which he rents mostly to whites. Considerably wealthy and has all the ego of a self-made man. Attempts to straddle the underworld and the respectable element at the same time. Started up the ladder as ice man, and was successively contractor, bondsman, policy racketeer and real estate owner. Activities as a bondsman paved way for his political and personal influence. Usually gets what he wants. Sometimes his personal desires benefit Negroes as a whole, but more often than not his political influence is used to foster his own personal interests. He would not hesitate to use his influence against the general race interests if the interests of the race conflicted with his personal needs. Alleged to have opposed Negro policemen secretly because Negro policemen would have interfered with his policy racket.

* * * *

An effort was made to start a civic club among Negroes in Covington, Georgia, not long ago. The movement was started by a young Negro who had just succeeded another Negro as the manager of a local Negro insurance agency. The police broke up the initial meeting, and the movement was abandoned. It is alleged that the replaced Negro manager had reported the intention of the Negro community to organize the civic club to the police, because when the members arrived at the church for their first meeting the police were there and advised them to go home stating that they did not need to participate in an activity of that kind.

* * * *

One Tennessean states: "I feel that Negroes should have compact independent political organization headed by men who would not 'sell out.' I think the leadership should come from the intelligentsia, but [should] be an unselfish type: freed from ambitions for personal aggrandizement. Negroes have been so often exploited by selfish leaders until the masses have become apathetic to their proclamations."

The Negro people in the mass are indeed often justifiably suspicious of their leadership, in view of the fact that it has so frequently betrayed them for small stakes.

White people, so a Birmingham leader believes, should never be told what Negroes are attempting to do politically. Pointing to a leaflet issued by a local organization announcing a mass meeting, in reference to a section reading:

> We can continue our efforts to win the right to vote so that our voices will be heard by the City Council and elected officials. That (he said) is what we want. But don't let them know it. They'll just close up everything tighter than before after this. We won't be able to get anything through.

He apparently meant that fewer Negroes would be registered by the Board as a result of this statement of aims by the organization. (Interview with a Negro dentist, Birmingham, Alabama, May 1940; Edward Strong's Birmingham memorandum.)

Negro political leaders on the whole on the local scene, he believes, have done nothing and are all for sale. To corroborate this statement he mentioned a "selling out" of Negroes some twenty-five years ago by the same men who are now recognized as among the older respected leadership. These men, he said, had charge of being impartial; they followed the policies of the whites, registering only Negroes of a certain class, turning away the majority, and accepting pay. These policies are continued by the leadership at the present.

A resident of Tuscaloosa spoke of a "fighting" Negro who was forced out of town:

> He was just indiscreet. He would talk poor white and Negro unity to poor whites who came into his store—they would agree and then go out and tell on him and call him a Communist. That's why he was chased away from here. He worked alone and there was no organization behind him.

The complaint is almost universal that the local Negro leadership is so venal and corrupt, so cheaply bought. There are, in every Negro community, a number of known and established hirelings, who do the bidding of their white paymasters—in politics, in labor relations, in the press, and even in education. It is common to hear Negroes despair of much future for the race unless a new honest, incorruptible, self-sacrificing leadership develops.

Generally the local Negro leadership is so poor that as one Negro citizen says: "What can be done about it? We got to have leadership. Somebody has got to come forward who knows the score and has the talent of persuasion and expose the bastards for what they are: lousy sewer rats, bloated with the blood of their own people. Before we can get to the real white ruling-class enemy, we've got to first back our way through a swarm of their black hirelings in our own group."

The deliberately opportunistic Negro leader, who sets about "getting ahead," if not too limited by personal principle, can often cut quite a figure for himself. For example, there is the Tennessee Negro leader who:

came from Georgia in 1934 with one suit, an old automobile, and a thorough knowledge of the numbers game. Started numbers and amassed a couple of hundred thousand dollars. Owns many cars, hotel, dining room, theatre, filling station, about two blocks of real estate and luxurious apartment. Thirty-five or forty years old. Former student at Morehouse. Invested $10,000 in a mayoralty campaign. On election day put his fleet of cars at mayor's disposal. Politics is instrument for safeguarding his racket from interference from law enforcement agencies. Makes no pretense of using his power in interest of race. In 1938 he opposed gubernatorial candidate who won election and then ordered a clean-up. He was arrested, given ninety days in jail. He got bitter and thought he had been double-crossed by those to whom he had given large sums of money, so he smeared many prominent officials during his trial. Served month of term and gave $1,000 bribe. Political power now overrated.

* * * *

Or there is the colorful "Gooseneck Bill" McDonald of Texas politics who allegedly made over a hundred thousand dollars a year as a professional politician, selling his patronage privileges to the highest bidder. As national Republican Committeeman from Texas about 25 years ago he handled much of the political patronage. Notwithstanding the authority he wielded in the state, no Negroes were ever appointed to any political position, not even in the postal service. Always sold his appointments and would say to Negro job seekers, "Boy, you can't pay the price I'm asking." All he was concerned with was how much he could make his national committee-manship pay in dividends. He had no social or racial scruples about seeking privileges for his people. Much of his wealth was accumulated at the expense of a rather naive white millionaire from New York who went to Texas with the intention of becoming a powerful political figure in that state. He chose McDonald as his political advisor. McDonald was successful, but not so the millionaire play-boy. It is said that when McDonald told his patron that he needed about twenty-five (meaning dollars, of course) in order to go to the State Capitol for a little political pow-wow, the play-boy wrote him a check for $25,000. Now he is president of the only Negro bank in Fort Worth and one of the city's leading citizens.

* * * *

San Antonio's Charlie Bellinger (now deceased) was one of Negro America's most colorful political leaders. Ascendancy as Negro leader came about through his success as a gambler. Made money on saloons when he first went to San Antonio in 1907–1908. Financed campaigns of Democratic candidates in the city, and personally footed the bill for the entire campaign among the Negroes. Contributed to Democratic state machine. In short, he bought power as a secondary aspect of purchasing protection for his gambling enterprises. What the race gained through Bellinger's activities was purely incidental, or rather, accidental. A menace to Negro progress because of the unrepresentative stooges he put in positions of responsibility through his influence in the City Hall. Though hailed as a philanthropist, he left nothing in his will to a single Negro charity. Left estate valued at $180,000, which appraisal was probably underrated by city officials in order to reduce the tax burden.

* * * *

A Negro clerical leader in a North Carolina town is often described as a "scavenger politician." Drunk half the time. Preaches to nearly empty church most of the time, but brags about the number of "niggers" he carries to the polls "all the time." For small handouts he campaigns vigorously, and while being interviewed he called the Mayor on a trivial matter merely to show his political power. Took interviewer to registrar's home in order to show his "friends." People admit he works hard at election time and gets out good number of Negro votes. His attitude: "Hurrah for me. The hell with everybody else."

The Negro ministers quite often have an unsavory reputation as leaders. They are among the most active political leaders in many communities and are not always celebrated for their courage and integrity by any means.

The Negro ministers in San Francisco, for example, are described as usually the henchman for political machines. Their reward might be some money for their churches or some slight share of patronage for their followers, mostly petty jobs. It is alleged that the ministers in Los Angeles are just hired to collect the Negro vote. A well-known businessman in Los Angeles once said that he had a list of Negro ministers to whom he gave money for their Christmas funds each year. He indicated that they were "on call." The ministers don't want to agitate or fight. The Negro ministers in St. Louis are backward and conservative, as a rule. Up to very recently they were, as a group, against trade unions. It is generally thought that they don't care much about the people. The allegation is made that the local Republican Party machine is running them. The ministers have been paid fifty or sixty dollars on more than one occasion by the politicos for their help. A short while ago the industrialists paid the ministers to fight labor unions.

Politics worms its way into all aspects of Negro leadership and organizational life. The organization and its leadership often become labeled as a party wheel horse and [their] usefulness is impaired. For instance:

The local branch of one of the national Negro organizations in St. Louis has degenerated to nothing more than a part of the Republican machine in the city. One of the representatives of the national headquarters of the same organization is described as a rank opportunist, who is even reluctant to speak for any group which cannot afford to pay for Pullman accommodations and tips.

* * * *

A prominent Negro leader of Nashville is in politics for what he can get out of it. Organization is impotent because it is Republican. More knowledge of local politics than any other Negro leader. Is grooming his organization for participation in Democratic primary, and he is subject to get on his feet politically again.

The Negro business man is often too smug and complacent to be an effective leader. The big Negro business men in Savannah, for instance, "just don't give a damn—they look out for themselves only." One observing citizen says, "You give a few Negroes a break, hand them a job, and all problems are solved."

The Negro property owner is motivated by his personal interests. For example, several prominent Negroes of Savannah owned property on unpaved streets and opposed a fight for having the streets paved in those Negro sections—on account of taxes.

The Negro leader is rarely ever economically independent, and even a small-income job is a temptation to him. One Kansas Citian (Missouri) says: "Every Negro who has come into any leadership at all here has jumped to accept a city job and thus automatically had his mouth closed, and his leadership possibilities negated. In the old days the Negro took his political reward by getting protection for his vices: today this is still more or less true."

Young Negro attorney for the Negro insurance company and Negro organizer for Republican Party in Duval County, Florida. Republican Congressional Committeeman. Convinced that since effort to get Negroes right to vote was lost in 1934, the political destiny of Negroes in Florida, and the South in general, lies in his alliance with Republican Party. Energetic, but obviously motivated by "self-interest."

* * * *

The executive secretary of the Jacksonville local of one of the Negro national organizations is a dynamic speaker, really interested in greater effective political participation on the part of Negroes. Makes lightning switches in party affiliations when it is expedient to do so. This puts him in bad odor with many old-line Negro Republicans.

* * * *

Representative of a Negro insurance firm in a North Carolina city and owner of a gas station. Powerful legionnaire, says he "could have had Oxley's job," but did not want it.[25] Quite popular with white legionnaires. Says, "I buss to them and manna falls my way." Negroes distrust him on account of his friendliness with whites. Has become rather inactive politically.

* * * *

Norfolk has a Negro woman leader who is a social worker, head of the Negro Women's Democratic Club. Not very personable, but energetic within her club of 150 women. Believes Negro women should participate more fully in politics. Not very popular among rank and file because it is believed by the masses of Negroes that she, like most of their other "leaders," is riding the administration's "gravy train," rather than politically active because of what the race stands to gain.

There are few Negro leaders who are not suspect immediately [should] they attain any eminence. The racial situation has created a vicious circle in Negro reasoning on leadership and the Negro leader is caught in it.

Director of Girls' Detention Home in a Tennessee city, President of Women's Clubs. Just another out-for-herself sister, who by her ingratiating manner is able to pull the political wool over the eyes of the gullible white politicians and get herself some small plum, or maybe just a $10 bill for voting a hundred head of Negroes.

* * * *

The Y.M.C.A. Secretary in a western city is described as a self-seeking, egotistic, cheap politician, with no interest in the race which does not serve his personal ends.

* * * *

Commander of the Local American Legion in a Tennessee city. Was put on city payroll in 1936, and since that time has been apologist for the city administration. His "job" is visiting doctor to the Negro Old Folks Homes. Also on staff of Negro Medical College. Republican, in national election and delegate to National Republican Convention in 1936. Influence on down-grade. Masses feel that he has been primarily interested in his own personal welfare. When a young Negro boy was murdered in jail recently, he wrote a letter to the Mayor which was released by him as a fake investigation, in an attempt to white-wash the sheriff from any responsibility.

* * * *

Among the leaders often regarded as "handkerchief heads" in a Louisiana town is the head of the local Negro college, who is also a Baptist preacher. His wife draws a salary at the college and he averages about $400 a month from his two commercial enterprises—the college and the Church. He represents the acme of reaction and has a "do-nothing-about-it" philosophy.

* * * *

A young Negro in a Colorado city insists that the present Negro leadership is very poor. He asserts that not a single Negro minister in the city can afford to fight because they are paid off either directly or indirectly. When an A.M.E. preacher had a recent drive for money for his church the mayor had every city employee make a contribution. Although this minister is a brilliant man, he keeps his southern manners. He does not sit down when he talks to white people—men or women. He knows the etiquette of race relations—that is his job. He says all the ministers think about is their jobs and how much they can make them pay. It is alleged that the A.M.E. preacher got $500 personally, plus $5 per day for his workers, to deliver this group. This same minister got his wife a job in the welfare set-up and his daughter in the school system. This daughter got the job over another very competent Negro woman who had it, but was ousted to make room for the preacher's daughter. It is alleged that the minister was a politician in the mid-West before he came West, and was run out of a city for some "dirty work." This cleric is described as a ruthless exploiter, and is said to be gaining unpopularity very rapidly. He masks as a non-partisan politically.

* * * *

It is said that a prominent Negro minister in Los Angeles gets about $50 a month for his political services. A Negro newspaper woman publisher is reputed to receive $100 a week for her newspaper. A Negro physician and an architect, both very prominent citizens, were placed on city commissions as a result of their political activity. The ordinary minister gets something like $100 for an election. The most prominent Negro minister in Los Angeles says, "The Negro Church has had a very great function. It keeps the Negro happy. Let the Negro shout and you have no trouble with him. The church is keeping them quiet, that is a fact. But this time is passing. The young Negro wants something." This same minister admitted that the ministers have controlled the Negro vote and that even now the church is taken into consideration at election time as the only *dependable* Negro vote.

* * * *

A Negro attorney in Houston says of a Houston Negro Democratic leader: "There is nobody he can't go to see. He represents himself to influential and gullible whites as the leader of all the Negroes and gets money from them under the pretense of projects to benefit Negro youth. In 1933 he collected over $200 worth of poll taxes and misappropriated the funds. He would do anything for money. He promotes jobs for Negroes and exacts a heavy toll. Yet, in the eyes of the white Houston he is the outstanding Negro leader."

This same leader was involved in something of a "fleece racket." He organized what he called the Harris County Young Negro Civic Club for the purpose of helping unfortunate Negro boys. Money was collected from several gullible whites and a few Negroes who were taken in by this "promoter's" line. When a prominent white man in Houston mentioned to his shoe-shine man that he was a contributor to the noble cause, the shoe shiner started making inquiries about this help for unfortunate Negroes. He wanted some of it, but alas, the organization was a "phony," no Negro youth had received any benefits—the promoter was the sole beneficiary of his own schemes.

Negro political leaders, who use their positions to protect their rackets, sometimes employ their influence to divert some good to the Negro community, especially with regard to Negro job holding. For example:

The editor of a Negro weekly in Tulsa is something of a politician, and has used his influence for years to protect his rackets. More recently, however (the past 18 months), his public political activities have centered around securing jobs for Negroes and more representation in the city departments. Aggressive, and used his contacts to get things done.

* * * *

It is reported that one of Chicago's most famous policy barons and a few lesser lights in the underworld furnished the funds to keep a W.P.A. project running for Negroes. (Dr. Myrdal's interview with Horace Cayton, Chicago, January 2, 1940)

* * * *

In two of the country's largest cities heavy contribution from the local vice lords precludes an attack upon their rackets by the largest and most influential civic organization leaders and preachers. In fact, more than one organization leader admits that without the support of the Negro underworld barons their organizations could not operate.

It is a very great asset for the Negro leader to have ready access to some influential white. Sometimes the Negro leader worms his way into the good graces of the powerful white leader and from that time on is able to impress the Negro community with the fact that he can "do things through Mr. Charlie." The white "Mr. Charlie" himself often realizes that he is in a position to designate Negro leadership, without being too particular about whom he selects.

Negro politician in Louisville. Has been selling city jobs for years, i.e., street cleaners, firemen, police. He has the ear of the Mayor and the Democratic city machine.

* * * *

One resident of Louisville says: "Our organization is lacking in desirable leadership; all the precinct leaders are appointed from the white Democratic Committee, and they select mostly the less representative Negroes—Negroes who have some following because of their connection with some racket."

* * * *

The Negro Democratic leaders of Louisville are of the old-line ward-heeler type who seek payroll jobs for themselves, and such race interest as they might have is purely a secondary consideration. Since about 1929 all non-elective city jobs have been under civil service, which has eliminated, in a large measure, much of the graft in politics and considerably reduced the importance of the ward heelers and their contact with the neo-underworld.

The old-line politicians are a survival from the halcyon days of Reconstruction. They still think within the scalawag–carpet bagger framework. Politics is to them a matter of horse-trading and votes are a commodity to be sold. They are necessarily Republican since they live only in the past.

Negro superintendent of a building in a North Carolina town. (Only one in town.) Proud of his job and the fact that he has been in politics 30 years. President of Senior Civic Association, he is old-line politician. Only too glad to follow white man's political dictates in return for commendation as a good fellow. Respected in community for his position.

* * * *

Buck Waller. Owner of small meat market. In Durham since 1911. Old-line political leader who listens to the white boss, extends his hand and delivers his people's votes. Has built up large following (300–400) which he has not organized into any political club, but corrals them near election time with the aid of "10 or 11 niggers." "I love money but don't bow to it. I am still recognized downtown as the power and the real father of Negro voting in Durham."

* * * *

A blacksmith and former chairman of Charleston County Republican Club. Strictly "old-line"—"born Republican till I die." Belongs to Tolbert faction and believes Republican Party is sole medium of Negro progress.

* * * *

An A.M.E. minister and an old-line Republican of Charleston. Ran for Congress in 1924. Believes the Republican Party is *the* party for the Negro. Although referred to by the people as a leader, he claims that his being a minister makes it impractical for him to participate in politics.

There are several "would-be" leaders in southern towns to whom politics is largely a personal and partisan thing. The only thing they agree on is—"We hate the Democrats. They don't want us. . . . We got to fight for our rights within the Republican Party."

A Negro attorney in Tulsa is one of the oldest Negro Democrats in the city, in contrast to most of his contemporaries who have swung over to the Democratic Party since the New Deal. As a politician he is purely a mercenary opportunist. He supports a candidate for the sole purpose of reaping a personal reward.

Type 4: Symbolic Leadership

The basis for leadership under this type is the position held by the leader. Influence and authority attach to the post rather than to the individual. For various historical and racial reasons the particular position has come to be regarded in the community as carrying with it a spokesmanship and responsibility for the Negro group. Though the occupant of the position may be a nincompoop, the tradition and prestige of the type persist, and the incompetent, unrepresentative incumbent blunders along under a heavy load of responsibility. The Negro schools of the South afford good examples of this sort of leadership. The white community tends to regard the head of the college or university, the principal of the school, as the titular head of the local Negro population. That the Negro community may hold little but scorn for the particular leader is of no relevance. It may often be true, of course, that the particular occupant of the office, by reason of his conduct and tactics would merit classification under one of the other type categories. It would be rare that a holder of such office would fall within the militant, aggressive Type 1 category, however. It is also true that the distinction between Type 4, the symbolic leadership, and Type 5, the prestige personality, is often difficult if at all possible to discern. The symbolic leadership is itself really a form of prestige leadership in that the holder of the office acquires a prestige which is reflected from the office which he holds. Educational administrators, preachers, lodge leaders, have, by virtue of their positions, an automatic investiture with leadership authority within the minds of both black and white communities.

There is a tendency of the North Carolina whites to accept President Shephard of the North Carolina State College for Negroes and [C. C.] Spaulding, head of the North Carolina Mutual Company, as Negro spokesman, but Negroes are beginning to refuse to petition whites alone—and are sending committees and delegations.

* * * *

Dr. J. E. Shephard. President of the North Carolina College for Negroes. Leadership based on prestige in educational world. Often referred to as "perfect diplomat." Shrewd in handling "big whites" in getting money for school. Interested in advancement of his college. Been in such a long and close relationship with whites that it is virtually impossible for him to push the Negro's cause. Believes in patience and advises: "We must go slowly, *slowly.*"

* * * *

The principal of the Negro high school and elementary school is a Negro leader in Opelousas. Though he has no certificate of attendance from any school, he has been teaching for 33 years. Received his appointment because his father used to work for the Superintendent's father. Negroes were promised a new school, but have not got it. It is believed that the principal advised against the erection of the new school for fear that he would not prove capable of managing a more modern plant.

* * * *

President of an Alabama Negro college could do much for the people should he take an active part in the government of the community. However, he has drawn himself into a shell and confines himself right to the educational field and that alone. He does dabble in some politics on a national scale, but not any that would affect the Negro citizenry of this section. Therefore, all of his efforts have gone for naught so far as the Negro people are concerned.

In the educational field, there have been leaders in Alabama. In more than one instance, leaders in this field could have gotten more recognition for the other members of the race just by speaking up, but in the crucial moment, they have always been known to go into a shell unless something affected them as individuals.

If those so-called leaders had asked for a number of things of government officials they would have been able to help their uncultured, unlettered and uneducated Negro brothers. Take, for instance, the late Dr. A. N. Parker (principal of the then Industrial High School, alleged to be the largest Negro high school in the world). He was a very fine man, but he kept himself in the field of education and thought very little of the affairs of the Negro politically. He could have said one little word that might have meant a lot for the Negro in this community. He did not act, I don't believe, from a selfish point of view; but it was done because his vision was so narrow. He usually followed the same formal routine without venturing to give the Negro a thrust of light. It is my opinion that he did not know that from his actions on the numerous occasions that he was selling the Negro out. Parker was considered a leader by the majority of white and Negro people. Whenever white people thought of the Negro and his progress, they thought of "Butch" Parker as he was known for a number of years.

* * * *

President of a Negro college in Tennessee. Accepted by many whites as spokesman for Negroes though in disrepute with many Negroes. Is Democrat and arch

Mary McLeod Bethune. (Photo by Carl Van Vechten, Carl Van Vechten Papers, Yale Collection of American Literature, Beinecke Rare Book and Manuscripts Library, Yale University)

Negro politician of the state. Prostitutes his political influence for purpose of obtaining state money for development of his school—this is key to every one of his political maneuvers. Academic freedom as alien there as it is in Berlin. Dictatorial personality. Maintains political influence by power he wields over his teachers' votes. Votes his teachers in solid bloc of 300. His job placements do his bidding. Will not hesitate to take position against best interests of race if it will improve his position with the white politicians who might direct some funds to his school. His political opportunism often puts him in tight spots. For instance, when the N.A.A.C.P. exposed Elmer Daves as a K.K.K., and memorialized President Roosevelt against his appointment as a Federal Judge, this man, though a member of the executive board of N.A.A.C.P. supported Daves on orders from a senior white political leader of the state. He drafted a telegram campaign to the President declaring Daves had the hearty endorsement of Tennessee Negroes.

* * * *

Negro woman president of a southern college. Accepted by whites as a very influential Negro leader and ideologist of the Negro group. Had done nothing to establish her prestige except run the school and affect a high degree of culture. At the first Southern Conference for Human Welfare, someone referred to her by her first name and she arose majestically and stated "for the sake of the record I am known as Mrs." It is quite possibly true that she is not an Uncle Tom in the true sense of the term, but it is equally true that many Negroes are very skillful in knowing just what to say and how to say it and when to say it to white folks. They appreciate that there is a certain type of "tolerated impudence" which they can get away with in the presence of whites and give the appearance of being courageous [to] naive Negroes. There is probably something in the thought that people take to this personality *because* she symbolizes the possibilities of Negro escape.

* * * *

A perfect example of the venality of Negro religious racketeers is "Prophet Goins," we will call him. Goins, in a lawyer's office telling dirty jokes on Christ while drinking gin. Bragging about the $14,000 house he bought his wife and how he rides around in a big car "with a nigger chauffeur to drive her while I drink my whiskey." He claims that his church pays him $350 per month and "all I can steal." He gives "readings" at $5.00 per. He exhibited a letter from a prominent government official "endorsing him." He says, "if the —— can recognize me, then all niggers have to." He is glib, ungrammatical, but shrewd. He was dressed in a dark coat and morning trousers.

The following observations of a very prominent Negro churchman are worth recording, not only for their frankness, but because his viewpoints are rather more realistic and progressive than those of the majority of Negro men of the cloth. It is an interesting bit of self-criticism.

From my view point, I would like to say that the Negro minister has not been as progressive along the lines of citizenship as he should have been. Information at my disposal indicates that we have over three hundred Negro ministers in Birmingham and I doubt very seriously whether one-third of this number are voters. There should be a definite program carried on by ministers to influence the people of the various churches to vote but at the present time no such program exists. Very little attention is given by the ministry to elections; here and there, however, you will find a minister who is personally interested in a white friend that he has known for years, stopping in the midst of his Sunday services to speak of him and his great qualities. Nine times out of ten it is a personal affair.

The Negro, since slavery, has been taught the value of white citizenship and the non-value of Negro citizenship. Although the church has done more than any other organization to break this attitude down, there is still plenty of room for improvement. The Negro minister, like the general run of our people, has the inferiority complex when it comes to political matters. He has not become politically conscious in Birmingham and in the South. He does not know the value of the ballot and if he does, he hasn't the courage to fight for it.

Many of the ministers here do not get the real meaning of politics; many of them look upon politics as something brought about by evil-thinking people or that it is a game for the lower strata of society. They seem not to think of politics as being the science of good government, but instead that it is something degrading, brought by unreligious people to achieve their own ends regardless of the cost. I think further that the white propagandists had prayed upon the Negro in such a manner as to keep him out of politics.

All of the achievements of the Negro in Birmingham have already come through the Negro church, but unless the Negro minister makes a contribution politically, the race is doomed.

The Negro minister here has also failed to become labor conscious. The matter of labor is one of the most vital questions that confronts the Negro preacher of today. He seems to think very little as to the attitude which he should take towards developing the Negro people as to their relationship with the various unions of the country. Many of the ministers are afraid to take a stand on account of the handout system on the part of the big corporations. By the handout system I mean that once a year the president of a corporation makes a donation to either the pastor [or] the church and the minister is afraid that he will lose the annual gift which is often times too small to be mentioned. If he were to stop to think that his salary and general upkeep of his church come from the laboring class, he would put more emphasis upon better wages for the laboring people which would mean better families and better preachers.

The Negro people in Birmingham have been kept out of the labor unions until recently when the CIO came here. The CIO offers to the Negro the largest opportunity of any organization in the United States for him to become really unionized and thus increase his general level of living. When our ministry shall have become educated to these facts, I believe that they will enter wholeheartedly the labor unions, and especially the CIO.

The CIO has done more, in my judgment, to better and promote interracial understanding in Birmingham than all of the other organizations combined. In all unions, excepting the CIO, there is discrimination.

I am sorry to say that I am unable to put my hands on any leading white people or white organizations that seem to be interested in interracial movements, excepting the church. But even in the church, an affiliation between the white and Negro ministers has been very scant. In many of the cities of the country, they have interracial alliances, but nothing of the kind is to be found in Birmingham. This accounts, perhaps, more largely for police brutality in Birmingham and in the surrounding areas than anything else. If the Negro and white ministers were to meet once a month together and study the various problems of the city as they relate to race conditions, there would be a better Birmingham. The only real interracial cooperation that is to be found anywhere in Birmingham is in the CIO labor unions. When it comes to such matters as these in Birmingham, Christianity is at a low ebb.

For instance, the Alabama Council of Democratic Clubs (white) recently put out the most calamitous statement that has been made here in recent years against the coming of Congressman Mitchell.[26] As long as such groups exist, interracial goodwill will continue to suffer.

The economic status of the Negro is far too low in Birmingham. We have around 125,000 Negroes in Birmingham, but with few, if any, outstanding Negro business enterprises. The economic status of the Negro will never be what it ought to be in Birmingham until there is a better support of Negro business. The Negro will never be too strong politically or otherwise until he becomes more business conscious. He must have faith in one another. He must believe that the sugar handled by the Negro business man is just as sweet as the sugar handled by the white man. And what is true in this one instance must be in a thousand other instances. The high-ups in the race must lead the way towards supporting Negro business. (Interview with Bishop P. G. Shaw, Birmingham, Alabama, May, 1940. Edward Strong's Birmingham Memorandum.)

Type 5: Prestige Personality

The prestige personality takes many different forms. In general the individual leader is looked up to because of his accomplishments, real or legendary, his talent or ability, his unusual success in some business, profession or art, the acclaim he wins from whites and/or Negroes, the glamour he reflects whether justified or not. Sometimes "pose," "front," mannerisms, affectations, "airs," affected culture, are valuable adjuncts in the attainment of "position" in the Negro community. The labor leader has a prestige in the Negro group connected with the mere fact of winning a higher degree, acquiring the titles of "Doctor," "Attorney," "Professor," and thus in a sense every Negro professional man is, in at least a minor degree, a "prestige personality." Attainments are apparently given a relatively higher rating in the Negro than in the white community. Negroes are still trafficking in "firsts," and the "first" Negro to win this or that degree, to be appointed to one position or another, the "youngest" Negro to have achieved something or other, are calculated to lend prestige to the individual. For some strange reason, perhaps because familiarity breeds contempt, the Negro community does not seem to make overmuch of the fact that a non-intellectual or self-made Negro attains a position of eminence and influence. Pride may be taken in his success, but Negroes never play up his slave, log-cabin or rail-splitting background, his lack of formal training, etc., though the individual himself may well be proud of it.

Success in business enterprise among Negroes is evidently sufficiently rare to cause a particular kind of glamour to accrue to the successful Negro business man. Prestige in the Negro community is a commodity of scarcity, and [because of] this a Negro girl clerk in the Library of Congress can rate a spot in the Who's Who in Colored America.

C. C. Spaulding, President of North Carolina Mutual Insurance Co., is almost unanimously acclaimed "leader" by Durham Negroes. This is really a result of the man's business acumen as reflected in the business institute he heads. Maintains friendly relationships with some powerful white financiers and has individually done much toward bettering standards of Durham Negroes. Though he seems to have interest of masses at heart his efforts have resulted in benefits to a selected few. In meeting of Durham Committee on Negro Affairs he said: "We must close now. . . . We must keep up our fight. . . . It's a good fight. . . . We've got to help these people some way."

* * * *

Leadership in Durham Committee on Negro Affairs is concentrated among North Carolina Mutual men whose streets are well paved and well lighted, and who are not really concerned by economic problems. One trade unionist on Committee. Labor is against it, but is afraid to speak out. Although paternalistically interested in "their" people, the organization has not spread its influence so that it is felt by the masses. No clear-headed leadership. One citizen says, "A few men in business here are making money, driving fine cars, living in palatial homes. They decided to let up and help out their people a little. Our leaders are too friendly with the white people to be real leaders. You cannot maintain friendship with the oppressors and attempt to still solve the problems of the oppressed."

* * * *

A white educator in North Carolina says that the crux of race relations is in the white dependence on Negro leaders like Spaulding. They come to him as "the King of Hayti," e.g.—when disturbance occurred after Louis-Schmeling fight, police got in touch with Spaulding and he came out and sent the trouble-makers home. This educator admits that such leadership has limitations, in that by its nature, it cannot demand, but only trade and compromise.

Possession of wealth, or merely ability to suggest it, is a sure-fire means of attaining high prestige and influence in the Negro community. It is no handicap in the white community, either.

Negro rights in Natchez, Miss., are represented mainly through Dr. Dumas, who occupies a unique position in the South despite the fact that Negroes do not vote. Through his intervention their petitions are given consideration. One of the wealthiest men in Natchez, and one of the largest tax-payers. Described as very superior diplomatic person and extremely popular and influential in the community. Has prestige and commands respect of even the local office holders.

The fact [of] having been the victim of racial persecution provides the basis for a special type of prestige and fame in the Negro world.

One of America's most famous Negroes (Dr. Sweet, of Sweet Case fame) who figures in the most publicized case involving civil rights for Negroes is said to never take part in any more race fights. He is now the highest exploiter of city funds for his private hospital in one of America's largest cities.[27]

* * * *

Banker and only Negro member of the Newport News Housing Authority. Younger than most. Claims not to be politically minded. Although there are no specific instances of his selling out, those interviewed were not so enthused over his leadership, but his success in business and official position afford him leadership qualities.

* * * *

Physician of Knoxville, Tennessee. A leader by virtue of position. Director of only Negro V.D. Clinic and only Negro staff member of Knoxville General Hospital. Conceited, cynical, in late thirties. Outspoken in relations with whites. Believes that ability will make its place.

* * * *

W. D. Hill, Executive in home office of North Carolina Mutual. Said to be hardest worker on Committee. Has Negroes' interest at heart, but does not have time or absolute willingness to sacrifice prestige to put this interest to work.

* * * *

M. Hugh Thompson, Attorney and head of extinct League of Independent Voters of Durham. Proud of North Carolina Mutual and is given to regarding politics as a matter to be fought solely between powerful groups of financiers. He refers in prideful tones to instances of shady dealings on the part of registrars in the following manner: "We just call up the Board of Elections and everything is all right." Interested in maintaining prestige.

* * * *

One of Jacksonville's Negro leaders is an insurance company executive and Republican committeeman from one of the precincts. Intensely interested in the return to power of the Republican Party and enthusiastic about Negro control of some of the Republican Party offices in Duval County. Old-line politician.

* * * *

The leader of Negro lodge in Alabama. "Is another so-called Negro leader, but he has done nothing concrete for the Negro. A large majority of the white people consider him the present leader of the Negro people. However, there are few Negroes that accept him as a leader of them. Adams has been a man to ride in on the success of other men. Negroes once owned the Pythian Temple, of which Oscar Adams is Grand Chancellor. During the period that Blount (his predecessor) was at the head of the organization, it prospered and was held in the esteem of the many Negroes throughout the state. He has torn the organization down to the point that few of the followers of the organization are at the present time interested in it. He is, I would say, a betrayer of the first sort. He will tear up any organization if he cannot get in the limelight and he only gets into these organizations because he wishes the limelight. He has never been known to build an organization, but is one of those individuals who rides in after it has been built.

When the time comes for the delegates to be elected to go away to the Elks National Convention, that is the one meeting that he attends a year."

Up until the last few years, Negro people who were looked upon as leaders led by virtue of their positions. If you were elected the head of the lodge, you became a leader in the community whether or not you made any major contribution to the community as a whole. Many of the leaders have been appointed by whites and thrust upon the Negro community. During the last few years, a more vocal militant leader has come to the front among Negroes.

The Negro professional men have a strong hold on the leadership position in the Negro community. They are in strategic position, and whether the Negro community actually trusts and respects them or not, their status as professionals—men with titles and degrees—assures them of an influence in the society that is often quite out of proportion to their abilities and contributions. The tradition that the Negro doctor is a "big man" still persists in the Negro race, though the Negro doctors have been notoriously narrow and stupid in their leadership outside of the field of their own chosen profession. The Negro professor is ordinarily too fearful of loss of his post to provide courageous, independent leadership, while the Negro lawyer, though often self-seeking and a shyster, is beginning to afford some of the most militant and forceful leadership of the group.

The Negro professional man is often terribly class conscious and snobbish. For example:

The Negro doctor of Chicago, a reactionary on health questions, bitterly complains about the southern Negroes coming up to Chicago and destroying the social position of the northern Negroes. He is a very prosperous female specialist.

* * * *

A dentist who is a member of Republican County Committee for Richland County, South Carolina, believes that if Negroes continue active with the Republicans, they can again become the political power in South Carolina. Whites accuse him of being interested only in the money he receives buying votes for delegates to conventions.

* * * *

A Negro attorney of Raleigh is already a leader who, according to one observer, "does his share of walking these streets and fooling the people." Suave, contained.

* * * *

A doctor is the most active political figure among Negroes of Winston-Salem. Ran for Alderman last election "to encourage the vote." Accused by a few of being a stooge for the corporations, but most of Negroes deny this. Right now is engaged in sending personal letters to all Negroes registered to prepare themselves for 1940. Intends to run again. Has quite a bit of influence.

* * * *

L. S. Palmer, High school principal of Newport News. Informed and active in civic groups. Secretary Virginia State Teachers Association, member Newport News Civic Association. Named by Richmond *Times Dispatch* last year as one of the outstanding men in Virginia. Honest, admired, respected and is immediately named a leader by those interviewed. Unusual in that Negro public school administrators are notoriously cautious and "safe."

* * * *

Professor at Charlotte high school. Outspoken opponent of buying and selling votes, but spoken of as an ardent poll worker by a few. President of Voters Alliance, and bitter because of factionalism which caused split and formed Voters League. Disturbed lest Negro's greed for authority muff his political chances. Ardently interested in intelligent voting and Negro's general welfare.

* * * *

Prof. Brier, Greenville, South Carolina, Teacher and president of local N.A.A.C.P. Implicated in recent registration campaign and K.K.K. incident. Not too militant, but very determined. Lost his teaching position because of his activities.

* * * *

Ex-President of Teachers' League, Knoxville, Tennessee. Hard working, but cautious young career man in the public schools. Advocates casting more votes, developing more business and forcing more Negro employment in white stores in Negro neighborhoods.

* * * *

Osie Davis, Highpoint, North Carolina, Former principal of high school. Only Negro in a city office—employed as "Boys Commissioner"—which job was given him after he was ousted from school job as a result of scandal. Was Republican, now ardent Democrat. Referred to by some as "race traitor," but he insists that his political faith is the only practical one to have in Highpoint. Due to "swing" with Democratic Party, he is very influential, and many Negroes feel safer when they are "on the good side" of Davis.

* * * *

Mr. Yokely, Highpoint, High School teacher and chairman of the Democratic Party Committee among Negroes. Ward worker for party, but laments the still large number of Negro Republicans in Highpoint. Seems honest enough, but party affiliation handicaps him among his own people.

* * * *

A group of Hampton Negro teachers organized a club a few years ago, which represents the liberal conservative group of those who regard themselves as "leaders." Program is to mold public opinion. Striving now to get a local bank to give them proper titles, emphasis propriety, etiquette, and sobriety.

* * * *

A Negro official in Democratic organization of Louisville. B.A. from Fisk University in economics; taught in C.W.A. adult education set-up in Tennessee. Engaged in social work there. Went to Louisville in 1936 and worked with insurance firm. Did election work for Democrats and became secretary of local Democratic club.

* * * *

Dr. J. B. Martin, Memphis, One of Church's aides, who admits that he (Martin) can do little for Negroes in Memphis because Crump is not indebted to him. Believes that effective Negro leadership in Memphis will come, not from politicians, but from progressive labor leaders.

* * * *

Dr. ——, head of an N.A.A.C.P. branch in a southeast state—a word manager without equal, and an intellectual snob. Not aggressive, and although his organization has 400 members, he cannot name a single achievement. Whether his members are qualified voters or not does not seem to interest him greatly.

* * * *

L. Marion Poe, Newport News, Negro woman attorney and first Negro woman to pass Virginia bar. Active and alert. Has served race for several years. Active member of Elks and interested in political unity for Negroes.

* * * *

A young Negro attorney, who is the head of the local N.A.A.C.P., is probably the most influential of the Negro political activities [sic] in Tulsa. Has important contacts with the administration as well as a large influential pull among the masses of Negroes. Typical ward-heeler type, but he has used his influence to some extent to secure certain jobs and city services for the Negroes as a whole.

* * * *

Mr. Fisher, Newport News, Attorney and president of the Young Colored Men's Democratic Club. Energetic and convinced of power of ballot and power of Newport News Negro if he were more integrated politically than he is now.

* * * *

Curtis Todd, Raleigh, Young Negro lawyer and state employee of State Employment Service. Is a bit disillusioned at seeing his race duped by its own leadership.

* * * *

A doctor from Louisiana is credited with establishing the Los Angeles branch of the N.A.A.C.P. about 15 years ago. He had a middle-class ideology and never wanted the organization to be a mass organization. This organization has been controlled by reactionary Republicans who never showed much interest in the common men.

* * * *

Attorney Chas. W. Anderson, Negro member of State Legislature of Kentucky. Ran for Legislature in Republican primary in April 1935 and defeated another Negro by 6-1 margin. Opposed by a Jew in general election, who ran as independent, and a Negro Democrat. Won over the latter who was closet rival, by 3-1. After election he was sued for fraud, non-residence, etc., by both unsuccessful opponents. Speaker of House appointed contest committee which declared him legitimate winner, and he was seated. Did not use radio, but depended upon street-corner speeches and rallies in churches and public halls. On Republican City County Executive Committee.

* * * *

Renchell Harris, Durham, President of the Bankers Fire Insurance Company, Secretary of Committee on Negro affairs. Interested in broadening power of the Committee, but prone to regard it as another business concern. Energetic.

* * * *

A fairly progressive Negro leader in Durham owns a large black dog named "Mister." He says that often whites come to his house and fail to give him a title, and he is unable to do anything about it because he "needs to use them." So he calls his dog, and when the white man answers, he blandly explains he was only calling his dog "whose name is Mister."

Negro undertakers are often very important individuals in the Negro community. They are among the most successful business men and are relatively better off than most of their group.

Mr. Haislip, Highpoint, Prominent undertaker and devoted Republican. An honest man, seemingly, has attempted political organization several times, but his attempts have been sabotaged by the Democrats. Seemingly a good man, intelligent enough, but not an astute politician.

* * * *

Leander Hill, Winston-Salem, President of Mutual Life Insurance Co. Not much formal education. Believes in one leader, and seems much in the "Bronze Mayor" idea. Active in local of Committee of One Hundred. Realizes the effectiveness of organization.

* * * *

An undertaker and official of the Young Men's Civic League, in Charleston. He is accepted by the people, but is really too indefinite about his ideas to actually lead. A Republican and ardent supporter of the Tolbert faction.

* * * *

A Negro realtor and old-line politician of Florida. Organizer of a Voters League in Jacksonville and a fraternal organization in Duval County. Not concerned with issues or trends, but only in number of members and party affiliation (Republican, of course).

* * * *

J. C. Crawford, Highpoint, Plumber, highly respected and chairman of the Negro Republican Committee. Hauls Negroes to polls diligently, hoping to restore the Republican Party. Thought of as one who believes in Lincoln Emancipation as reason enough to live, eat and die Republican. Although he is probably paid for campaign activities, gives impression that he corrals the vote on basis of principle that Republicanism is the political faith for Negroes.

* * * *

McClain, Winston-Salem, Mortician, youngster. Goes around personally encouraging Negroes to register and vote, urging them to be unafraid. Enthusiastic and well trained. Shows promise.

* * * *

"Dall" Haywood, Raleigh, Mortician and power in Precinct 16. When asked about youth, he said, "They are busy dressing and dancing. For a drink, a free shindig at a piccolo center and a barbecue, they'll vote." He is a grasper who is riding the political bandwagon.

The philosophy of a Savannah Negro business man, who represents a class, may be summed up as follows:

Has the tendency of the Negro middle-class—intelligent and professional Negroes—to defend themselves. Such Negroes merely rationalize an essentially aristocratic (or oligarchic?) philosophy, springing from their own measure of success—thus they are "successful" because of their own unusual ability. Energy, application, and common sense—these are the middle-class virtues which the "common" Negro lacks. There is also a tacit admission of the superiority of the white man, rationalized on the basis of better background and contacts than the common Negro has.

* * * *

It is charged that N.A.A.C.P. leadership in Richmond, which is almost entirely Negro professionals, has been characterized as weak, personally pre-occupied, socially myopic, "society" leadership. Not resourceful. Retains legalistic, scholar's approach to the Negro's problems.

* * * *

A Negro politician in St. Louis has a Democratic machine of his own, and is described by Dr. Myrdal as "pretty decent." He is supposed to be beyond the control of the Mayor and other party officials. He gets jobs for Negroes, and is described as one of the few Negro leaders "anchored in the masses."

* * * *

A resident of St. Louis accuses the local N.A.A.C.P. of being a predominantly "bright skinned" organization whose leadership is mostly concerned about eating and drinking with whites.

The Negro labor leader, the non-intellectual leader from the masses, is still a small company among the Negroes. There is developing slowly a new leadership which has a labor orientation and which devotes its major attention to the Negro working class.

A young Negro organizer of a labor union, which has 200 members, represents the better type of leadership in Tampa, Florida. Quiet spoken, but an unstinting labor worker, and believes that it is his pressing duty to convince Negroes of the importance of cooperating with unions and the Community League, in order to further their aims.

* * * *

Despite the fact that he is an old man and a Seventh Day Adventist preacher, Rev. —— is an outspoken and respected leader of Tampa. Is president of both the Negro Voters League and the local N.A.A.C.P. Sincere and honest, but still is reluctant to dismiss the importance of the Republican Party [to] Negroes in the South. Is not blind to the shortcomings of the Republicans, and has denounced them on more than one occasion for their seeming abandonment of the Negro, but invariably counsels that they are still the ones to look to for help. Referred to as a "leader" by all the Negro citizens.

* * * *

An official of a laborer's union who is tremendously interested in more active participation of union members in the political life of the city. Independent in his politics, clear on issues. Gives promise of becoming a real political force in Jacksonville.

* * * *

F. D. Lucy, President of East End Voters League and retired ship-yard worker, has been an active resident of Newport News for 50 years. Prudent, retired and slow to express himself, but is well informed. Convinced of the power of the ballot.

* * * *

The son of a small-town preacher, who is a former laborer in the Creosote Plants and Longshoremen, is the Negro section organizer of the Communist Party. He is a leader in the West Heights Civic Club and is active in the N.A.A.C.P. Youth Council.

* * * *

Ernest Young, Greensboro, New tailor shop operator. President of an organization City Brotherhood. Not very well lettered and not so well fixed financially, but gives promise of leadership. Though genuinely interested, he is not racialistic. Labor champion. Disgusted with old-line leadership.

* * * *

A railway clerk is head of one of the national organization locals in Norfolk. Jovial, "Irish politician" type. Gets chief support from "lower" Negro—who is looking for leaders, but those who don't look down on him. He says of average Negroes, "He says he is 'as good as anybody,' but knows that he isn't, but will follow a leader who doesn't make him feel his inferiority."

Claims success as a leader because he is one of the common folks—they all call him by his first name—"Jerry." He is head of the local Elks Lodge. He says that the college-bred boys are self-seeking and ambitious in a personal way, and really wreck organizations. Realizes he is in delicate position on account of his job. Says that Negroes with jobs don't want to be bothered with problems of other Negroes.

* * * *

A Negro proprietor of a beer parlor and ardent supporter of Solomon in Miami. Though not highly educated in the formal sense, he is unusual in that he has ideas on a program for the political organization and activity of Negroes. Is doing his best to foster cooperation.

* * * *

Rev. ——, President Knoxville N.A.A.C.P. Pro-labor social view. Honest, active and his influence is increasing. Has active interest in getting Negroes to pay poll tax, vote and join labor unions.

* * * *

H. H. Price, Richmond, Virginia, resident for 25 years. One-time publisher of "Colored Republican," "Progressive Citizen," "Daily Sentinel," all erstwhile Richmond papers. Organized Civic Association of Chesterfield County, which conducted continuous campaign to get Negroes to pay poll taxes and register and vote. Believes focal point of Negro problem is for Negro to put all his political emphasis on local elections. Says, "We have fooled around all these years dickering in national politics and got nothing because we ain't enough to count in national elections. We must build up locally before we gain any hearing in national politics. . . . The secret of Negro success in the South as a whole lies in affecting an alliance with the whites."

Type 6: Negro Leaders [Who] Are Designated by Whites

Much of Negro leadership in the North as well as in the South is either the product of direct white designation, or must depend largely upon white approval. The formula is simple. The white man holds the purse-strings, he is in the position of political and organizational power, and the Negro, greatly lacking in all of these, must depend upon the whites for support. Thus Negro organizations, institutions and causes are almost entirely dependent upon white financial backing. Negro politicians have to rely upon political machines. Negro school heads are dependent upon school boards, educational officials and boards of trustees which are either entirely white or where whites have the authoritative voice. Even Negro preachers are given to realization that whites hold mortgages on their churches, or make eagerly accepted contributions to them, [and] while the Negro ministers are not designated by or subject to white approval, their attitudes and conduct are very often influenced by what they think white reaction might be.

This white control and influence over Negro leadership is intimately related to white economic and political power and Negro lack of it. The criteria applied to Negro leaders whom whites designate are not subject to detailed definitions; usually, however, they conform to the white patterns of thought concerning the Negro, with a view to the interests and services desired by the whites. The Negro leader designated by whites may be a very able, thoroughly conscientious person, a buffoon, or just a faithful servant. The white selection is often not subject to any rational motivation; the Negro leader selected may be chosen merely because the whites think one Negro leader is as good as any other, or because a Negro has tickled the vanity of some responsible white man, or because it is thought that a faithful servant ought to have some such reward. I presume that an important aspect of this picture concerning the selection of Negro administrators will be presented in Mr. Wilkerson's memorandum on Negro Education.[28]

Richmond Negroes have received their leaders from their white rulers. The Interracial Commission is busily engaged in selecting, grooming and promoting Negro leadership. The only obligation the aspiring leader is under is to the "good white folks" who promote his campaign so that he will do everything in his power to frustrate all genuine movements which may take root among the Negro people and that seek to tilt the balance of "racial harmony" away from the status quo toward equal rights.

* * * *

A Negro of Louisville is Democratic district leader of over 37 precincts. Although he is the only Negro district leader, Negroes had no choice in his election, because he was appointed by the white Democratic Committee.

* * * *

In speaking of a prominent Negro Republican politician, who happened to be from his state, a well-known Senator from the deep South said enthusiastically, "Oh yes, —— is a *good* nigra. He is brilliant, of good character and he will sit here and talk to me and will condemn the bad qualities of the nigra just as freely as I will. He is not afraid to say what is wrong with the nigra. He is an honest man."

* * * *

In Suffolk, Virginia, the Negro janitor of the white bank went to the bank president and said, "We colored people want our own bank." The president endorsed the idea and promised to help. The white bank President put up a good deal of money, helped put up a building, and turned over all the colored depositors to the new Negro bank. Then he made the janitor president of the new Negro bank. Then came the depression, the bank failed, the Negro bank president went back to the dust from whence he came to his janitor's job. The Negro depositors went back to the white bank too. The Negro president, however, had lived high and handsome while it lasted—big car, good clothes, cigars, and all. Only the unfortunate depositors were unhappy.

* * * *

Editor of a Negro weekly in Tennessee. Appointed in late 20's as truant officer by Commissioner of Education, in return for delivering 1,000 votes. Seeking to capitalize further on his political control, he organized the Colored Voters League which was composed of the chairman of each Negro ward club. This league was a move to create a monopoly of the entire Negro vote in order to effect a greater bargaining unit with the candidates. But this unification of the Negro electorate in support of a single group of candidates spelled no advance for the Negro people. The Negro editor-politician and his cohorts effected this united front only in order to get a maximum prize in selling the total Negro vote. They would hold a meeting and decide who to support and for what price (vote to highest bidder), then would split up the money for the total vote among them. Organization finally broke up when leader took too much of the pie. Negroes' social needs meant nothing to these opportunists. Opponent of Negro editor's white patron ran and won on plank of ridding the Education Department of "Nigger" politician's control. Although Negro progressives resented the injection of the race issue in the campaign, they took the opportunity to oust the Negro politician and voted for the Negro baiter. During C.I.O. strike at Foundry, this same leader acted as company stooge and urged Negroes back to work. Looked upon as "oily, slick, double-crosser." His strength has depended upon the support of his white backer.

* * * *

A Negro business woman and civic worker in Birmingham complained:

> I haven't been in the civil leagues enough to pass judgment on their leaders. But I wonder sometimes if these people want to do as much good as they claim or if they are concerned with loaves and fishes for themselves. For instance, there is one young man who is being slated to head the Slossfield Health Center. But it is the white people who want to put him there. Is he prepared? Of course he isn't. And that is the way it has been for years. The key jobs in education and other fields are given to Negroes because whites like them rather than because they are capable.

The following comments on Negro leadership by Negroes who are themselves in positions of leadership and responsibility in Negro communities are cited merely because they are fairly typical of many of the views frequently expressed in Negro circles.

A Negro lawyer in Houston says, "I believe the greater pressure exerted the more a man can accomplish. Negroes will have to learn to like themselves and stop abhorring what is Negroid. The preachers and teachers are to blame for a lot of the sense of inferiority that we exhibit as a people. . . . Our preachers are still too much with 'Heaven and Hell.' I believe like Shakespeare said, 'Put money in my purse.' We've got to get something on the land, then we can force respect."

* * * *

In New Orleans, where there is a distinct caste system, a Creole high school instructor observes, "There is a difference in the traditional culture as between uptown and downtown colored groups in New Orleans. The downtown population has a traditional culture which the 'uptown' group cannot understand; when leadership comes from 'uptown' it is bizarre as only it can be from an uncultured group. Until something is done whereby this group which has the culture comes out and takes the leadership, it can only be bizarre, and only the 'downtown' group has the culture, the necessary elements for progress." (The "downtown" group is the mixed-blood or so-called "Creole" population; "uptown" is the "Negro" group.)

* * * *

The former editor of the official publication of one of the national organizations delivered a lecture to a Negro group in a mid-western city. The lecture had a fairly optimistic tone as far as it related to the Negro's position in the United States. Once off the platform, however, the lecturer revealed a very pessimistic attitude to his individual friends. When questioned about his private pessimism and his public optimism, he frankly admitted that he could not be "heartless" enough to strike a pessimistic note to an audience of hopeful Negroes.

* * * *

The former head of a national organization local in Savannah avers that the Negro ministers are no help to a progressive organization, because they have gone to the white man so many times that they cannot participate in a frontal attack—they are obligated.

* * * *

In Savannah several prominent Negroes formed a Committee. Attorney M. A. Norrell, former editor of *Richmond Planet,* about 55 years old, embittered, cynical, ex-leader. Says: "Negroes will never get anywhere in politics or anything else. They are too damned content and jealous. They just born to exploit—you wasting your time trying to do something with 'niggars.' They ain't got no will to want to do for themselves. I know. I spent thirty years trying to help 'em and every time you get to a pressure point they turn and run and leave you facing the fire. The hell to 'niggars.' Go make yourself some money, son, and leave 'niggars' alone—they'll kill you."

* * * *

In New Orleans, the principal of a Negro school, an intellectual and social snob, exposes the theory that the Negroes are destined to play an important role in the coming struggle between fascism and communism. It seems clear from the recorded interview with this man that in his bitterness against the inequities of white America he would use the masses to seek revenge and settle accounts—but that within the Negro world he looked upon himself as superior, both in lineage and culture—a hearty aristocrat.

* * * *

When asked what persons he considered leaders of the Negro people in Birmingham, a prominent, well-educated young Negro observed:

> Frankly speaking there are no Negro leaders in Birmingham. There are some who have been known for a number of years as leaders; however, they fall way short of being leaders. Those that have long since been accepted as so-called leaders have used the confidence and faith of those not quite so fortunate to exploit them economically. Negroes here have been sold out to their political enemies in a number of instances.

* 3 *

Life Histories Analysis

Purely as an experiment, a number of letters were sent out to prominent Negroes and whites in the interracial field, selected more or less at random except for some attention to occupational and geographical distribution, requesting that short autobiographies of about 2000 words each be prepared. The autobiographies were to devote themselves strictly to the eight questions listed in the letter. (Copies of the letters sent to Negroes and whites are appended in Appendix III.)[29] This was a heavy request and I was surprised to get returns, many in very full form, from 36 Negroes and 14 whites. The objective was to get to the individual leader's own picture of: (1) His family background, social and economic; (2) Early factors or incidents which aroused his consciousness of the racial problem; (3) Nature of obstacles it was necessary to overcome and types of social repression experienced; (4) The factor or related factors in the life of the individual primarily responsible for his elevation; (5) Extent to which contacts with Negro or white individuals in key positions have played a role in the individual's progress; (6) Nature and value of the educational training received; (7) Effect which the racial situation has had upon the individual's personal social philosophy; (8) Extent to which the individual's career has been influenced or controlled by the racial situation.

Of the 36 life histories returned by Negroes, 22 have been considered sufficiently to the points raised to be used. These have been summarized in the following pages, very hurriedly, with a view toward indicating the nature of the responses gotten. An intensive study of the group of histories might reveal certain patterns as to backgrounds, contacts and attitudes, but no serious attempt to do this is undertaken here, since the sampling should be considerably greater to have real meaning, despite the fact that these are representatives of the uppermost rungs of the Negro leadership ladder. In this instance the main objective, anyway, has been merely to test the possibilities of getting data in this way rather than through the orthodox but not too revealing questionnaires, and to suggest some of its possibilities as source material for a really thorough-going analysis of Negro leadership.

The occupational distribution of the 22 leaders whose histories are herewith summarized is as follows:

College Presidents	5
Politicians	3
Government employees	3
Professors	2
Editors	2
Organization leaders	2
Jurists	2
Churchman	1
Journalist	1
Musician-Composer	1
Total	22

Not all of these gave information covering all questions. At least seven of them are descended from slave parentage. Practically all come from Negro middle-class families which stressed the typical middle-class virtues of thrift, industry, honesty. None stress lowly origins. The obstacles they have had to overcome are of many varieties, but in general are subsumed under poverty and prejudice. A good many, either directly or indirectly, have indicated that contacts with whites have been an important influence in their careers, and some have indicated their deliberate purpose to cultivate friendly relations with whites. They had race impressed upon them at an early age for the most part and in the many usual ways. They tend generally to admit that race has been a dominant influence in their thinking, and also upon their careers. In some instances, their careers have been a direct result of the racial situation.

1. *Family Background—Social and Economic*

A Negro National Organization Executive; Born in Richmond, Va., 1885. Father a slave—Mother free. Father a graduate of Colgate in 1876. Mother graduate of Howard in 1880. Father taught theology at Union University. Mother, teacher of music at Hartshorn Memorial College.

Charles S. Johnson. (Photo by Carl Van Vechten, Carl Van Vechten Papers, Yale Collection of American Literature, Beinecke Rare Book and Manuscripts Library, Yale University)

A prominent Negro educator of Alabama; Born in Washington, D.C. Youngest of six children. Orphaned at age of two. Went to Texas when 7 years old. Father and Mother were graduates of Prairie View College and school teachers in Calvert, Texas. When family migrated to Washington, D.C., father was employed as government messenger. While there, father studied law and passed bar just before his death. Family's economic status none too good. Father left Texas for Washington in hope of getting much better job than he obtained. Expected this because of staunch support he had given Republican party as editor of Negro weekly newspaper in Calvert, Texas.

A prominent Negro Republican politician's mother and father were both slaves, who lacked education, but nevertheless strived to accumulate something from a meagre existence.

A young Negro woman organization leader in Norfolk, Virginia, was born in that city in 1908, the eighth of a family of nine. Her parents were descendants of some of the first Virginia families, and she states that this fact made her family one of the first in their social group. The father of this family was a retail merchant, and was considered a "good liver" because he owned his home and provided well for his large family.

An eminent Negro attorney, who is now the Dean of the outstanding Negro college of law, was born in Knoxville, Tennessee. The Dean's father, a native Ohioan, came to Washington, D.C., during the nineties and entered the government service as a clerk. Although eligible to practice pharmacy, as a result of training received at Howard University's evening school, the father remained in the government service until his death in 1921. The mother of this outstanding attorney and educator is a member of an Alabama family of independent tradespeople and artisans, and after completing two years of college work, began teaching, and continued in this work until her marriage.

A prominent Negro educator and sociologist was born in Clifton Forge, Virginia, the son of a Baptist minister of West Indian descent. The mother of this Negro was a member of a proud West Virginia family.

An outstanding Negro attorney and member of the legislature of Ohio is the son of thrifty, hard-working people. His father was a native of Kentucky and his mother was born in Tennessee. The family was poor, but industrious.

America's leading Negro woman educator, executive and now government official was born of slave parents near Mayesville, South Carolina in July, 1875. This prominent woman's early formal training was received in a little mission school maintained by the Presbyterian Church about four miles from her home. Further training was received at Scotia Seminary in Concord, North Carolina, at the State College at Orangeburg, South Carolina, and at the Moody Bible Institute at Chicago. The pioneer in Negro education started what is now one of the leading southern colleges for Negroes, in a small cottage with cast-off furnishings and $1.50 in cash.

A Negro bishop is the son of middle-class parents who were home owners with a moderate income. The family was considered socially prominent in the community. This bishop's father was also a clergyman and a teacher who had a strong feeling of race pride. The bishop's mother is described as 12.5% Negro and who had strong anti-Caucasian sentiments.

A Negro army officer, who is now a Federal government official, is a native of Boston, Mass. This gentleman received his early training in the public schools of Boston and Cambridge and the Prospect Union Preparatory School. Two years were spent at Harvard as a special student. During the World War this official was commissioned a First Lieutenant and served as morale officer with the General Staff of the United States Army.

The holder of a high judicial position in the City of New York was born in December, 1878, in Franklin County, Alabama, of parents who had been slaves. This Negro, who is a judge of New York's Municipal Court, was forced to leave his family at the age of 15 in an effort to obtain an education, since his parents were too poor to provide the proper facilities.

The editor of one of the oldest Negro weeklies in New York, and former Alderman of that city, was born in Loudoun County, Virginia, in 1857. This Negro's father was a white man, son of one of the state's leading families, and his mother was a slave, but never referred to that fact. The editor was born in the "big house," and was taken to the District of Columbia at a very early age.

The head of a leading Negro institution of higher learning in Georgia was born in 1900 at Salisbury, North Carolina, and taken to Louisville, Ky., when less than a year old. This educator received all of his early formal training in southern schools, up to and including a college course at Livingstone College in Salisbury, N.C. During the summer while in school, this man worked at various jobs in order to obtain funds for his school years, e.g. bell boy and Pullman porter. Along with his educational career, this young college head is a minister, and for a few years was the active pastor of a Methodist Church.

Another Negro woman educator and founder of a small southern institution was born in North Carolina in 1883, but was carried to Cambridge, Mass., at an early age, and was reared there. Although this outstanding Negro woman's grandparents were slaves, they were fortunate in having benevolent owners, who are credited with giving the family a "splendid economic start." This woman describes her mother as a far-seeing sensible woman, who told her to "try to make friends of those southern white people for they can make you or break you."

A noted Negro journalist was born in Providence, Rhode Island. This columnist's mother was originally Catholic, but changed to Episcopalian because of dissatisfaction with the Catholic attitude toward Negroes. The parents of this Negro once operated a hand laundry in Syracuse, and at other times were cooks in various hotels. The journalist states that his family belonged to the upper-class Negroes, socially and economically, and that his first recollections are of a fine home, beautifully furnished, and with a general atmosphere of plenty, although everybody worked.

A young Negro, who has been serving in an administrative capacity under the New Deal regime for the past seven years, was born in Washington, D.C., in 1907. This official's father was a postal clerk, and his mother was a graduate of the Minor Normal School. In the home was the usual stress of middle-class virtues, i.e., thrift, honesty and industry. There seems to have been an assumption that this gentleman and his brother were to receive a college education.

An eminent Negro composer of popular music was born in Florence, Alabama, in 1873, a descendant of slave parents.

A not so widely known editor of a successful little Negro paper in Tampa, Florida, was born near Dawson, Georgia. This publisher's parents separated when he was quite young, and he had a stepmother who he thought was his mother for many years. The school term in the community was three months out of the entire year, and the editor's father sent him to school for only three weeks of one of the terms. When the father met with reverses as a sharecropper, he moved, leaving his son to live with a friend. The editor slipped away from this home and went to live with his father's sister. Conditions in this last abode were more satisfactory, and the young publisher-to-be felt the ambition to prepare himself for life.

A very high-ranking government employee, whose position is a permanent, civil service job, was born in Texas of hard-working, systematic parents, one of ten children. According to this official, industry seemed to have been the watchword of his family's household, the members of which were taught to regard all manner of work as honorable. Even as a youngster of seven years, this government official engaged in running errands, shining shoes, etc. Punctuality, honesty, efficiency, and reliability were constantly emphasized in the home, and practiced as much as possible.

The head of a Negro college in Kentucky was born in 1897 in the west end of that state, the only son of 7 children. This educator's father was a prominent man in the community and was generally spoken of as a leader, although he had begun life as an ordinary day laborer. The mother of this family "took in laundry," but paid strict attention to the training of her children. Both parents insisted upon the best possible education for their children. The white people of the community were among the first to recognize the father's leadership qualities, and conceded him the position of Negro "Mayor" given him by his friends. This energetic father was something of a politician too, having made an unsuccessful campaign for the city council of his town. Prudent investments in the town's estate resulted in economic independence for the father and his family.

An eminent Negro educator, who has been a noted Dean of America's leading Negro university and who is now at the head of another institution for higher learning, is the son of parents who were both slaves in their early days in Virginia. This educator's father became a teacher and minister. The father's duties as an Episcopal minister kept the family on the move, and consequently the College head saw much of the United States, as a youngster.

A well-known Negro educator and Dean in one of the Virginia Negro institutions was born in 1884 at Ninety-Six, South Carolina. The father of this man was a minister and teacher, and his mother was one of the first Negroes to be certified to teach in South Carolina's public schools. The mother died when the Dean was two years old. Then the Dean went to live on the farm of a great-uncle who was constantly urging an education for the youngster, and doing all he could to see that the young man obtained one.

A popular and likeable Negro publisher of Cincinnati, Ohio, was born in Richmond, Virginia, in 1865. Both parents of this character were born slaves, and were each grandchildren of their parents' owners. The father at one time was a racehorse jockey of note, but later turned to hotel and caterer's work. The father soon gained a reputation as an expert mixer of mint juleps, and the publisher under discussion calls him a famous "Mixicologist." This same "mixicologist" bought the freedom of himself, the publisher's mother and their oldest son. These parents not wealthy, but considered "well off" after a while, and insisted upon providing educations for the children. When this publisher went to work with his father at one of his best-known hostelries which was patronized by many of the country's most prominent whites in all fields, the old man told his son, "Son, you will hear lots you never heard before, see lots you never saw before. Keep you eyes and ears open, and above all things, study white folks. You won't have to study colored folks, 'cause you will know them anyhow."

Reflecting over this advice, the publisher and editor says, "That last remark was the only mistake I have ever known him to make in giving advice. Years have shown me that he should have said, "Study colored folks, for you will know white folks. They always set in accordance with their interest, while colored folks generally are guided by their feelings or emotions."

2. Early Factors or Incidents Which Aroused Individual's Consciousness of the Racial Problem

The Negro National Organization Executive: Consciousness of problem aroused by activities of several Negro leaders in Richmond to develop race pride and political influence, and combat racial discrimination. Father's fight to get Negroes in Richmond's Negro public schools as teachers.

Prominent Negro educator of Alabama: 1. Separate school systems; 2. White boy in small Texas town spit in his face when he refused to buy soda water. Restrained from fighting this offender by an older cousin, who warned him that the white boy's father would probably shoot him if he hit the boy.

The outstanding Negro Republican politician was a member of the only Negro family in the village in which he was born, and when he was only five years old his white playmates reminded him of the fact that he was a "nigger," and could not attend their schools and churches, nor could he eat with them. These white youngsters also told him that he could never be a sheriff or governor in his state, since he was a "nigger."

Consciousness of the race problem was brought home to the young woman leader in Norfolk when a superintendent of schools in one of Virginia's counties refused her a teaching position which had been offered her before he knew she was not white. The superintendent was apologetic, and instead of the job originally offered, she was urged to take a position in the best Negro school in the county, which paid more than the Negro teachers were receiving, but less than the original job. She admits she was angered, hurt and indignant.

While pointing out that he could not remember when he was not aware of racial discrimination and attitude in the South, the Dean of the best-known Negro law school states that he did believe that the individual Negro who insisted upon decent treatment would usually be treated accordingly.

The well-known sociologist and educator got his first inkling of the racial problem from an intra-racial source, when his mother's relatives always expressed sympathy for him and his brothers because they were "so dark." The first real consciousness of the racial situation, however, came to this man when he was sent to one elementary school in Philadelphia, while his white neighbor and playmate went to another.

The Ohio legislator states that his racial consciousness was first aroused when he began his elementary school training, and has been aroused ever since.

Consciousness of the racial problem came to the eminent Negro woman educator when she realized the difference in treatment of Negroes by the northern white missionaries and the southern white people.

The Negro bishop lists several factors as instrumental in arousing his racial consciousness. Among these are: (1) strong racial sentiments in his family; (2) early life in small towns of Western Tennessee; (3) the sight of the naked body of a Negro dangling from a tree in Tennessee; (4) residential segregation in places in which he lived; and (5) the Jim Crow street-car system in Memphis.

The woman educator and founder of the school in North Carolina claims that the story of how an old white woman, who was a distant relative, told her mother, "Caroline, if there be anything like a colored lady, I want you to be one," was her first real knowledge of a difference in the races. Another instance which aroused this woman's race consciousness was the lecture she received from a prominent white woman in Cambridge after she had formed a committee of the handful of Negro students in the school which she attended, and arranged a dance to which all her Negro friends were invited. The affair was a social success, but its sponsor was admonished for staging a segregated affair, and impressed with the fact that the better-class whites were striving to eliminate all forms of segregation.

The Negro journalist claims that his consciousness of "race" was not as a "problem," but was obtained through Negro historical material on great Negroes such as Douglass, Sojourner Truth, etc. Having lived in a mixed neighborhood during his early life, this journalist claims that his early contact with the "race problem" was purely through hearsay; and when he was called "nigger" at the age of 8 he was "shocked and ran home in tears." As he grew older, however, this man became increasingly aware of the various subtle forms of discrimination.

Some realization of the existence of the race problem came about when the Negro government official was forced to ride the street car to a Negro school, although there was a white school within two blocks of his home. The consciousness of the race situation was further aroused in this Negro when, after winning an oratorical contest in his high school which was sponsored by the Capital's leading daily, two white judges who were sent to the school during the city-wide run-off were inattentive to the point of being discourteous.

The Negro composer of popular music, which seems to never grow old, states that he had no real idea of the race problem until he heard a candidate for the governorship of Alabama make a campaign speech in which he "heaped bitter vituperation on my race, receiving applause from followers for whom I had the highest regard."

The high-ranking government employee under the Federal civil service recalls that he was first made aware of the race situation when he read "*K Lamity's Harpoon*," a publication put out in Austin, Texas, the purpose of which was to vilify the Negro race, incite riots, create prejudice, and "keep the Negro in his place." Reading some of Ben Tillman's speeches and listening to discussions of the Jim Crow street-car law were other instances which aroused racial consciousness.

The head of the Negro college in Kentucky was first made aware of the racial situation when he was quite a boy. The incident responsible for this was the expulsion of a successful Negro barber from the community. It seems that the barber had built up a successful business of such proportions as to incur the jealousy of some of the whites. The fact that he had a white woman as a regular client, and attended her in her home, was used as an excuse to order this successful Negro businessman out of town. When the barber failed to comply quickly enough, and gave evidence of some reluctance to leave his established business, a mob formed and compelled him to flee. In his flight, this unfortunate man sought refuge at the home of our Negro educator. This made a deep impression upon the young man.

The college head whose father's duties as a minister carried him to several places was first made conscious of the racial problem when he was called "nigger" by some young whites in Annapolis, Maryland, when he was about six years old.

The Dean of the Virginia college remembers his racial consciousness being aroused first when, while very young, one of his white playmates brought him bread and butter out of his house for the Dean to eat under a tree in the yard. For some time the white boys and our Negro notable had been going freely in and out of each other's houses, eating and drinking. Then occurred the tree episode. The Dean states that at that age he gave it no immediate thought, but when he mentioned it at home the same night, he was told very firmly to never let it happen again. Then the Dean saw the light. Another incident which brought home to this educator the fact that a race problem existed was an over-heard conversation between two white store clerks in South Carolina in which both professed a low opinion of a "nigger," but one was willing to treat him as a human being, while the other insisted on persecuting him.

3. Nature of Obstacles Individual Has Had to Overcome and Types of Social Repression Experienced

Negro National Organization Executive: Principal obstacles are outgrowths of general thought of white American public that the Negro should not be given equal status with whites in the body politic. Philanthropists do not give to worthy Negro causes. Negroes often "let you down" by submitting to unfavorable compromises when much more could be gained if they held out a little longer. The Negroes' economic position is too unstable to stand much pressure. Hostility of Negro leaders who branded any social welfare effort in the interest of Negroes as an attempt to segregate them.

Prominent Negro educator of Alabama: Obtaining education under handicap of low funds. Being one of few Negro students at Iowa State College, together with working way through, led to some social repression. Some of this was undoubtedly due to personal reticence.

The Negro Republican leader states that his "racial identity" has been his highest hurdle in life.

Besides a bone infect[ion] which left her a cripple, the militant young woman in Norfolk cites the bitter disillusionment caused by the realization that merit is not the chief requisite for success as her chief obstacles.

The sociologist and educator admits that the factor of race had borne down heavily upon him by the time he had finished college, but ascribes it more to the apathy and truckling of Negroes than to actual repression from whites. Then, according to this gentleman, he has had a tendency to "cut off his nose to spite his face."

The Negro member of the Ohio legislature was compelled to work his way through school, and at the same time contribute to his family's support, and claims that he has experienced nearly every type of social repression that the average Negro has confronted.

The well-known Negro woman educator lists (1) the lack of finances, (2) meeting and combatting prejudice in the deep South, and (3) the opposition to Negro education as the most important difficulties to be overcome in her rise to prominence.

The chief obstacles which have confronted the Negro bishop have been (1) financial reverses after the death of his mother when he was 13 years old, (2) church politics, which he characterizes as very realistic and formidable, and (3) his efforts to exercise self-restraint without losing his self-respect.

The head of the North Carolina educational institution, who ranks high among Negro women, has had numerous unpleasantnesses on account of the Jim Crow policies on transportation facilities. Many of these have been humiliating, and on two or three occasions, dangerous. On many occasions, this woman has dressed and undressed in her Pullman berth rather than create trouble by coming into contact with prejudiced whites in the dressing rooms.

Among the early obstacles confronted by the noted Negro journalist and columnist was that of securing employment in his home town where the Jim Crow employment system embittered him.

The Negro composer of popular music indicates that his chief obstacles in life were extreme poverty, and a sort of social ostracism among his own people who looked upon show people and musicians as social outcasts.

The Florida editor cites extreme poverty when a young man as his most serious obstacle.

The employee under the civil service appointment ranks precedent or custom as the chief obstacles in his path of progress, i.e., most of his immediate superiors seemed reluctant to break an established precedent by giving a Negro a merited promotion.

The noted head of the Negro college in Maryland, while not listing any specific obstacles, does complain of the fact that he had to forego his regular senior year in college because of lack of funds, work a year, and then complete his course.

Financial difficulties were mentioned by the Virginia Dean as his most pressing difficulty in early life.

4. Factor or Related Factors in Individual's Life Considered Primarily Responsible for His Elevation

Negro national organization executive: Self-confidence. One must believe in the principle underlying his work. The confidence of others. Grateful to certain individuals—teachers, staff and board members and other associates in public life—for their confidence and interest in his life's work. Hard work is another factor. Cultivation of Negro and white friendships in key positions.

Prominent Negro educator of Alabama: A fortunate chain of circumstances, along with a willingness and desire to be of larger usefulness when possible.

The national Negro Republican leader states that his desire for elevation was aroused by the fact that his father was a member of Mississippi's legislature; two Negroes were elected in the United States Senate from the state; his father was a delegate to Republican National Convention; and his brother graduated from college.

Although her physical disability is necessarily a handicap, the young Norfolk woman considers it primarily responsible for what success she has attained in life. She admits that she makes a conscious effort to compensate for her physical infirmity by determining to do everything which had been said she could not do.

Contacts with the Harvard Law School are credited with being the chief factor in the professional advancement of the leading Negro educator and attorney. The appointment of this Negro as Assistant Solicitor in the Department of Interior in 1933 was a direct result of his Harvard contacts. Subsequent appointment as Federal District Judge in the Virgin

William Hastie. (Scurlock Studio Collection, Archives Center, National Museum of American History)

Islands may also be indirectly traced to the same connections. Without attempting to evaluate its influence, the Dean notes the fact that in each case in which he was appointed to public office there had been a period of agitation by Negro pressure groups. The Dean believes this circumstance to be an indication of the political expediency that prompted some recognition to individual Negroes which would either lessen the clamor or increase the political prestige of the appointing party among Negro voters.

The sociologist who is wont to "cut off his nose to spite his face" ascribes what success he has made to hard work and "luck."

The Ohio solon attributes much of his success to his rigid home training in the principles of the Golden Rule. The Bible and the Church are also regarded as having had much influence on the success of this leader. Finally, this man believes that the public has confidence in his integrity.

The noted woman educator attributes most of her success to the early influence of white missionaries and hard work in connection with the establishment of a promising junior college and teacher training institution.

The bishop outlines the factors primarily responsible for his elevation in the following terms:

a) The will to achieve. The old "I'll show them" spirit.
b) The ambition (not as yet well realized) to "do something" about the racial situation.
c) What those of the Christian persuasion called "faith."

After pointing out that her mother's plans for her were her chief inspiration, the Negro woman educator of North Carolina states: "My New England training in the grammar, high and normal schools, thorough in detail, the associated influences and the private study in music, art and drama, the fine friends in that coveted literary circle of New England, the Boston people who through organized and individual effort like the Sedalia Club, which was 'open Sesame' to people of culture and wealth, my welcome into the clubs, homes and churches added to my store of knowledge and experience. . . . My summers at Howard University and Simmons, my years of study at Wellesley, my association with the National Board of the Young Woman's Christian Association, my visits and stay upon the campuses of colleges like Smith, Mt. Holyoke, and others where I was asked to lecture to classes and assemblies, my frequent visits to and participation in the Northfield summer and winter programs . . . are responsible for my larger education which has made possible the masses of my educational and cultural endeavors."

Figuring prominently in the circumstances which have made for his measure of success, according to the Negro writer and journalist, was the fact that his early environment was "proud, iconoclastic and nonconformist," and that his people thought for themselves. Along with this, this man claims that he learned honesty, sincerity, loyalty and personal pride.

The Negro administrator in the Federal Works Agency ascribes his rise to his present position to circumstances beyond his control. He lists these circumstances as: (1) the emergence of the Negro as a more important factor in the American political scene; (2) the election of a national administration with generally liberal tendencies; and (3) the presence in positions of authority of persons predisposed to secure fair treatment for Negroes and anxious to use trained persons in their offices.

Early home training and a capacity for work are mentioned as the chief contributing forces to the success of the employee of the Federal government with the high civil service status.

5. Extent to Which Contacts with Negro or White Individuals in Key Positions Have Played Role in Progress

Negro national organization executive: Where the objective is to gain larger consideration for Negroes in important social matters, it is absolutely necessary to gain the support and sympathy of leaders in other fields. Thus efforts have been made to cultivate friendship of all those in a position to help.

Prominent Negro educator of Alabama: To the greatest extent possible, from the inspiration received from a teacher in his chosen field in Texas, to college administrators and key persons in private foundations who have made possible advanced study. Has been generously helped in this manner.

Contact with Booker T. Washington and his associates, together with opportunities to visit the courts, legislatures, and Congress, played an important role in his efforts to move upward, according to the well-known Mississippi Republican leader.

A young Negro woman organization leader in a Virginia town expresses the opinion that her contacts with Negroes in key positions have had little or no elevating qualities as far as her progress is concerned. She states, "Truth to tell, had I allowed myself to listen to them, I fear I would have gone far in the other direction. My experience has been that Negroes in key positions have been put there, or kept there, to keep others out of positions that might be had with a little effort. Especially have I found this true in politics."

The outstanding Negro attorney and educator attributes his success in public life chiefly to his contacts formed at the Harvard Law School.

In regard to this question, the prominent Negro sociologist and educator says, "I do not know. When first I started working, I tried courting the favor of people who might help. The tactics sickened me and I quickly dropped them. I do have friends in both groups who have been helpful, but in many instances they were not in unusual positions."

The prominent Negro in Ohio's legislature admits that there is something to the old adage that "it is not what you know, but whom you know," and expresses lasting appreciation to those of his friends, Negro and white, who have favored him.

The Negro woman educator believes that her progress upward has been materially aided through her contacts with leading Negro and white educators throughout the country. This same personage also values her many contacts gained through her affiliation and participation in many liberal and progressive movements and organizations.

The bishop's response to this question is worth quoting. He says, "If in 'key positions' implies the conscious employment of 'pull,' I must be immodest enough to plead 'not guilty.' For myself I have disdained this, although I do not condemn it in others. Perhaps it has merely been a chronic case of exaggerated ego. Within the past 25 years I have never applied for a position affording salary remuneration. Undoubtedly, however, persons of influence have, of their own spontaneous volition, spoken kindly of me in strategic situations."

Although not mentioning specific beneficial contacts, the former New York City alderman cites an instance in which he was able to frustrate his dismissal from a government job in Washington, D.C., by contacting his Congressman and Senator. This same man claims to have gained a valuable knowledge of the "game of politics" while employed as messenger to the Secretary of the Treasury under President Hayes. In this capacity, the noted editor and politician had an opportunity to see enlightening correspondence and observe the tactics of the cream of America's always abundant crop of politicians.

The Negro school head in North Carolina attributes a goodly portion of her success to her valuable contacts among Negroes and whites alike.

The Negro journalist, while admitting that contacts have played a certain part in his career, expresses the feeling that almost all he has ever attained came because it was known that he had the qualifications for the job.

The Negro composer expresses the opinion that his introduction to two of America's outstanding cornetists in the music instrument factory of E. G. Conn was most fortunate, and claims that in a half-hour's conversation with these personages, he learned more about the cornet (his instrument) than he could have in many years spent at a music school.

The Florida publisher ascribes the major portion of his success to his ability to keep in close contact with all well-meaning people, both white and Negro.

The Negro government employee under the civil service regulations admits that by exhibiting desirable characteristics while employed as a mere messenger he has formed acquaintances with many whites who have been in a position to aid or hamper his promotions.

6. Nature and Value of the Training Received

Negro national organization executive: Education secured in public schools of Richmond, Va., Virginia Union University. Graduate work in Social Sciences at Cornell—M.A. Attended lectures at New School for Social Research.

Prominent Negro educator of Alabama: Regards basic principles involved in his training as having great value. (He is veterinarian.)

The training received in college, the preparation for the legal profession, and five years experience as a college professor are considered indispensable as a factor in the development of the Republican politician.

The ambitious young woman in Norfolk is particularly thankful for her training in economics and debating, and contends that while the former gave her an insight into the present economic situation and general system, the latter taught her to analyze situations.

The Negro sociologist characterizes his formal college training as "atrocious," but regards his graduate training in economics and sociology, plus his experience in education, social work and research, as invaluable.

The Negro legislator in Ohio places a high valuation on his training and experience at the Cheyney Training School for Teachers.

The woman educator and prominent public figure characterizes her formal education as meager, but valuable, particularly that obtained at Scotia Seminary, where the teachers exemplified a spirit of sacrifice and courage. According to this woman, her experiences during the founding and development of her junior college have proved most valuable.

The Negro bishop states that the most valuable aspect of his elementary education in his southern community was its personal guidance. Speaking of his entire formal training, the Bishop expresses the opinion that the practical prestige value of the degrees may have often outweighed the intrinsic value of the training itself.

We have already seen the statement of the Negro woman educator of North Carolina, who regards her New England formal training as a tremendous asset.

The Negro journalist received little formal education, but did serve in the army, which afforded some valuable discipline.

Although he attended only an elementary school in Florence, Alabama, the famous Negro composer contends that this is where he learned the fundamentals of music, and formulated the desire to put them to good use.

The editor of the Negro newspaper in Florida received his formal training in the high school of his home, and at the Howard Normal School at Cuthbert, Ga., correspondence courses in theology from Morris Brown, and editorial work from Columbia. This Negro claims to be a close observer of men and events, and opines that he has learned far more since leaving school than he learned while in school.

Since first entering the government service as a messenger, the Negro who now occupies a high position under the rules of the Federal civil service has acquired legal training and knowledge in other specialized fields, anticipating that at some future time he might be called upon to put them into play. This is exactly what has happened, so naturally this man regards his education in particular fields as invaluable.

The Dean of the Virginia institution says of his education, which is quite extensive from a formal point of view, "The struggle to get an education was the best part of my education. I have spent more than $10,000 on my education and had the good fortune to earn every dollar of it."

7. Effect Which Racial Situation Has Had upon Personal Social Philosophy

Negro national organization executive: Racial situation has helped crystalize personal social philosophy. Believes racial and group prejudices are moulded to accommodate themselves to the desire of one group to have economic advantage over another, and that fundamentally people do not hate other people because they are of different color or possess different physical characteristics.

Prominent Negro educator of Alabama: Believes racial situation caused him to develop a set of social values. He says: "They have been inculcated in a philosophy of race, and pattern of behavior that I daresay would have come far less into my thinking otherwise. For example, I regard an understanding of minority technic [*sic*] a matter of first importance."

The Negro Republican from Mississippi reflects that rather than embittering him, the racial situation has made him receive his racial obstacles and difficulties "philosophically."

The young woman organization leader in Norfolk cites the racial situation as the definite reason for the formulation of her social philosophy, which, in her own words, is: "I am so low down that kicks must of necessity start me upward."

The sociologist and educator claims that in recent years he has become intolerant of the programs of race organization whose roots seem stuck in "race relationism" rather than in basic programs of economic and social reform and reconstruction.

Ohio's Negro Assemblyman believes that inter-marriage and the amalgamation of the races is the only hope for the Negro in this country.

The woman educator and prominent public figure maintains that the racial situation has not warped her thinking, and that her faith in American democracy is the basis for a very optimistic attitude.

The Negro churchman admits that the racial situation has been an important conditioning influence on his social thinking and behavior, and while confessing occasional bitterness, believes that as the years pass he will think with an increasing degree of objectivity.

The Negro woman educator of North Carolina claims to hold no ill will or resentment toward the white race, and although she has been compelled to accept segregation because "... my people who need what I have to give live in larger numbers in the land of segregated ideals ... my philosophy is that position or place can never segregate mind or soul. ..."

The Negro journalist discounts the influence of the racial situation as a controlling influence, contending that psychologically he would probably have been the same without the racial situation.

The Negro administrator believes that his identification with a minority group has had much to do with his social philosophy, and claims that it has contributed much toward his combined interests in labor problems and liberal movements and programs.

The Negro composer states that he bases his philosophy upon an old lesson in an equally old elementary text book, i.e.,—"No excellence without great labor." This famous Negro says that, being a Negro, he thought that this axiom was exceptionally fitting.

The publisher of the Florida weekly expresses the belief that in spite of the social conditions of this country, the Negro can rise and make himself felt. In order to do this, however, the Negro must have the utmost faith in himself.

The Negro civil service employee outlines the effect of the social situation upon his personal social philosophy in the following terms:

It is my belief that the racial situation in this country will never be improved materially except through some miracle such as war. The education of all races would, in time, accomplish much, were it not for the fact that the economic situation is growing more acute. Regardless of the white man's tendency to be fair and just, it will be difficult to convince him that he should give the Negro preference in employment, all other factors being equal. The Negro may organize and be in a position to demand a certain share of employment, and he may vote intelligently and in sufficient numbers to demand certain rights and privileges, but until then he is at the mercy of others; others who are better organized and more intelligent than he, and who are working most effectively against him. Where the Negro has migrated and found employment, he is despised as a competitor. Prejudice, therefore, has spread with his migration. Even though these conditions did not exist, and were it possible to wipe out prejudice overnight, I am of the opinion that the Negro as a race is not capable of existing in a world where only the fit survive. Too few are trained for the contemporary scene; too few realize the responsibilities of life; too few can stand the tests required of a despised minority group; and too many have as their patterns the white man whose income and resourcefulness are several times his own, and with whose background there can be no comparison. These faults of the Negro are the natural results of slavery, forced isolation, separate and poor schools, and discrimination in general; but in his fight for existence, his faults, and not the causes thereof, are the determining factors. No one wants an insolent, untrained, or unreliable associate or employee, even though that associate or employee is not responsible for his condition. Neither do the Negroes of the upper stratum feel that they should adopt a policy other than that of *laissez faire*; neither can they see the necessity for assuming additional burdens. They, too, are intolerant and unsympathetic; and they, too, look at conditions as they exist, and not at the causes thereof. With the proper training, I feel the Negro might justify his existence, just as other races have done, but this will require generations. Whether the race dies before it succeeds, is the question. In view of the growing prejudice against millions not taught methods of combating the same, a prejudice which affects every phase of life, I cannot hold much hope for the Negroes' future until they are trained in the light of existing conditions as well as legal theories; until they are convinced that work is more important than play; until they are willing to make sacrifices; until they are capable of doing those things which competition demands of us all; and until they realize the seriousness of life's situation in general. These shortcomings are especially true when unemployment is so prevalent. The fact that it is difficult for a Negro to secure employment should not be attributed to prejudice alone. Too many Negroes are unreliable and incompetent; they do not attempt to improve their conditions; they render poor services and resent the slightest reprimands; they consider their social lives far too important; they give up places of employment when there is no justification; and too many of them start out with the thought that advantage is to be taken of them. These faults are not to any particular class of Negroes; some of them apply to the professional and business classes, as well as to others. All of which results in the Negro being a non-entity in practically every phase of life; it commands no respect in the financial, business, or political world. The race excels in a couple of fields only, and this because a certain few were willing to fight life's battles as they existed; because they were willing to work hard, make sacrifices, and forget social ambitions; and because they saw the necessity for future financial security even while in the midst of world-acclaimed triumphs.

Evidence of the imprint made upon his social philosophy by the race situation is presented in the following statement from the head of the Kentucky Negro college:

Though not agreeing with the illogical basis of racial segregation and deploring the sacrifices which must be made by my group, I recognized the fact that it existed, and that customs and inbred beliefs of centuries could be removed only by a slow evolutionary process. . . . While segregation exists it should be used by the Negro to develop and extend his own leadership.

8. *Extent to Which Career Has Been Influenced or Controlled by Racial Situation*

A Negro educator merely states: "I am sure that the racial situation has been a dominant influence in my career."

Although admitting that the racial situation has made him bitter on occasions, Mississippi's foremost Republican leader believes that it has made him generally more tolerant and liberal in his racial views. This Negro admits that the "spirit of antipathy" early turned into a desire to excel other races in the matter of competition.

As a staunch advocate of the proper and effective use of the voting franchise by the Negro voter, the Norfolk woman believes that the ballot is the chief weapon to use in attempts to improve conditions arising out of the racial situation. This young lady contends that while the racial situation may indirectly influence her career, she will never allow it to be a controlling factor.

The law school Dean expresses the opinion that the racial situation is largely responsible for his recognition, both among whites and Negroes, and frankly believes that being a Negro has been an asset to him in this connection.

The sociologist believes that the racial situation was the reason for his determination to find out whether or not he could function outside of an area of race employment. This was done by taking several state and federal civil services examinations simply as a test of ability. When his ranking satisfied him as to his ability, he refused the job offered, but later on accepted a civil service appointment as a safe-guard against any "whims of the racial situation as might occur." Later, when dealing with young Negro graduate students, this educator has sought to provide them with tools that will enable them to fight an aggressive social battle.

The Ohio Assemblyman admits that the racial situation has definitely figured in his determination to always bear in mind that in public life his primary purpose is to represent the best interests of his people. However, this gentleman emphasizes that this determination does not blind him to the general problems confronting all citizens.

The noted Negro woman educator says: "My career has been influenced by the race situation to the extent that I've devoted the greater proportion of my life to the cause of my people. This control has given me a larger opportunity since leadership is so sorely needed among my group. The problem of races has produced leaders which otherwise might have been lost in the general melting pot. . . ."

The Bishop ranks religion and race as the dominant influences in his life.

The Negro editor and former Alderman of the City of New York states that he has never allowed prejudice to interfere with going after what he wanted. He further states that he has helped whites as well as Negroes, and has never let prejudice interfere with getting things done.

The woman educator who received most of the benefits offered by the New England culture states:

> Recognizing the need of a cultural approach to life, believing absolutely in education through racial contacts, I have devoted my whole life to establish for Negro youth something superior to Jim Crowism by bringing the two races together under the highest cultural environment that will increase race pride, mutual respect and confidence, sympathetic understanding, and Interracial Goodwill.

Though admitting that the race situation has forced him into a "segregated mold," the Negro journalist and writer contends that he has not been rendered provincial in outlook, and says: "While I hate the segregated system and the whole civilization that has been built upon it, I am not blind to the shortcomings of the colored brethren, and appreciate that they would act the same as the whites if positions were reversed."

The Negro government official in the Federal Works Agency expresses the belief that his racial identity has been more of an attribute than a detriment to his advance in his government work.

Evidently the racial situation was a tremendous factor in the success story of the famous composer, for he says:

> As a day laborer in various fields, I have suffered the hardships of the man farthest down. Knowing that slavery gave birth to the spirituals, I

had sufficient musical education to write the idioms and snatches of sorrow songs that grew out of a nominal freedom, and to mold them into a mournful yet happy pattern which I called the blues.

The Negro occupying the high-ranking civil service position states that while retarding his progress in many respects, the racial situation has also been the cause of a certain amount of advancement. In explaining this seemingly paradoxical statement he states:

> My experience has been most unusual. For a number of years I worked under a supervisor who feared competition. He was promoted to his position by reason of his political affiliations. As a result of this fear, no white person with originality, training, or ambition was permitted to remain in the division long enough to gain any kind of foothold, for fear he would become a competitor of this supervisor; with me it was different. Realizing that the racial and political situation precluded my ever becoming his competitor, I was retained in the division, was assigned law work, and have reaped some of the benefits automatically resulting from such an assignment. Had I been white, I don't feel that I would have been permitted to remain in the division long enough to gain the knowledge I now have of the work. In other words, very unusual conditions made it possible for a Negro to get an unusual position.

Although not disclosing what effect the racial situation has had upon his career as an educator, the Maryland college head does point out that the reason he became an educator, rather than fulfilling his heart's desire by becoming an engineer was the fact that he realized the very limited possibilities the latter field offered members of his race.

The racial situation has inspired the Virginia educator to try his hand at interracial work, and he has done much along this line.

White Leaders in the Interracial Field

Of the 14 life histories submitted by white interracialists, 11 have been summarily analyzed and the digests of them are presented below. Of those considered, two are Y.M.C.A. officials, three are from an important formal interracial organization, three are foundation officials, one educator, one government official, and one Negro protest organization leader. All of them did not present material relevant to each of the queries raised, but whenever they have done so their views are recorded. The points about which they were requested to weave their abbreviated life histories are the following:

    I. Family background.
    II. Early consciousness of race problem.
    III. Active interest in racial problem.
    IV. Obstacles encountered in interracial activity.
    V. Advantages or handicaps due to interracial activity.
    VI. Effect of race situation on personal social philosophy.
    VII. Reactions of friends and [of] relatives to interracial activity.
    VIII. Personal adjustments necessary because of interracial activity.
    IX. Nature of activities engaged in.

A successful lawyer, and an official in one of the leading Negro protest organizations, was born in New York City in March, 1878. The father of this outstanding character was a successful merchant, an importer and grower of tobacco, and a generally respectable and conservative citizen, who was also active in the New York Chamber of Commerce. This champion of the Negro's cause received the usual advantages common to such an environment, including extensive travel and excellent formal education, and by the year 1900 he had received his A.B., M.A., and L.L.B. from Columbia University. In this same year this gentleman entered the legal practice in New York City, and has been so engaged ever since.

One of the nation's leading clergymen, who is also an educator and philanthropist, was born in New York in 1874. This national figure was one of a family of merchants and bankers who long have been recognized in the field of philanthropy.

An eminent surgeon, educator and trustee of the leading institution of higher learning for Negroes was born in up-state New York in 1869 of English parentage. The father of this man was somewhat notorious as a "free-thinker," and an opponent to class distinctions. The father is also credited with having smuggled more than a few runaway slaves into Canada. *Uncle Tom's Cabin* was read and re-read aloud by the father.

The head of an education foundation in the South was born in Boston, but adopted by an Englishman who came to this country and went to Virginia after living in New York about 13 years. After this adopted father's first wife died he married a southern white woman who had violent prejudices, but had no "dislike for Negroes." This administrator spent his childhood on the farm, where his principal associates were the Negro laborers on his father's tobacco farm. The custom was to give a drink of whiskey to the hands at the end of each day's work. The administrator had the whiskey distributing job. It was thought that this was a good way to build up good will among the men. The father is described as a kindly old gent who never used the word "nigger." The administrator attended all private schools.

An outstanding interracialist and present government official was born in Atlanta in 1902. His parents were not wealthy, but "comfortably well off." His father was a business man and his mother had a broad interest in social and political affairs as a result of her father's public life as editor of one of the South's leading newspapers.

An interracial-educator was born in South Africa in May 1879 of middle-class English parents, who emigrated to South Africa in search of better economic advantages. Although the family had its economic trials and tribulations, it was considered as among the better social classes in the colony. The family employed a number of native servants, with whom, according to this informant, he and his three brothers and two sisters [were] on terms of condescending friendship. He played with the servants and learned some of their language. He states in this connection: "I suppose I always regarded myself as the young master, but this did not prevent me from liking my native playmates. . . ." When about 12 years old, his father and mother made it clear to him that he was growing up and could no longer afford to have natives as his friends. Because his father was a "kind, but firm, disciplinarian and treated both his children and his servants in a truly Roman style," this interracialist was not aware of developing any feelings of superiority.

A foundation official and educator was born in 1887 in Nebraska, and as a youngster was reared in Wyoming. When seven years old he was taken to Kentucky, when he lived with his grandparents on a farm. He attended a mixed college—Berea—and never thought anything strange about Negroes and whites learning together.

A woman interracialist of Charleston, South Carolina, is a descendant of an old, land-holding and slave-owning family, which was considered influential up to the Civil War. In this family the slaves as well as the children were "very spoiled." This woman was ten days old when a Negro woman with a baby was brought to their home to nurse her. During her childhood this woman grew up in the mountains of Georgia on her grandfather's farm. There was a most cordial relationship here between the Negroes and whites, and the youngsters credit the Negroes with guiding them to their etiquette, morals and religion. After struggling along trying to acquire an education there was a brief period of teaching in order to make a "little money."

A prominent educator and member of one of the best-known education boards was born and reared in Cumberland County, Virginia, a county with more Negroes than whites. There was always at least one Negro family on the family's farm, and this gentleman has had association with Negroes all his life. This eminent educator states: "I was one of ten children. Everybody was poor and we were all poor together— white and black. I did not have a mammy nurse."

A director of interracial work in two Southern states was born in Tennessee in 1879, the fourth child in a family of eight. His maternal ancestors were [from] North Carolina, while his father's people were Virginians.

The head of the Interracial Commission was reared on a plantation with several Negroes who were very kind and congenial. He claims that his father never had any feeling that Negroes were inferior, and neither has he. This gentleman thinks that the unusually cordial relationship between his family and the Negroes on the farm gave him something of an advantage on the racial question. The first formal introduction to a Negro as man-to-man occurred when he was introduced to "Mr. Napier."

An outstanding interracialist from Texas admits that his parents accepted the traditional race mores without question, but that their deep religious convictions tempered their attitude.

Soon after 1900 the head of the nation's leading Negro national organization became interested in settlement work, and for a number of years was engaged in such work among the recently arrived immigrants. Somewhat later this gentleman became concerned with the problems of the unprotected girl, and served on the legal committee of the New York Probation Association. It was during this work that the realization dawned that the Negro was by far the most helpless, aggrieved and exploited group in America, that his plight was desperate, and that he was on the road to being deprived of all his manhood rights. It was thought that the latter was inimicable [*sic*] to democracy itself. In 1910, this leader's brother helped incorporate the National Association for the

Advancement of Colored People, and enlisted his aid as a member of the New York Vigilance Committee, which served as the New York branch of the N.A.A.C.P. Soon after he became a director of the national organization. In addition to this, the discovery of deplorable health conditions of Negro troops during the World War made a deep impression upon this man.

The clergyman-educator and philanthropist was first interested in the race problem as a result of several factors. In the first place, two of his aunts were engaged in actual philanthropy, and were quite friendly with Booker T. Washington, who was often the topic of family discussions. In addition to this influence, this man's mother was actively interested in a Negro orphan asylum in New York, and several members of the family were interested in Liberia. In about 1905 a trip to Tuskegee seemed to heighten an interest in the race problem. Then the Phelps-Stokes Fund was put into operation in 1910, and this race benefactor was made an official of the Fund Board. In addition to these factors, the acceptance of trusteeships of Negro institutions and the General Education Board stimulated a keen interest in the Negro situation, especially from an educational angle.

Listening to his father read *Uncle Tom's Cabin* aroused the consciousness of the noted surgeon and trustee to the existence of the racial situation. The first real close-up on racial discrimination, however, occurred in his hometown when a group of touring Negro singers were refused accommodations in the village hotel. The trustee's brother and his wife arranged accommodations for these singers at their home and at the homes of some friends. Many of the townspeople criticized this action.

The foundation head had his first inkling of the race situation when as a student at William and Mary he supported, along with the rest of the students, President Tyler's defense when he was criticized throughout the South for sending his daughter to Wellesley College while Booker T. Washington's daughter was there. The main stimulus for the interracial work of this administration was his appointment as principal of a Negro elementary school in Richmond at the age of 21.

The interracialist, now employed in the federal government, was first impressed with the existence of the racial situation when he attended a lynching while at the University of Georgia. The active interest in the problem, however, was stimulated at a meeting of the Liberal Club at Harvard University where Dr. Du Bois was the guest speaker. This interest was further stimulated while he was in attendance at the London

School of Economics, where he studied with foreign students from all points of the globe, and thought how absurd it was that the line seemed to be drawn on American Negroes alone. This man gained his first knowledge of the Interracial Commission in Atlanta when he reviewed Oldham's *Christianity and the Race Problem,* and decided that he might put into practical operation some of his theories through the agency in his home town.

After college, the interracialist-educator was made superintendent of schools in his native town, but was not in charge of the native schools. However, he met the author of "Black and White in Southeast Africa," and together they formed the Native Affairs Reform Association, which was the first non-political body to study the question of white and black relationships in the country. The work of this body was spurred by the outbreak of the Zuhr Rebellion of 1906, and the general feeling among the townspeople that reform in Native Administration was badly needed. In 1920, General Smuts, Prime Minister of the Union of South Africa, anxious to have the native question out of party politics, created the Native Affairs Commission, and this educator was made one of the commissioners.

The foundation official and educator spent considerable time in the Orient, Pacific Isles, and Eastern Europe, and necessarily came into contact with many races. Interest and friendship for these many races was aroused as he sensed organized opposition to them and discrimination against them.

The South Carolina woman interracialist went to Sweden when she was quite a young woman, and suddenly realized that color was a barrier in no other place than America. The lady claims that the short period she spent in Sweden broadened her outlook in many ways, and had a lasting influence on her character. Harriet Stowe's *Uncle Tom's Cabin* had its effect, too. When approached by one of her friends later in life, and asked to become an active member of the Interracial Commission, this woman eagerly accepted, and with a few white and Negro women launched the Charleston Committee on Better Race Relations.

The educator and foundation official states that in his early background there was no consciousness of a "problem," but there was a well-defined difference between the races. In the country there was a gallery which was built for Negroes. There sprang up a separate Negro church, and Negroes were pulling away from the white church. The incident which impressed race consciousness on this educator's mind came late in his college career. The President Tyler–Booker T. Washington's daughter–Wellesley College affair broke when he was a senior at William and Mary, and he presided over a meeting of the student body which adopted a resolution relative to the absurdity of the attacks upon Tyler, and upheld him. The foundation head says: "This was the first time I had seen the issue raised in a political way, and it made me conscious of the way people with political interests could use the race issue."

The head of the Interracial Commission broke with the church, and to this day belongs to none, on account of the failure of the church to apply the proper Christian principles to the racial situation.

The eminent clergyman-educator and philanthropist designates the lack of the knowledge of the facts on the part of the general public as the one obstacle encountered frequently in his interracial activity.

The director of the Commission's work in North Carolina and Virginia confesses that his prejudice was his main difficulty, and gives credit to Mrs. Bethune as one of those responsible for dispelling the traditional beliefs as to the Negro's criminal tendencies and general worthlessness.

The well-known leader of the Negro organization, while not claiming any special advantage or disadvantage as a result of his interracial activities, does express the belief that his activities in connection with improving the lot of the Negro soldier resulted in several recommendations for promotion in the Army being ignored. Other than this there is no evidence of unfair treatment on account of interracial activities.

The educator and philanthropist contends that his interracial activity has been of tremendous value to him, in that it has broadened his field of interest and sympathy.

In a statement regarding his personal social philosophy after many years of interracial work, the noted educator and philanthropist says:

> I do not believe that intermarriage between any widely separated racial groups is generally advisable, and think that in the interest of race pride of a good type, the system of separate social life of different racial groups is normally advisable, but feel that there is no reason whatever why representatives of such groups, whether they be Chinese, Japanese, Jewish, *Negro,* German, French or *American* should not meet occasionally to discuss their problems and to break bread together. (Italics in original.)

The Atlanta interracialist states that his career has been shaped by his eleven years of service with the Interracial Commission and the interest in that work.

The foundation head has simplified things to an appreciable degree with this: "Since I have identified Negro progress with general progress in the South and in the nation, I have been concerned with southern problems of all sorts—with the white as well as the colored."

The Texas interracialist claims that his belief in the sacredness and value of the individual has been moulded by the racial situation, and vice versa.

While pointing out that some of his friends and relatives have been either amused or sympathetic with his interracial activities, the organization head denies any hostility on their part.

The widely known philanthropist disclaims any knowledge of any criticism of his interracial activity from any one of his family, but admits that such activity on the part of his wife, who is a southerner, might have been commented upon unfavorably by some of her relatives. The belief is also expressed that undoubtedly some of the citizens of the nation's Capital think that they have gone in a little too strongly for activities in behalf of Negroes.

The noted surgeon and trustee recalls that upon his first trip to Tuskegee Institute some young Alabama whites deliberately created dust on an Alabama road on which he and his wife were being driven by a Negro official of the Institute and another Negro. When the gentleman protested and rebuked these "ignorant, ill-bred" whites, they scoffed at him, and ridiculed him as a "nigger lover." This gentleman is, and has been, connected with some of the finest medical centers in the country, in both a professional and official capacity; while connected with one of the most exclusive medical institutions he had exacted the assurance from certain other officials that Negro graduates from the Medical School would be accepted as interns in the institution's hospital facilities. When two qualified Negroes were not given internships for an obviously trumped-up reason, this man resigned his official position in the institution, which he had held for many years—making it very emphatic that he disapproved of such bigoted conduct on the part of the institution. This was obviously a sacrifice few would make. Another incident involving this same personage occurred on a boat, when an intoxicated white woman rang the service bell and cursed and berated the Negro servant who answered the call after a little delay. After calling the servant a "damned lazy nigger" this woman called the ship's officers and demanded the boy's dismissal. At this juncture the trustee took up the defense of the Negro and cleared him of any offense. After the complaining woman left the scene, the officer said, "Well, we have to bawl out these nigger boys just to please some of these overbearing white people."

The education foundation head has this to say:

I have not suffered in my relationships with southern whites because of the nature of my work and my attitudes on the question. I eat meals with Negroes frequently, but I don't advertise the fact. I don't mention it to any of my relatives unless they ask me directly, and an admission of this fact would not affect my relations with my relatives or with my intimate friends.

The interracialist characterizes the reaction of his relatives to his interracial activities as "affectionate tolerance"; but that of his friends varies from enthusiasm to skepticism, and that of his acquaintances from praise to bitter hostility. So far as personal adjustments because of interracial activities are concerned, this gentleman says: "I have pursued the course that my conscience dictated and left it to other people to make whatever adjustments were necessary."

The foundation official remembers no hardships whatever on account of his interest in "unusual races."

The South Carolina interracialist avers that she has been severely criticized socially, and but for the standing acquired in the community before going into the work, it might have been a serious handicap.

The Chairman of the Interracial Commission states that many southern Congressmen hate him, and that one well-known senator evidenced resentment at eating dinner with him at the White House recently. According to this gentleman, he is berated as a race traitor and a "nigger lover."

The Texan says:

This work has brought me into many very delicate and difficult positions. It has caused its full share of criticism and heartache. Some of my white friends have berated me for going too fast; some of my colored friends have called me names because I would not go faster, but as I look back over it, I wouldn't have missed it for the world, and the joys have far exceeded the hardships.

In response to the query as to the nature of some of the activities engaged in, the philanthropist lists the following: 1) arranging for the meeting of about ten leading white men and ten leading Negroes when General Smuts came to this country; 2) leadership in the movement for the Encyclopedia of the Negro; 3) membership in Conference on the Christian Mission on Africa at La Zoute.

The work of the Atlanta interracialist has found him as Secretary for the Georgia and Florida Committees on Interracial Cooperation for two years, Assistant to the Director of the Phelps-Stokes Fund, and Associate and Director for Studies of the Rosenwald Fund, and a Director of the Commission on Interracial Cooperation.

The foundation official and educator has been largely concerned with the improvement of Negro and southern institutions; southern rural education for both whites and Negroes; fellowships for Negro and white Southerners; and the promotion of Negro health.

South Carolina's interracialist has conducted speaking tours throughout the eastern and mid-Atlantic states; and has held classes in race relations in several communities.

The educator and foundation executive states that he was selected to the Board of the James Teachers Fund on the advice of Dr. R. R. Moton.

* 4 *

Leadership Schedules

An identification schedule containing 88 names of prominent Negroes and including a few whites of prominence in the interracial field was drawn up with a view toward experimentally testing the extent to which Negro leaders are known to Negroes. (See Appendix II, for sample of this schedule). The schedule included prominent Negroes in several different fields of activity, covering education, organization leaders, political leaders, newspaper publishers and journalists, artists and popular entertainers, radicals and insurrectionists, churchmen, business leaders, scientists and authors. The schedule called for multiple identification as to (1) race, (2) living or dead, and (3) occupation or activity for which individual is best known. A total of 896 of these schedules were completed. They were submitted to the group from which most favorable scores might be anticipated—Negro college students. Negro college students, largely, in the social science classes at Howard University (Washington, D.C.), Atlanta University (Atlanta, Ga.), Dillard University (New Orleans, La.), Prairie View State College (Prairie View, Texas), North Carolina State College for Negroes (Durham, N.C.), Shaw University (Raleigh, N.C.), Tuskegee Institute, Miner Teachers College (of Washington, D.C.), and Kentucky State College (Frankfort, Ky.) submitted to the test.[30]

These schedules have not yet been fully tabulated. The columns involving racial and living or dead identifications have been worked over, but time has not permitted the analysis of the occupation percentage scores.

My assumption has been that Negro leadership has not impressed itself greatly upon the consciousness of the Negro population. There is nothing in the returns from this explanatory effort which would greatly disturb that view. Though the schedule was employed only with Negro students in Negro colleges, who it can be assumed have had more contact with Negro history materials than any other group of Negroes, who read the Negro press, and who are alive to the activities of Negro organizations, the returns do not suggest any great knowledge of leading Negro personalities.

The table attached indicates the results of the tabulation of racial identifications by occupational or activity groups. No similar table has been prepared for the living or dead column due to lack of time. Since the occupational identifications have not been worked up, nothing can be said of those results here.

The analysis of the racial identifications as indicated in the table shows that, as might be suspected, the Negro artists and entertainers are best known. Individuals such as Marian Anderson and Paul Robeson were correctly identified racially by 93.8 and 93.1 [percent,] respectively. For this group of six as a whole, including one pugilist, the percentage right was 78.6. It should be noted, however, that there were individuals in other group categories who were identified by a higher percentage than any in this top group. Frederick Douglass was identified correctly on 96%, Booker T. Washington on 95.5% and George Carver on 94.1%. The percentage rate for the artists and entertainers group would undoubtedly have been much higher if some of the more popular figures such as Duke Ellington, "Cab" Calloway, "Bojangles" Robinson and Ethel Waters had been included—not to mention Joe Louis. On the other hand, it would be difficult to name any living Negro political figure who receives more publicity than Arthur Mitchell, the only Negro Congressman, who was identified by only 69.3%; or a more active organizational leader than Walter White, with only 59.7%. The returns on the churchmen, though next highest, are not representative, for only two such figures were included, Father Divine with 95% and Richard Allen with 39.6%. The organization leaders group percentage was only 36%, despite the fact that some of the biggest leaders were included: Walter White of the N.A.A.C.P., Marcus Garvey, Eugene Kinckle Jones and A. Philip Randolph. The group of educators were identified racially by only 49.1%, with such figures as Booker T. (93.5), Mary McLeod Bethune (89.3), Carter Woodson (87.0) and W. E. B. Du Bois (78.6). The small group of radicals was far down the list with a percentage of only 28.6%, with Ben Davis, Jr., leading at 36.3%, rather surprisingly over Angelo Herndon at 33.4%, John P. Davis, Secretary of the National Negro Congress, at 25.3% and James Ford, perennial vice-presidential candidate of the Communist Party, at 19.5%. The explanation for the readier identification of Ben Davis, Jr., may be found in the fact that his father had

Arthur W. Mitchell. (Scurlock Studio Collection, Archives
Center, National Museum of American History)

been a widely known Republican politician and former National Republican Committeeman from Georgia. Nat Turner's race was known to
only 58.1% while 95.4% were correct on the Scottsboro boys.

Of the white leaders who loom most prominent in the Negro world,
Julius Rosenwald, the Jewish philanthropist whose death is still
mourned by Negroes, ranked highest in the racial identification with
72.4% correct. Harriet Beecher Stowe of *Uncle Tom* fame was next with
41.7%, and John Brown with 40.5%. The active interracial leaders,
such as Arthur Spingarn, president of the N.A.A.C.P., Will Alexander,
head of the Commission on Interracial Cooperation, Edwin Embree of
the Rosenwald Fund and others had low scores with 36.8%, 11.2%,
and 7.9%, respectively.

A rough table indicating the breakdown of those racial identification scores is attached. The rank order needs revision since it is given in totals rather than per cents. This affects only a few names, however, and resulted from the addition of some names to a subsequent schedule, after the first schedules had been used. The error is a relatively slight one.[31]

* 5 *

Conclusion

Two studies of Negro leadership have been made which are good examples of what Negro leadership studies ought not to be. (cf. *Negro Leaders,* by Harry W. Greene, West Virginia State College Bulletin, Series 23, No. 6, Nov. 1936; and *Virginia's Contribution to Negro Leadership,* Extension Department, Hampton Institute, 1937.) The first of these makes a mild attempt to analyze the educational and social background factors of 150 prominent Negroes whose life sketches are carried in national directories. It makes simple tabulations of the birthplaces of these leaders, the colleges and universities they attended, their informal educational contacts, their organizational affiliations, their professions or vocations, and their religious denominations. When all the shouting is over, it is shown that most of them came from small towns in the South but now live in big ones; they attended the best schools, they are mainly in educational work, they belong to learned societies, many are ministers, etc. No attempt is made to analyze the basis for their elevation, the dynamics of leadership among Negroes, the techniques employed to attain power and to preserve it, nor of their general attitudes on general and Negro problems. The Virginia study merely presents a long list of names with bare biographical facts, and no analysis at all.

Negro leadership is a largely local phenomenon and even in the local communities its influence seldom filters down to the masses of black people. Quite often it does not even impress itself upon the "classes." Negro leadership has not developed well the techniques for really reaching the masses of people, nor have those appeals been developed which can really arouse them in the mass. There is a fundamental realism lacking in the approaches of Negro leaders. They are great platform artists, many of them, but they have not permitted themselves to strike at the heart of the Negro's suffering here. The trouble is that so much of the leadership is middle class in its thinking and living, and inevitably harps upon those disabilities which are of far more importance to the limited number of middle-class than to the vast majority of working-class Negroes. Lynching, equalization of teachers' salaries, admittance to white universities, court cases, etc., are sensational and evoke admiration from the Negro elite, but they leave the masses of Negroes and their problem of daily bread untouched.

The Negro leadership just is not making an imprint upon the thought and action of the Negro mass world. It doesn't reach into the rural areas in which dense hordes of Negroes eke out an existence under the cruel lash of racial oppression. It doesn't force its way into the dark ghettoes of our cities. The Negro children are unaware of it and they grow up groping for guidance, for a basis of understanding, for a strong arm of support against the fury of race hatred.

An experience in a little one-room, one-teacher, Negro school in a rural area in Georgia is symbolic of an ominous truth. Only one of the eager students knew, or thought he knew, of Booker T. Washington. He said that Washington was a white man who was president of the United States. No one knew Walter White, John Hope, Du Bois, or Moton. No one had heard of the N.A.A.C.P. One boy identified Carver as a "colored man who makes medicine." Several could identify Joe Louis, Ella Fitzgerald, Henry Armstrong and Fats Waller. One, with unconscious satire, informed that "the Constitution of the United States" is a "Newspaper in Atlanta."

The material presented in this memorandum, though hurriedly and roughly assembled, should give some idea of the lack of respect among Negroes for their leaders and the bases for it. The objective was merely to provide some insight into what the Negro thinks and says behind the scenes about the quality of his leadership. Much of this expression is quite probably the product of gossip, biased appraisal and personal grudges, but by and large, it is symptomatic of a fundamental disregard among Negroes for the Negro leadership.

The picture thus presented is a rather gloomy and disreputable one. It is not by any means suggested that the generality of Negro leadership is as venal, corrupt, dishonest, fawning, opportunistic and crudely materialistic as many of the appraisals suggest. There is a great deal of Negro leadership that is honest to a fault, sincere and conscientiously devoted to the betterment of the race. In many instances it is confused, misguided and inept, but it means well. Yet there is no real leadership in the sense of powerful personalities who can command enthusiastic followings. The Negro minority is in dire need of a strong and clear-headed leadership to steer it through the dangerous rapids of current domestic and international affairs. The very complications of the Negro's racial position make it difficult for him to comprehend clearly the full significance of events as they relate to his interests. Racial thinking is an obstacle to clear thinking, and the Negro is easily and often led astray. No group can be so easily violated ideologically as that which blindly seeks escape.

But it will take more than strong and intelligent Negro leadership to save the Negro a decent future in this world. The dice which are determining the world's future—and therefore the Negro's as well—are not in the hands of black men. The Negro alone can do little or nothing to control world events and this is the arena in which the Negro's stakes in the civilized world are being fought for. But the Negro can play his part in shaping the course of events by the nature of his alliances. His force is an important one, not alone, but when allied with other and stronger groups. Negro leadership is needed that will see and understand this clearly, that will clarify Negro thinking, that will be able to exhort and enlist the full force of Negro numbers and energy behind the forces that are fighting to preserve the only kind of world in which the Negro can have a future that is worth living to see—a world devoted to democratic practices.

Finally, the Negro leader, himself, though elevated, remains a Negro, subject to all of the humiliations and many of the disabilities suffered by his lowly black followers. The Negro leader, with an advantaged status, tends to emphasize the humiliations rather than the privations, for it is the humiliations that he often feels most bitterly about. For example, an important Negro leader and big business man in the South owns a building in which one of his business enterprises is located. A part of this building was rented to white operators of a soft-drink stand. The Negro business leader rushed out of his office one day and bought a coca cola at the stand. Without thinking, he began to drink it on the premises and was rudely put out of a part of his own building. The Negro leader commands no general respect from the white community. His acceptance as a group leader is observed only by that part of the white population which understands that he has a function to perform, and an always relatively small group of liberal-minded and tolerant whites. In his relations with the mass of whites the Negro leader, no matter how great his name, must keep to the Negro's "place."

In the final analysis, it would seem that the relative success of the Negro leader, and of the white leader who is sincerely devoted to the "solution" of the race problem, must be judged in terms of his ability to lead the Negro people toward an ever-widening horizon of decent, respectable life in America, to immersion in the mainstream of that life, to acceptance in the society as a full, unqualified and respected citizen on a level of absolute equality with all other citizens. This must be the unequivocal goal. There is room, surely, for variation in tactics, for deviation, for reasons of immediate tactics and strategy, to this or that by-road, but the goal must never be lost sight of, the direction must ever remain clear. There is no "place" for the Negro or his leaders other than the place of all full-blown Americans.

Appendix I

General but Incomplete List of Negro Leaders Employed for Guidance in Leadership Memorandum

Abbott, Robert S.
Publisher Ed. of Chicago Defender. Politics: Independent, Chicago, Ill.

Adams, Frank W.
Asst. U.S. Attorney, Wash., D.C.

Adams, George C.
Lawyer, Politics: Rep. Chicago, Ill.

Adams, Oscar W.
Editor of Birmingham Reporter. Politics: Independent, Birmingham, Ala.

Adams, Stanley H.
Registrar, Johnson C. Smith University

Adderly, Quinton Jerome
High School Principal, Lakeland, Fla.

Aiken, Clarence L.
Clergyman, Atlantic City, N.J.

Aiken, Mrs. Cora M.
Principal, Colored School, Cheswold, Del., Dover, Del.

Akins, Mack W.
High School Principal, Raleigh, N.C.

Alexander, Ernest R.
Physician, N.Y.C.

Alexander, Royal C.
Dentist, Politics: Rep. Orange, N.J.

Alexander, Raymond Pace
Lawyer, Politics: Rep. Phil., Pa.

Alexander, Mrs. Sadie
Lawyer, Phil., Pa.

Alexander, Walter G.
Physician, Independent Dept. Orange, N.J.

Alexis, Lucien V.
Principal High School, New Orleans, La.

Allen, Cleveland G.
Lecturer, Journalist, Republican, N.Y.C.

Allen, Graves M.
Lawyer, Republican, St. Louis, Mo.

Allen, Nimrod B.
Social Worker, Republican, Columbus, Ohio.

Allen, Willard N.
Grand Master Masons, Republican, Balt., Md.

Allison, Andrew J.
Fisk Univ. Alumni Sec. Rep. Nashville, Tenn.

Allison, James M.
Physician-Surgeon, Rep. Chicago, Ill.

Alston, J. H.
Asst. Dean, Prairie View State College, Politics: Independent, Balt., Md.

Amos, Thomas H.
Clergyman. Politics: Independent, Asbury Park, N.J.

Anderson, Blanche W.
School Principal. Politics: Independent, Phila., Pa.

Anderson, Charles W.
Collector Internal Revenue, N.Y.C.

Anderson, Elmo M.
Exec. Sec. Catholic Bd. of Mission Work, N.Y.C.

Anderson, Forrest B.
Lawyer, Rep. Kansas City, Kansas.

Anderson, Louis B.
Lawyer-Alderman. Rep. Chicago, Ill.

Anderson, Mrs. Myrtle R.
Lawyer, N.Y.C.

Anderson, Peyton F.
Physician. Dem. N.Y.C.

Anderson, Clarence R.
Lawyer. Rep. Seattle, Wash.

Anderson, Subbeal S.
Dentist. Independent, N.Y.C.

Anderson, Violette N.
(Mrs. Albert C. Johnson)
Lawyer. Rep. Chicago, Ill.

Anderson, William E.
College prof. Rep. Langston Univ. Okla.

Andrews, William T.	Lawyer, Dem. N.Y.C.
Anthony, Lucie B.	Physician-Educator-County Supervisor. Rep. Sumter, S.C.
Archer, Samuel H.	President, Morehouse College. Rep. Atlanta, Ga.
Armond, Walter A.	Principal of Brewer Normal School. Greenwood, S.C.
Arthur, George R.	Member, Staff Rosenwald Fund. Rep. Chicago, Ill.
Asbury, John C.	Lawyer. Rep. Phila., Pa.
Atkins, Cyril F.	Educator, Wiley College, Independent. Marshall, Texas.
Atwood, Rufus B.	President, Ky. State Industrial College. Frankfort, Ky.
Ayer, Mrs. G. E. J.	School Principal, N.Y.C.
Bagley, Caroline	Lecturer and Author, Rep. Brooklyn, N.Y.
Bagnall, Robert W.	Director and Lecturer, N.Y.C.
Bailey, Robert L.	Lawyer. Asst. Attorney General. Rep. Indianapolis, Ind.
Baldwin, Damon O.	Physician. Rep. Martinsville, Va.
Banks, Myrtle N.	Teacher, Social Worker, Evangelist. Rep. New Orleans, La.
Banks, W. Rutherford	Educator, Prairie View State College. Prairie View, Texas.
Barons, Robert B.	Lawyer–Special Counsel. Rep. Columbus, Ohio.
Burnes, W. H.	Physician. Rep. Phila., Pa.
Barnett, Claude A.	Director, Associated Negro Press. Chicago, Ill.
Barnett, Constantine O.	Physician. Rep. Lakin, W.Va.
Barnett, Leonard	High School principal. Rep. London, W.Va.
Baskerville, Erasmus L.	Clergyman, Editor. Charleston, S.C.
Bate, Langston F.	Educator. Lincoln Univ. Jefferson City, Mo.
Battle, Wallace A.	Field Sec. Am. Church Institute. Socialist, N.Y.C.
Baxter, Daniel M.	Clergyman–business manager. Rep. Phila., Pa.
Bean, Theresa C. B.	Rural school supervisor. Wadesboro, N.C.
Beamon, Reginald E.	Dentist. Rep. Cincinnati, Ohio.
Bearden, Mrs. Besaye J.	Journalist. Dem. N.Y.C.
Beaubian, George H.	Asst. U.S. Attorney. Rep. Hempstead, L.I.
Bell, William A.	Rep. Birmingham, Ala.
Bell, William Y.	Clergyman-instructor, Memphis, Tenn.
Benjamin, Edgar P.	Bank President and lawyer, Rep. Roxbury, Mass.
Bennett, Stephen U.	Lawyer, Independent. Rep. Yonkers, N.Y.
Berry, Joseph C.	High School Prin., Rep. Charleston, S.C.
Berry, R. J.	Editor and publisher, Louisville, Ky.
Bethune, Mrs. Mary McLeod	Pres. of Bethune-Cookman College, Daytona Beach, Fla.
Beverly, Robert H.	Physician-Surgeon, Dem. Springfield, Ill.
Bias, John H.	Educator, State Normal School. Rep. Elizabeth City, N.C.
Biggers, Charles A.	President, Business College, Rep. Austin, Texas.
Billupe, Pope A.	Lawyer, Rep. N.Y.C.
Blackburn, E. Marsellus	Teacher-prin. Rep. Dover, Dela.
Blakemore, Elijah P.	Lawyer, Rep. Chicago, Ill.
Blanton, John O.	Bank pres. Rep. Louisville, Ky.
Blanton, Joshua E.	Educator, Rep. Denmark, S.C.
Blyton, Jesse B.	Educator, Accountant. Independent, Atlanta, Ga.
Bledsoe, Howard H.	Asst. Attorney Genr'l. Dem. Detroit, Mich.
Blount, William M.	Physician, Assemblyman. Rep. Kansas City, Kansas.
Bolton, Lemiel D.	Editor, Independent. Jacksonville, Fla.
Bond, Horace M.	Dean, Dillard Univ., New Orleans, La.

Bond, Roy S.	Lawyer, Baltimore, Md.
Bonner, Frederick D.	Public Accountant, Independent, New Bedford, Mass.
Boone, Alexander L.	Clergyman, Rep. Cleveland, Ohio.
Boone, Theodore S.	Clergyman, Editor, Author. Rep. Fort Worth, Texas.
Bousfield, Mrs. Maudelle B.	Educator, Prin. Republican. Chicago, Ill.
Bousfield, Midian Orthello	Insurance Co. Pres., physician. Independent, Chic., Ill.
Bradley, Isaac F.	Lawyer, Rep. Kansas City, Mo.
Bradshaw, William M.	Asst. Attorney Genr'l. Rep. Topeka, Kans.
Brokenburr, Robert L.	Lawyer, Rep. Indianapolis, Ind.
Brooker, E. Luther	Educator, Clark Univ. Atlanta, Ga.
Brooker, Stella B.	Educator, Independent, Atlanta, Ga.
Brooks, Walter H.	Clergyman, Wash., D.C.
Brown, Dr. Charlotte Hawkins	Educator, Palmer Memorial Inst. Sedalia, N.C.
Brown, Lawrence G.	Physician, Rep. Elizabeth, N.J.
Brown, Lucian S., Jr.	College Pres. Brulmert Institute. Dem. Chester, S.C.
Brown, S. Joe	Lawyer, Rep. Des Moines, Iowa.
Browning, James B.	Educator, Wash., D.C.
Bullock, Matthew W.	Lawyer, Rep. Boston, Mass.
Burroughs, Asa Morris	Lawyer, Chicago, Ill.
Burrell, J. Neton	Lawyer, Assemblyman. Rep. Newark, N.J.
Carter, Elmer	Editor, Independent. N.Y.C.
Carver, George Washington	Educator, Scientist. Tuskegee Inst.
Clark, Joseph S.	Pres. of Southern Univ. Rep. Baton Rouge, La.
Clement, George C.	Bishop, Dem. Louisville, Ky.
Clement, Rufus E.	Pres. of Atlanta Univ. Independent. Louisville, Ky.
Cobb, James H.	Municipal Judge, Wash., D.C.
Cobb, Robert S.	Lawyer, Rep. Jefferson City, Mo.
Comither, Arthur L.	Exec. Sec. Y.M.C.A. Rep. Brooklyn, N.Y.
Conners, William R.	Exec. Sec. Urban League, Negro Welfare Assoc. Independent, Cleveland, O.
Cullen, Countee	Poet. Rep. N.Y.C.
Daniel, Robert P.	Pres. Shaw Univ. Raleigh, N.C.
Daniel, Vattel E.	Dean, Wiley College, Rich., Va.
DePriest, Oscar	Realtor, Rep. Chicago, Ill.
Dogan, Matthew W.	Pres. Wiley College, Marshall, Texas. Rep.
Du Bois, W. E. B.	Activist, educator, author
Dungee, Roscoe	Publisher, Editor, Independent, Oklahoma City, Okla.
Elay, Robert J.	Exec. Sec. Brooklyn Urban League, Rep. Brooklyn, N.Y.
Falls, Arthur Grand Pro	Physician, Rep. Chicago, Ill.
Fennel, Emory N.	Dean School Education, Va. Seminary & College, Lynchburg, Va.
Ferguson, Thomas J.	Bank official. Rep. Atlanta, Ga.
Fleming, George J.	Journalist, N.Y.C.
Foster, A. L.	Exec. Sec. Urban League, Chicago, Ill.
Fowler, Stephen H.	Y.M.C.A. Secretary, Rep. Fort Worth, Texas.
Fox, J. T.	Dean, Houston Jr. College, Houston, Texas.
Francis, Robert C.	Professor, Lincoln Univ. of Mo. Berkeley, Calif.
Franklin, Chester A.	Editor, Independent, Kansas City, Mo.
Frazier, E. Franklin	Sociologist, Wash., D.C.
Gandy, J. M.	Pres. Va. State College. Rep. Ettrick, Va.

Garvin, Charles H.	Physician. Rep. Cleveland, Ohio.
Gibbs, William W.	Physician. Rep. Chicago, Ill.
Giles, Roscoe C.	Physician. Rep. Chic., Ill.
Gillespie, Chester K.	Lawyer, Assemblyman, Rep. Cleveland, Ohio.
Glass, D. R.	Pres. Texas College, Tyler, Kansas.
Gore, George W., Jr.	Dean, Tenn. A. & I. State College, Nashville, Tenn.
Granger, Lester B.	Social Worker. Independent, N.Y.C.
Graves, Lemuel E.	Sec. of Insurance Co. Independent, Raleigh, N.C.
Green, Aaron W.	Y.M.C.A. Sec. Rep. Wilkes-Barre, Pa.
Greene, Harry W.	Dean, W.Va. State College. New Bern, N.C.
Gregg, J. A.	Bishop, Rep. Kansas City, Kansas.
Gregory, Montgomery	Prin. of School. Rep. Atlantic City, N.J.
Grey, Edgar M.	Journalist, Rep. Augusta, Ga.
Hale, William J.	Pres. Agrc. and Ind. State College, Nashville, Tenn.
Hall, Charles E.	Government employee. Bureau of Census, Rep. Wash., D.C.
Hall, Egerton E.	Clergyman. Plainville, N.J.
Hamilton, West A.	Printer. Rep. Wash., D.C.
Hancock, Gordon B.	Educator, Rich., Va.
Harris, Abram L.	Educator, Wash., D.C.
Harris, Mrs. Judia J.	Educator, Athens, Ga.
Harris, Marquis L.	Dean, Samuel Houston College, Independent, Austin, Texas.
Harris, Nelson H.	Teacher, Raleigh, N.C.
Harrison, G. Lamar	College prof. Cincinnati, Ohio.
Hawkins, John C.	Lawyer. Rep. N.Y.C.
Hawkins, William A.	Lawyer. Independent. Rep. Balt., Md.
Hayes, Robert B.	Dean, New Orleans Univ. Rep. New Orleans, La.
Haynes, George E.	Sociologist. Rep. N.Y.C.
Henry, Edward W.	Magistrate. Rep. Phila., Pa.
Heywood, J. W.	Clergyman. Knoxville, Tenn.
Hill, Leslie P.	Educator. Rep. Cheyney, Pa.
Hill, T. Arnold	Dir. of Industrial Relations, N.Y.C.
Hinton, William A.	Clinical pathologist. Canton, Mass.
Holmes, Dwight O. W.	Pres. of Morgan College. Independent. Baltimore, Md.
Hood, Solomon P.	Minister to Liberia. Rep. Trenton, N.J.
Hopkins, Wayne L.	Exec. Sec. Phila. N.A.A.C.P. Rep. Phila., Pa.
Houston, Charles H.	Lawyer, Wash., D.C.
Houston, Gordon D.	Educator, Rep. Wash., D.C.
Howard, Perry W.	Lawyer, Rep. Wash., D.C.
Hubbard, Christopher C.	Educator, Rep. Sedalia, Mo.
Hughes, Langston	Poet, author. N.Y.C.
Hunton, Mrs. Addie W.	Sociologist, author. N.Y.C.
Jackson, Alexander L.	Realtor, Rep. Chic., Ill.
Jackson, Ida L.	Dean of Women, Tuskegee Inst. Rep. Oakland, Calif.
Jackson, Juanita	Special Asst. to Sec. N.A.A.C.P. Independent, N.Y.C.
Jason, William B.	Pres. Lincoln Univ. of Mo. Jefferson City, Mo.
Jeffries, Christina A.	Asst. Exec. Sec. Urban League. Pittsburgh, Pa.
Jernagin, William H.	Clergyman, Wash., D.C.
Johnson, Charles S.	Sociologist, Nashville, Tenn.
Johnson, Edward A.	Lawyer, N.Y.C. Rep.
Johnson, Everett W.	Social Worker. Rep. Toledo, Ohio.
Johnson, Mordecai W.	Pres. Howard Univ. Wash., D.C.
Johnson, Reginald A. N.	Exec. Sec. Urban League. Independent, Atlanta, Ga.

Jones, Eugene Kinckle	Social worker. Flushing, L.I. Rep.
Jones, Lawrence C.	Educator, Piney Woods, Miss.
Jones, Robert E.	Bishop of M.E. Church, New Orleans, La.
Jones, William H.	Dean, Tillotson Women's College, Rep. Austin, Tex.
Just, E. E.	Educator, Wash., D.C.
Kemp, Thomas S.	Educator, Clergyman, Rep. Wash., D.C.
King, Beasley Y.	School prin. Rep. Crockett, Texas.
King, L. Melendez	Lawyer, Rep. Wash., D.C.
King, Willis J.	Pres. Gammon Theol. Sem. Indepd't. Rep. Atlanta, Ga.
Lacey, George C.	Lawyer, Dem. Cleveland, O.
Lampkin, Foster R.	School supervisor. Rep. Columbus, Ga.
Lane, Isaac	Bishop of C.M.E. Church. Rep. Jackson, Tenn.
Lawrence, Pauline J.	Social worker, Realtor, Rep. Chic., Ill.
Lee, J. R. E.	Pres. of Fla. A & M College, Tallahassee, Fla.
Lenus, Rienzi B.	Pres. Brotherhood of Dining Car Employees, Independent. Rep. N.Y.C.
Lightner, Lawrence H.	Official of fraternal organization. Editor. Rep. Denver, Colorado.
Lipscomb, Mrs. Mary S.	Teacher, Atlanta, Ga.
Locke, Alain L.	Educator, Wash., D.C.
Lang, Charles S., Jr.	Pres. Edward Waters College, Jacksonville, Fla.
Longe, George	School prin. New Orleans, La.
Lucas, J. Gray	Asst. U.S. Attorney. Dem. Chic., Ill.
Lyon, Ernest	Clergyman, diplomatist. Rep. Balt., Md.
McCracken, Frederick D.	Realtor, Rep. St. Paul, Minn.
McCrorey, Henry L.	Pres. Johnson C. Smith Univ. Rep. Charlotte, N.C.
McDonald, A. W.	Educator. Rep. Galveston, Texas.
McDuffie, Emanuel M.	Educator. Laurinburg, N.C.
McKane, Alice Woodby	Physician, author. Rep. Boston, Mass.
McKay, Claude	Author. N.Y.C.
McKinney, Theophilum E.	Dean, Johnson C. Smith Univ. Independent. Charlotte, N.C.
Mamors, Monro A.	Physician. Author. Rep. Los Angeles, Calif.
Mallory, Arenia C.	Educator. Lexington, Miss.
Malone, Robert N.	Pres. Southwestern Life Ins. Co. Independent. Pine Bluff, Ark.
Maloney, Arnold A.	Clergyman. Independent, Wash., D.C.
Martin, Alexander H.	Lawyer, Rep. Cleveland, O.
Mason, James E.	Clergyman. Rep. Ithaca, N.Y.
Matthews, John F.	Educator, Independent, Institute, W.Va.
Matthews, Ezekiel Z.	Educator, Rep. Roanoke, Ala.
Matthews, William W.	Bishop A.M.E. Zion Church. Rep. Wash., D.C.
Miller, George F.	Clergyman. Socialist, Brooklyn, N.Y.
Miller, Herbert T.	Exec. Sec. Y.M.C.A. Phil., Pa.
Miller, Kelly	Educator, Wash., D.C.
Minkins, John C.	Journalist, Rep. Pawtucket, R.I.
Mitchell, Arthur W.	Congressman, Dem. Chic. Ill.
Mitchell, John A.	Educator, Rep. Columbus, O.
Mitchell, W. H., Jr.	Y.M.C.A. Sec. New Orleans, La.
Molette, Lemuel S.	Asst. State Educ. Supervisor. Fort Valley, Ga.
Montgomery, Charles H.	Pres. La. Collegiate Inst. Rep. Shreveport, La.
Moore, Blake E.	High School prin. clergyman. Independent, Columbia, Mo.

Moore, Fred R.	Alderman, publisher, N.Y.C.
Moorland, Jesse E.	Clergyman, Brooklyn, N.Y.
Morris, Edward H.	Lawyer, Rep. Chic., Ill.
Morsell, Samuel R.	Y.M.C.A. Sec. Independent. Rep.
Morton, Ferdinand	State Civil Service Commissioner, Dem. N.Y.C.
Moss, Richard M.	Exec. Sec. Urban League. Independent. Pittsburgh, Pa.
Morton, R. R.	Educator. Rep. Tuskegee Inst. Ala.
Murphy, Carl J.	Editor-publisher. Dem. Balt., Md.
Murray, Peter M.	Physician, N.Y.C.
Nash, W. E.	High school prin. Progressive. Athens, Tenn.
Nelson, William S.	Pres. Dillard Univ. Independent. New Orleans, La.
Oldfield, Mrs. Blossie B.	Publisher and owner of Chattanooga Defender, Chattanooga, Tenn.
O'Neal, Edmund J.	Training School Prin. Selma, Ala.
Overton, Boyd W.	Y.M.C.A. Sec. Independent. Cincinnati, Ohio.
Oxley, L. A.	Social worker. Dem. Raleigh, N.C.
Pace, Harry H.	Lawyer. Dem. Chic., Ill.
Paige, Miles A.	Lawyer. Magistrate. N.Y.C.
Parker, Thomas O.	Pres. Provident Benefit Assn. Rep. Chic., Ill.
Parker, Walter N.	Lawyer. Rep. Jacksonville, Fla.
Patterson, Frederick D.	Pres. Tuskegee Inst.
Payne, Fitz-Melvin C.	Physician. Rep. Tulsa, Okla.
Perkins, Lamar	Lawyer. Rep. N.Y.C.
Perry, William A.	Educator. Rep. Brunswick, Ga.
Petioni, Charles A.	Physician. Dem. N.Y.C.
Pickens, William	Educator, author. N.Y.C.
Poe, Lavinia F.	Lawyer, Rep. Newport News, Va.
Poole, William T.	Mortician. Rep. Pittsburgh, Pa.
Powell, A. Clayton	Clergyman. Rep. N.Y.C.
Presnell, J. N.	Physician. Rep. Knoxville, Tenn.
Preston, W. A.	Clergyman. Editor. Rep. Texarkana, Texas.
Ragland, John M.	Exec. Sec. Urban League. Rep. Cincinnati, O.
Randolph, A. Philip	Editor, author. Socialist. N.Y.C.
Randolph, Joseph B.	Pres. Claflin College. Rep. Orangeburg, S.C.
Ransom, Reverdy C.	Bishop of A.M.E. Church. Independent. Oceanport, N.J.
Rasbury, Levie	Pres. Kingston College. Rep. Kingston, N.C.
Reid, Barney F., Jr.	Clergyman. Cincinnati, Ohio.
Reid, Ira DeA.	Industrial Sec. N.Y.C.
Rhodes, Eugene W.	Editor. Lawyer. Rep. Phila., Pa.
Richardson, Clement	Pres. Western College. Independent. Kansas City, Mo.
Richardson, Clifton F.	Editor. Houston, Texas.
Richardson, Henry J., Jr.	Lawyer. Dem. Indianapolis, Ind.
Richardson, Percy S.	Physician. Independent. New Rochelle, N.Y.
Ricks, Edgar E.	Clergyman. Rep. Newark, N.J.
Ridley, Gloria R.	Social Worker. Independent. Boston, Mass.
Ridley, John R.	Banker. Rep. Newport News, Va.
Ringer, Thomas J.	County Training School Prin. Rocky Point, N.C.
Rivers, Joseph D. D.	Publisher. Denver, Colo.
Roberts, Carl G.	Surgeon. Rep. Chic., Ill.
Roberts, Eugene F.	Physician. N.Y.C.
Robinson, Gladis B.	Educator. Rep. Chic., Ill.

Robinson, William H.	Educator. Atlanta, Ga.
Robinson, William J.	Publisher, managing editor. Rep. Detroit, Mich.
Rogers, Elmer L.	Editor. Pub. Rep. Springfield, Ill.
Rogers, Garfield D.	Undertaker, realtor. Rep. Bradenton, Fla.
Rogers, Joel A.	Author. N.Y.C.
Ross, Martha H.	Educator. Rep. Cincinnati, Ohio.
Roxborough, Charles A.	Lawyer. Rep. Detroit, Mich.
Royall, John M.	Realtor. Rep. N.Y.C.
Rush, Mrs. Gertrude E.	Lawyer. Rep. Des Moines, Iowa.
Russell, Alfred P., Jr.	Dentist. Rep. Roxbury, Mass.
Sampson, David S.	Publisher. N.Y.C.
Sanders, William W.	Exec. Sec. Nat. Assn. of Teachers in Colored Schools. Rep. Charleston, W.Va.
Schuyler, George S.	Author. N.Y.C.
Scott, Emmett J.	Educator. Rep. Wash., D.C.
Scott, John R.	Dentist. Rep. Miami, Fla.
Scott, Robert T.	Deputy Circuit Court Clerk. Rep. St. Louis, Mo.
Seabrook, James W.	Pres. of State Normal School. Independent. Fayetteville, N.C.
Shaw, Benjamin G.	Bishop of A.M.E. Zion Church. Rep. Birmingham, Ala.
Shaw, Charles A.	Insurance exec. Independent. Houston, Texas.
Shaw, George C.	Clergyman. Rep. Oxford, N.C.
Shaw, J. Beverly F.	Clergyman. Rep. Los Angeles, Calif.
Shepard, James E.	Educator. Rep. Durham, N.C.
Simon, Hubert V.	Author. Independent. Chic., Ill.
Simpson, Abram	Pres. of Allen Univ. Independent. Columbia, S.C.
Simpson, James T.	Clergyman, lawyer. Republican. N.Y.C.
Sims, David H.	Bishop of A.M.E. Church. Independent. Newark, N.J.
Singleton, John A.	Dentist. Republican. Omaha, Nebr.
Smith, Aaron	Lawyer. Democrat. N.Y.C.
Smith, Allen A.	Clergyman. Teacher. Rep. Kingston, N.C.
Smith, Alvin D.	Editor, publisher. Rep. Cincinnati, Ohio.
Smith, Byrd Randall	Pres. of Mary Allen Jr. College. Independent. Crockett, Texas.
Smith, Frank B.	Lawyer. Rep. New Orleans, La.
Smith, James H. L.	Clergyman. Rep. Chic., Ill.
Smith, Robert L.	Bank Pres. Educator. Rep. Waco, Texas.
Smith, Rutherford B. H.	Deputy prosecutor. Dem. Indianapolis, Ind.
Smith, Thomas J.	Clergyman. Dayton, Ohio.
Smothers, James W.	School prin. Rep. Malokoff, Texas.
Spaulding, C. C.	Insurance Co. exec. Durham, N.C.
Stalmaker, Calvin K.	Clergyman. Social worker. Rep. Toledo, Ohio.
Stewart, Mrs. Sallie W.	Ex-pres. of National Assn. of Colored Women, Evansville, Ind.
Stocks, Gilbert T.	Circulation mgr. of Houston Informer. Rep. Houston, Tex.
Strauss, Mrs. Mattye O.	School prin. Rep. Paducah, Ky.
Summer, Francis B.	Educator. Rep. Wash., D.C.
Tate, V. Morse	Educator. Detroit, Mich.
Tatum, Robert J.	School prin. Rep. Beaumont, Texas.
Taylor, Abruthens A.	Dean, Fisk Univ. Independent. Nashville, Tenn.
Taylor, Mrs. Birdie S.	Social worker. Rep. Topeka, Kans.
Taylor, Daniel B	Physician. Rep. Phila., Pa.

Taylor, Davie E.	Publisher, editor. Independent. Los Angeles, Calif.
Taylor, Halley B.	Clergyman. Rep. Wash., D.C.
Taylor, Robert L.	Lawyer. Rep. Chic., Ill.
Taylor, Thelma C.	Newspaper mgr. Topeka, Kans.
Terrell, Mary Church	Lecturer, writer. Wash., D.C.
Thomas, Benjamin E.	Businessman. Dem. N.Y.C.
Thomas, George J.	Clergyman. Rep. Winston-Salem, N.C.
Thomas, Jesse O.	Social worker. Atlanta, Ga.
Thomas, Joseph C.	Funeral director. Rep. St. Louis, Mo.
Thomas, Julius A., Jr.	Exec. Sec. Urban League. Independent. Louisville, Ky.
Thompson, Hugh	Lawyer. Independent. Durham, N.C.
Thompson, John L.	Lawyer. Rep. Des Moines, Iowa.
Tompkins, Richard W.	Deputy Recorder of Deeds. Rep. Kansas City, Kans.
Tobias, Channing H.	Sec. Nat. Council Y.M.C.A. Independent. N.Y.C.
Toney, Charles E.	Municipal court judge. Dem. N.Y.C.
Toney, Lee A.	Supervising school prin. Rep. Macdonald, W.Va.
Toomer, Jean	Author. N.Y.C.
Townsend, Arthur M.	Denominational Sec. Rep. Nashville, Tenn.
Trenholm, Harper C.	Educator. Montgomery, Ala.
Trent, William J.	Pres. Livingston College. Rep. Salisbury, N.C.
Tucker, Charles R.	Clergyman, lawyer. Independent. Louisville, Ky.
Turner, Maxie L.	Supervisor of Schools. Warsaw, N.C.
Turner, Thomas W.	Educator. Hampton Institute, Va.
Underwood, Edward N.	Physician. Frankfort, Ky.
Utley, Samuel M.	Physician. Rep. Nashville, Tenn.
Valentine, William R.	Prin. Bordentown State School—Bordentown, N.J.
Vann, Robert L.	Editor, pub. Dem. Pittsburgh, Pa.
Vass, Samuel N.	Clergyman, Rep. Nashville, Tenn.
Vaughn, Marey E.	Editor, publ. Murfreesboro, Tenn.
Vernon, Villial T.	Bishop, A.M.E. Church. Rep. Detroit, Mich.
Walden, Austin T.	Lawyer, Rep. Atlanta, Ga.
Walker, Mrs. Hattie Brown	Librarian. Independent. Cincinnati, Ohio.
Walker, J. E.	Physician. Ins. Exec. Rep. Memphis, Tenn.
Walker, Thomas H. R.	Clergyman. Rep. Jacksonville, Fla.
Walker, William R.	Lawyer. Dem. Newport News, Va.
Walker, Owen N.	Physician. Dem. Brooklyn, N.Y.
Walls, N. J.	Bishop of A.M.E. Zion Church. Chicago, Ill.
Walrond, Eric D.	Writer. N.Y.C.
Walton, Lester A.	Journalist, diplomatist. Dem. N.Y.C.
Ward, A. Wayman	Clergyman. Repl. Chic., Ill.
Warfield, William A.	Physician. Wash., D.C.
Waring, Dr. M. Fitzbutler	Physician. Chic., Ill.
Warrick, Ennis C.	Dean, Wilberforce Univ. Rep. Wilberforce, Ohio.
Washington, Forrester B.	Dr. Atlantic School of Social Work. Rep. Atlanta, Ga.
Washington, George	Clergyman. Independent. Columbus, Ohio.
Washington, John M.	School prin. Rep. Huntington, W.Va.
Watson, James S.	Municipal court judge. Dem. N.Y.C.
Weaver, Seymour N., Jr.	Clergyman. School prin. Griffin, Ga.
Webb, James R.	High School prin. Rep. Madison, N.J.
Wells, Eva T.	Social Worker. Rep. Chic., Ill.
Wesley, Charles H.	Educator. Wash., D.C.
West, William B.	Dean of Men. Howard Univ. Rep. Washington, D.C.
Wheatley, Laura D.	Civic Worker. Rep. Balt., Md.

White, Walter	Sec. N.A.A.C.P. Independent, N.Y.C.
Whyte, George B.	School prin. Rep. Balt., Md.
Williams, Lacey K.	Clergyman. Chic., Ill.
Williams, Paul R.	Architect. Rep. Los Angeles, Calif.
Williams, William T. W.	Educator. Rep. Tuskegee, Ala.
Wilson, George D.	Educator. Independent. Talladega, Ala.
Wilson, J. Finley	Grand Exalted Ruler, LRRAE of W. Wash., D.C.
Wingfield, Judge Randolph	Educator. Mount Meigs, Alabama.
Winston, George B.	Y.M.C.A. Sec. Rep. Wichita, Kansas.
Womack, Arthur W.	Clergyman. Rep. Indianapolis, Ind.
Wood, Francis M.	Dir. of Schools. Rep. Balt., Md.
Woodson, Carter G.	Author, editor. Wash., D.C.
Wright, John C.	Educator. Rep. Daytona Beach, Fla.
Wright, James A.	Clergyman. Rep. Hartford, Conn.
Wright, John M.	Deputy County Treas. Topeka, Kans.
Wright, Louis T.	Physician. Independent. N.Y.C.
Wright, Richard R., Jr.	Bishop A.M.E. Church. Rep. Capetown, South Africa.
Yergan, Max	Y.M.C.A. Sec. N.Y.C.
Young, Mrs. Mattie D.	Y.M.C.A. Sec. Rep. St. Louis, Mo.
Young, Plumber B.	Editor and publisher. Rep. Norfolk, Va.

Appendix II
Leadership Schedule Tables

TABLE I

Racial Identification of Negro Leaders by Occupation Groupings
(Based on returns from leadership schedules)

	% correct racial identification
Organization Leaders	35.0
Walter White	59.9
Marcus Garvey	51.0
Charles Houston	36.8
William Pickens	23.7
A. Philip Randolph	21.2
Eugene K. Jones	18.4
Newspapers	22.6
George Schuyler	25.1
Ralph Matthews	24.5
Carl Murphy	22.3
Robert Vann	22.2
Claude Barnett	19.1
Politics	34.3
Frederick Douglass	96.0
Arthur Mitchell	69.3
Emmett J. Scott	57.0
William H. Hastie	53.5
Armond Scott	36.4
Jane Bolin	31.0
Lt. Lawrence Oxley	30.4
Crystal Bird Fauset	25.4
Robert Weaver	23.5
John R. Lynch	19.1
Robert R. Church	13.6
Melvin Chisum	10.0
Homer Brown	8.0
Elmer Carter	7.5
Church	67.3
Father Divine	95.0
Richard Allen	39.6

(continued)

TABLE 1 *(continued)*

	% correct racial identification
Education	49.1
Booker T. Washington	95.5
Mary McLeod Bethune	89.3
Carter G. Woodson	87.0
W. E. B. Du Bois	78.6
Kelly Miller	76.1
Nannie Burroughs	70.1
Robert R. Moton	62.8
Frederick D. Patterson	53.6
Alain Locke	49.7
E. Franklin Frazier	37.6
John Hope	33.9
John Gandy	28.9
Charles S. Johnson	28.0
Abram L. Harris	27.5
Rufus Clement	25.4
Ambrose Caliver	23.5
Monroe Work	23.3
William Hale	22.3
Ira DeA. Reid	20.3
Entertainment	78.6
Marian Anderson	93.8
Paul Robeson	93.1
Henry Armstrong	89.5
Roland Hayes	86.5
William C. Handy	59.6
Bert Williams	49.1
Radicals	28.6
Ben Davis, Jr.	36.3
Angelo Herndon	33.4
John P. Davis	25.3
James Ford	19.6
Science	58.5
George Washington Carver	94.1
Benjamin Banneker	71.4
Ernest E. Just	60.8
Matthew Henson	41.7
Paul Williams	24.7

TABLE I *(continued)*

	% correct racial identification
Artists, Writers	52.3
James Weldon Johnson	89.9
Phyllis Wheatley	88.8
Langston Hughes	80.6
Harry T. Burleigh	62.3
Countee Cullen	56.0
E. Simms Campbell	53.1
Benjamin Brawley	43.4
Richard Wright	35.4
Claude McKay	26.7
William Grant Still	20.5
Zora Neale Hurston	18.1
Business	
C. C. Spaulding	60.4
Victims	
Scottsboro Boys	95.4
Insurrectionist	
Nat Turner	58.1

TABLE 2
Racial Identification of Negro Leaders, Total Rank across Occupations
(Based on returns from leadership schedules)

#	Negro Leaders in Rank Order	Number Correct Racial Scores	%	Number Incorrect Racial Scores	%	Number Blank Racial Scores	%	Howard and Atlanta Universities Number Correct Racial Scores	%	Number Incorrect Racial Scores	%	Number Blank Racial Scores	%	Tuskegee, A&T, Prairie View, Kentucky State, Miners Teachers College Number Correct Racial Scores	%	Number Incorrect Racial Scores	%	Number Blank Racial Scores	%
1	Frederick Douglass	860	96.0	9	1.0	27	3.0	487	96.4	6	1.2	12	2.4	343	95.8	2	.6	13	3.6
2	Booker T. Washington	855	95.5	3	.3	38	4.2	481	95.2	2	.4	22	4.4	343	95.8	1	.3	14	3.9
3	Scottsboro Boys	718	95.4	2	.3	33	4.3	349	96.4	2	.6	11	3.0	337	94.1	0	—	21	5.9
4	Father Divine	715	95.0	3	.4	35	4.6	349	96.4	2	.6	11	3.0	334	93.3	1	.3	23	6.4
5	George W. Carver	843	94.1	2	.2	51	5.7	476	94.3	2	.4	27	5.3	336	93.9	0	—	22	6.1
6	Marian Anderson	840	93.8	2	.2	54	6.0	477	94.5	2	.4	26	5.1	332	92.7	0	—	26	7.3
7	Paul Robeson	834	93.1	1	.1	61	6.8	479	94.8	1	.2	25	5.0	323	90.2	0	—	35	9.8
8	James Weldon Johnson	806	89.9	7	.8	83	9.3	451	89.3	4	.8	50	9.9	325	90.8	3	.8	30	8.4
9	Henry Armstrong	802	89.5	8	.9	86	9.6	467	92.5	6	1.2	32	6.3	302	84.3	2	.6	54	15.1
10	Mary McLeod Bethune	800	89.3	4	.4	92	10.3	457	90.5	2	.4	46	9.1	317	88.5	2	.6	39	10.9
11	Phyllis Wheatley	796	88.8	7	.8	93	10.4	448	88.7	2	.4	55	10.9	317	88.5	4	1.1	37	10.4
12	Carter G. Woodson	780	87.0	6	.7	110	12.3	430	85.1	3	.6	72	14.3	321	89.7	3	.8	34	9.5
13	Roland Hayes	775	86.5	3	.3	118	13.2	468	92.7	3	.6	34	6.7	277	77.4	3	—	81	22.6
14	Langston Hughes	722	80.6	27	3.0	147	16.4	421	83.3	10	2.0	74	14.7	270	75.4	16	4.5	72	20.1
15	W. E. B. Du Bois	704	78.6	16	1.8	176	19.6	400	79.2	11	2.2	94	18.6	274	76.5	5	1.4	79	22.1
16	Kelly Miller	682	76.1	22	2.5	192	21.4	417	82.6	5	1.0	83	16.4	235	65.6	16	4.5	107	29.9
17	Benjamin Banneker	639	71.4	38	4.2	219	24.4	398	78.8	21	4.2	86	17.0	214	59.8	16	4.5	128	35.7
18	Nannie Burroughs	628	70.1	9	.8	261	29.1	366	72.5	3	.6	136	26.9	246	68.7	4	1.1	108	30.2
19	Arthur Mitchell	621	69.3	9	1.0	266	29.7	364	72.1	4	.8	137	27.1	237	66.2	5	1.4	116	32.4
20	Robert R. Moton	563	62.8	9	1.0	324	36.2	319	63.2	3	.6	183	36.2	222	62.0	5	1.4	131	36.6
21	Harry T. Burleigh	558	62.3	28	3.1	310	34.6	340	67.3	15	3.0	150	29.7	202	56.4	11	3.1	145	40.5
22	Ernest E. Just	544	60.8	38	4.2	314	35.0	380	75.2	17	3.4	108	21.4	158	44.1	19	5.3	181	50.6
23	C. C. Spaulding	541	60.4	85	9.5	270	30.1	334	66.2	37	7.3	134	26.5	198	55.3	41	11.5	119	33.2
24	Walter White	537	59.9	41	4.6	318	35.5	354	70.1	25	5.0	126	24.9	158	44.1	15	4.2	185	51.7

#	Name																		
25	William C. Handy	534	59.6	18	2.0	344	38.4	319	63.2	12	2.4	174	34.4	197	55.0	6	1.7	155	43.3
26	Nat Turner	521	58.1	50	5.6	325	36.3	302	59.8	27	5.3	176	34.9	197	55.0	21	5.9	140	39.1
27	Emmett J. Scott	511	57.0	18	2.0	367	41.0	354	70.1	8	1.6	143	28.3	151	42.2	10	2.8	197	55.0
28	Countee Cullen	502	56.0	23	2.6	398	41.4	302	59.8	15	3.0	188	37.2	168	46.9	8	2.2	182	50.9
29	F. D. Patterson	480	53.6	18	2.0	398	44.4	259	51.3	10	2.0	236	46.7	208	58.1	7	2.0	143	39.9
30	William H. Hastie	479	53.5	19	2.1	407	44.4	365	72.3	10	2.0	130	25.7	108	30.2	6	1.7	244	68.1
31	E. Simms Campbell	476	53.1	13	1.5	397	45.4	299	59.2	6	1.2	200	39.6	162	45.2	7	2.0	189	52.8
32	Marcus Garvey	457	51.0	42	4.7	424	44.3	300	59.4	26	5.1	179	35.5	132	36.9	14	3.9	212	59.2
33	Alain Locke	445	49.7	27	3.0	429	47.3	368	72.9	11	3.4	126	24.9	68	19.0	13	3.6	277	77.4
34	Bert Williams	440	49.1	27	3.0	403	47.9	286	56.6	17	3.6	202	40.0	144	40.2	8	2.2	206	57.6
35	Benjamin Brawley	327	43.4	23	3.1	501	53.5	203	56.1	13	2.2	146	40.3	113	31.6	9	2.5	236	65.9
36	Matthew Henson	374	41.7	21	2.3		56.0	261	51.7	11		233	46.1	99	27.7	8	2.2	251	70.1
37	Richard Allen	355	39.6	52	5.8	489	54.6	200	39.6	34	6.7	271	53.7	137	38.3	15	4.2	206	57.5
38	E. Franklin Frazier	283	37.6	27	3.6	443	58.8	228	63.0	14	3.9	120	33.1	51	14.3	13	3.6	294	82.1
39	Charles Houston	330	36.8	30	3.3	536	59.9	235	46.5	18	3.6	252	49.9	93	26.0	13	3.3	253	70.7
40	Armond Scott	326	36.4	14	1.6	556	62.0	232	45.9	8	1.6	265	52.5	92	25.7	6	1.7	260	72.6
41	Ben Davis, Jr.	325	36.3	18	2.0	553	61.7	207	41.0	8	1.6	290	57.4	115	32.1	7	2.0	236	65.9
42	Richard Wright	317	35.4	81	9.0	498	55.6	158	31.3	39	7.7	308	61.0	148	41.4	37	10.3	173	48.3
43	John Hope	304	33.9	47	5.2	545	60.9	207	41.0	26	5.1	272	53.9	85	23.8	18	5.0	255	71.2
44	Angelo Herndon	299	33.4	24	2.7	573	63.9	212	42.0	13	2.6	280	55.4	75	21.0	9	2.5	274	76.5
45	Jane Bolin	278	31.0	36	4.0	582	65.0	182	36.0	21	4.2	302	59.8	95	26.6	13	3.6	250	69.8
46	Lawrence Oxley	272	30.4	29	3.2	595	66.4	184	36.4	13	2.6	308	61.0	82	22.9	14	3.9	262	73.2
47	John Gandy	259	28.9	23	2.6	614	68.5	187	37.0	13	2.6	305	60.4	71	19.8	9	2.5	278	77.7
48	Charles S. Johnson	251	28.0	11	1.2	634	70.8	136	26.9	6	1.2	363	71.9	101	28.2	4	1.1	253	70.7
49	Abram Harris	207	27.5	20	2.6	526	69.9	178	49.2	8	2.2	176	48.6	27	7.5	10	2.8	321	89.7
50	Claude McKay	239	26.7	38	4.2	619	69.1	156	30.9	27	5.3	322	63.8	72	20.1	10	2.8	276	77.1
51	Rufus Clement	228	25.4	8	.9	660	73.7	145	28.7	4	.8	356	70.5	80	22.4	4	1.1	274	76.5
52	Crystal Bird Fauset	228	25.4	29	3.2	639	71.4	192	38.0	16	3.2	297	58.8	33	9.2	11	3.1	314	87.7
53	John P. Davis	227	25.3	22	2.5	647	72.2	169	33.5	15	3.0	321	63.5	54	15.1	6	1.7	298	83.2
54	George Schuyler	225	25.1	86	9.6	585	65.3	151	29.9	43	8.5	311	61.6	63	17.6	40	11.2	255	71.2
55	Paul Williams	221	24.7	11	1.2	664	74.1	144	28.5	6	1.2	355	70.3	68	19.0	5	1.4	285	79.6
56	Ralph Matthews	184	24.5	7	.9	562	74.6	119	32.9	5	1.4	238	65.7	63	17.6	2	.6	293	81.8
57	William Pickens	212	23.7	30	3.3	654	73.0	145	28.7	15	3.0	345	68.3	53	14.8	14	3.9	291	81.3

(continued)

TABLE 2 (continued)

		Number Correct Racial Scores	%	Number Incorrect Racial Scores	%	Number Blank Racial Scores	%	Howard and Atlanta Universities						Tuskegee, A&T, Prairie View, Kentucky State, Miners Teachers College					
								Number Correct Racial Scores	%	Number Incorrect Racial Scores	%	Number Blank Racial Scores	%	Number Correct Racial Scores	%	Number Incorrect Racial Scores	%	Number Blank Racial Scores	%
#	Negro Leaders in Rank Order																		
58	Ambrose Caliver	211	23.5	20	2.2	665	74.3	161	31.9	12	2.4	332	65.7	45	12.6	6	1.7	307	85.7
59	Robert Weaver	211	23.5	13	1.5	672	75.0	154	30.5	6	1.2	345	68.3	51	14.2	7	2.0	300	83.8
60	Monroe Work	209	23.3	37	4.1	650	72.6	115	22.8	22	4.3	368	72.9	88	24.6	15	4.2	255	71.2
61	William Hale	200	22.3	54	6.0	642	71.7	122	24.2	37	7.3	346	68.5	75	20.9	15	4.2	268	74.9
62	Carl Murphy	200	22.3	46	5.1	650	72.6	144	28.5	32	6.3	329	65.2	56	15.6	12	3.4	290	81.0
63	Robert Vann	199	22.2	24	2.7	673	75.1	136	26.9	17	3.4	352	69.7	53	14.8	7	2.0	298	83.2
64	A. Philip Randolph	190	21.2	22	2.5	684	76.3	131	25.9	14	2.8	360	71.3	46	12.8	7	2.0	305	85.2
65	William Grant Still	184	20.5	23	2.6	689	76.9	112	22.2	9	1.8	384	76.0	60	16.8	14	3.9	284	79.3
66	Ira DeA. Reid	153	20.3	11	1.5	589	78.2	113	31.2	3	.8	246	68.0	35	9.8	8	2.2	315	88.0
67	James Ford	176	19.6	65	7.3	655	73.1	121	24.0	40	7.9	344	68.1	49	13.7	23	6.4	286	79.9
68	John R. Lynch	171	19.1	104	11.6	621	69.3	104	20.6	69	13.7	332	65.7	57	15.9	34	9.5	267	74.6
69	Claude Barnett	144	19.1	22	2.9	587	78.0	55	15.2	15	4.1	292	80.7	83	23.2	6	1.7	269	75.1
70	Eugene Kinckle Jones	165	18.4	14	1.6	717	80.0	134	26.5	10	2.0	361	71.5	27	7.6	3	.8	328	91.6
71	Zora Neale Hurston	162	18.1	37	4.1	697	77.8	109	21.6	21	4.2	375	74.2	47	13.1	16	4.5	295	82.4
72	Robert R. Church	122	13.6	14	1.6	760	84.8	83	16.4	9	1.8	413	81.8	37	10.3	4	1.1	317	88.6
73	Melvin Chisum	90	10.0	21	2.3	785	87.7	58	11.5	12	2.4	435	86.1	32	8.9	9	2.5	317	88.6
74	Homer Brown	72	8.0	9	1.0	815	91.0	58	11.5	4	.8	443	87.7	13	3.6	5	1.4	340	95.0
75	Elmer Carter	67	7.5	23	2.6	806	89.9	50	9.9	14	2.8	441	87.3	16	4.5	9	2.5	333	93.0

TABLE 3
Racial Identification of White Leaders, Total Rank across Occupations
(Based on returns from leadership schedules)

#	White Leaders in Rank Order	Number Correct Racial Scores	%	Number Incorrect Racial Scores	%	Number Blank Racial Scores	%	Howard and Atlanta Universities						Tuskegee, A&T, Prairie View, Kentucky State, Miners Teachers College					
								Number Correct Racial Scores	%	Number Incorrect Racial Scores	%	Number Blank Racial Scores	%	Number Correct Racial Scores	%	Number Incorrect Racial Scores	%	Number Blank Racial Scores	%
1	Julius Rosenwald	545	72.4	68	9.0	140	18.6	251	69.3	39	10.8	72	19.9	266	74.3	26	7.3	66	18.4
2	Samuel Liebowitz	327	43.4	25	33.0	401	53.3	194	53.6	13	3.6	155	42.8	116	32.4	72	20.1	170	47.5
3	Harriet Beecher Stowe	374	41.7	259	28.9	263	29.4	192	38.0	131	26.0	182	36.0	164	45.8	118	33.0	76	21.2
4	John Brown	363	40.5	191	21.3	342	38.2	226	44.7	115	22.8	164	32.5	104	29.1	28	7.8	226	63.1
5	Arthur Spingarn	277	36.8	76	10.1	400	53.1	159	43.9	46	12.7	157	43.4	119	33.2	12	3.4	227	63.4
6	Will Alexander	100	11.2	76	8.3	722	80.5	45	8.9	47	9.3	413	81.8	39	10.9	25	7.0	294	82.1
7	Thomas T. Jones	94	10.5	100	11.2	702	78.3	62	12.3	64	12.7	379	75.0	32	8.9	34	9.5	292	81.6
8	Edwin Embree	71	7.9	44	4.9	781	87.2	37	7.3	29	5.8	439	86.9	31	8.7	14	3.9	313	87.4
9	Jackson Davis	64	7.1	100	11.2	732	81.7	27	5.3	65	12.9	413	81.8	36	10.1	32	8.9	290	81.0
10	Guy Johnson	52	5.8	96	10.7	748	83.5	34	6.7	63	12.5	408	80.8	17	4.7	31	8.7	310	86.6
11	Mary White Ovington	41	5.4	57	7.6	655	87.0	25	6.9	32	8.8	305	84.3	14	3.9	23	6.4	321	89.7
12	Clark Foreman	44	4.9	17	1.9	835	93.2	27	5.3	15	3.0	463	91.7	16	4.5	2	.6	340	94.9
13	Thomas Elsa Jones	30	3.3	32	3.6	834	93.1	18	3.6	29	5.7	458	90.7	10	2.8	3	.8	345	96.4

Notes

1. The memoranda mentioned here are "Conceptions and Ideologies of the Negro Problem" and "Extended Memorandum on the Programs, Ideologies, Tactics, and Achievements of Negro Betterment and Interracial Organizations."

2. Pinckney Brown Stewart (P. B. S.) Pinchback (1837–1921), politician. Born in Mississippi to a white planter and a freed slave, Pinchback traveled to Ohio as a youth to receive his education. After working aboard boats in the South and Midwest, he traveled back to the South during the Civil War and enlisted with the Union forces. Harassed about his race, he turned his attention to politics. In 1867, he developed a Republican club in the Fourth Ward of Louisiana and quickly ascended the state ranks to become president pro tem of the state senate in 1871. Following a brief period as lieutenant governor and later acting governor after an impeachment, Pinchback was involved in numerous contested elections at the state and national levels. By 1883, he was appointed surveyor of customs in New Orleans. In 1890, he moved to Washington, D.C., where he lived the rest of his life. W. Augustus Low and Virgil A. Clift, *Encyclopedia of Black America* (New York: McGraw-Hill, 1981), 677.

3. Charles H. Wesley (1891–1957), historian, educator, administrator. Born in Louisville, Kentucky, Wesley received his BA from Fisk University in 1911, his MA from Yale University in 1913, and his PhD from Harvard University in 1925. He joined the faculty of Howard University in 1913 and remained for nearly thirty years, during which he occupied many positions including professor, departmental chair, and dean of the graduate school. In 1942, he went to Wilberforce University where he served as president, and in 1947 he became president of Central State University (Wilberforce, Ohio). In 1965, he was named president emeritus of Central State and became director of the Association for the Study of Negro Life and History. He published, among many titles, *Negro Labor in the United States, 1850–1925* (New York: Russel and Russel, 1927). Low and Clift, *Encyclopedia of Black America*, 850.

4. William Edward Burghardt Du Bois (1868–1963), author, editor, educator, activist. Born free in Great Barrington, Massachusetts, Du Bois received a BA from Fisk University in 1888. He earned a second BA in 1890, an MA in 1891, and a PhD in 1895, all from Harvard University. He taught at numerous colleges and universities including Wilberforce University, University of

Pennsylvania, Atlanta University, and Howard University. As a prominent sociologist, he authored numerous scholarly works including the mentioned *Black Reconstruction* (1935). A life-long activist and social critic, Du Bois helped found the Niagara Movement in 1905, which led to the establishment of the National Association for the Advancement of Colored People (NAACP) in 1909. At the NAACP, Du Bois was the director of research and in that capacity edited the association's magazine, *Crisis,* from 1910 to 1932. After a long history of political engagement with various leftist organizations, including the Communist Party, Du Bois increasingly came under governmental surveillance in the later stages of his life and went into exile in Accra, Ghana, in 1961, where he died at the age of ninety-five. Low and Clift, *Encyclopedia of Black America,* 326–28.

5. Booker T. Washington (1856–1915), educator, author. Born into slavery in Virginia, Washington spent his childhood working, first in tobacco fields and then, after emancipation, in the coal mines of West Virginia. He worked his way through Hampton Institute in Virginia, an institution that offered a vocational education to its students. Washington took the Hampton model and applied it to a school of his own making: Tuskegee Institute in Alabama (founded in 1881). Tuskegee soon became the darling of northern white philanthropists, and Washington rose to national prominence. His address at the Atlanta Cotton Exposition in 1895 and the publication of his autobiography *Up from Slavery* in 1901 cemented his place as the dominant figure in black America. He called on blacks to accept the racial practices of the South and asked in return that white southerners invest in black labor. He was the leading advocate for vocational or industrial education until his death in 1915. At the height of his fame and power he regularly advised U.S. presidents on race matters and had virtual control over patronage positions in the federal government. Documenting the American South Web site, "Booker T. Washington," http://docsouth.unc.edu/washington/bio.html.

6. When Bunche wrote this, he did not know the final structure of *An American Dilemma,* but he did know the other work that was being pursued on its behalf. The contents of *An American Dilemma,* however, bear out Bunche's assertion. The ninth part of the book (out of eleven total) is titled "Leadership and Concerted Action" and contains within it ten chapters covering, among other things, "The Protest Motive and Negro Personality," "Negro Popular Theories," "The Negro Church," "The Negro School," and "The Negro Press."

7. Marcus Garvey (1887–1940), Pan-Africanist and founder of the Universal Negro Improvement Association (UNIA). Garvey was born in St. Ann's Bay, Jamaica. He left school in 1901 and immersed himself in black nationalist politics while working as a printer and traveling throughout Central America. He moved to England in 1912 and returned to Jamaica in 1914. Upon his return he, along with future wife Amy Ashwood, established the UNIA. Together, they dedicated the organization to uplifting blacks throughout the world through self-

help politics and economics. Garvey moved the UNIA to New York City in 1916, remarried in 1919, and built the largest mass movement among African Americans to date. Garvey sought to become a captain of industry through developing the Black Star Line. The steamship project was an economic failure almost from the start even though the idea of developing independent commercial economies via the high seas inspired the masses. Garvey was investigated and harassed by the U.S. government and eventually indicted and arrested for mail fraud in 1922. Garvey was imprisoned in 1925 and deported in 1927. The UNIA struggled without Garvey's presence and leadership. Garvey struggled himself, unable to start new careers in Jamaica and London over the remaining thirteen years of his life. Judith Stein, *The World of Marcus Garvey: Race and Class in Modern Society* (Baton Rouge: Louisiana State University Press, 1986), 1–6.

8. Frederick Douglass Patterson (1901–1988), educator, philanthropist. Orphaned at age two, Patterson was raised by his sister. He received a DVM from Iowa State College in 1923 and an MS in 1927. In 1932, he received his second doctorate from Cornell University. He taught veterinary science at Virginia State College before he started his twenty-five-year tenure at Tuskegee University in 1928. At Tuskegee, he was a professor of veterinary science as well as president of the school from 1935 to 1953. In 1944, he founded Tuskegee's School of Veterinary Medicine. He cofounded the United Negro College Fund that same year. In 1987, President Ronald Reagan bestowed the Presidential Medal of Freedom on Patterson. Tuskegee University Web site, "Legacy of Leadership," http://www.tuskegee.edu.

9. "Mayor of Harlem" is an honorary title given to Bill "Bojangles" Robinson in 1939 in recognition of his fame, contributions to the arts, and long-standing roots in Harlem. This is an honorific title that has been "bestowed" or even claimed outright by long-time Harlem residents since then. Black neighborhoods in other American cities also participate in a similar tradition.

10. Asa Philip Randolph (1889–1979), labor leader and civil rights activist. Randolph was born in Crescent City, Florida. The child of deeply religious parents, Randolph left home in 1911 for New York City. While working odd jobs in New York, Randolph was exposed to cadres of radical political activists. He befriended Chandler Owen and together they publicly declared an affinity for socialist politics. Randolph and Owen established the *Messenger*, a socialist periodical that promoted the International Workers of the World. The *Messenger* was said to have "attacked everybody." Owen left the paper in 1923, frustrated by the near-constant federal surveillance and the temporary revocation of the paper's mailing permit due to its radical politics. Randolph maintained the periodical, but its message moderated once he was elected president of the Brotherhood of Sleeping Car Porters (BSCP) and the *Messenger* became that union's official journal. As head of the BSCP, Randolph fought for union recognition and membership in the American Federation of Labor. Randolph eventually won the

fight for recognition and was recognized as the most important labor leader in black America. He was elected the first president of the Popular Front–style National Negro Congress but publicly resigned when he concluded that the Communist Party controlled the organization. In 1941, he threatened a march on Washington unless Franklin Roosevelt desegregated the military and opened up defense factory jobs to black workers. Roosevelt responded with Executive Order 8802, which established the Fair Employment Practices Committee. Randolph continued to agitate for the desegregation of the military through his new organization, the March on Washington Movement. Paula Pfeffer, *A. Philip Randolph, Pioneer of the Civil Rights Movement* (Baton Rouge: Louisiana State University Press, 1990), 6–44; Anthony Appiah and Henry Louis Gates, *Africana: The Encyclopedia of the African and African American Experience* (New York: Basic Civitas Books, 1999), 1292.

Father Divine, a.k.a. George Baker (1880?–1965), religious leader. Little is known about Divine's early years. A migrant from the South, Divine fashioned his early career as an itinerant preacher who promoted a "New Thought" ideology that advocated communal wealth and self-reliance. He founded the Universal Peace Mission movement, and it still serves as the organizational foundation of his religious practices. Originally based in Long Island, New York, Divine moved the headquarters of the movement to Harlem, where he quickly became famous for his day-long communal banquets at different Peace Mission homes at which throngs would arrive for a free meal and hours-long homilies. His fame and philosophy spread, and he quickly developed a national base of white support. Institute for the Study of American Religion, http://www.americanreligion.org/cultwtch/frdivine.html.

11. George Washington Carver (1864–1943), botanist. Born in Missouri, he was kidnapped along with his mother, and both were sold as slaves in Arkansas. After securing a return from his owner, Carver worked his way through high school and earned both a BS and MS from Iowa Agricultural College. Carver first headed the college's greenhouse, then was persuaded by Booker T. Washington to go to Tuskegee Institute in 1896. Carver concentrated his research on the industrial uses of the peanut, sweet potato, pecan, and cotton. Frequently honored by many organizations for his humanitarian works and research, Carver was named a Fellow of the Royal Academy of England in 1916, given the NAACP's Spingarn Medal in 1923, and awarded the Roosevelt Medal for distinguished service to science in 1939. Low and Clift, *Encyclopedia of Black America*, 218.

12. Walter Francis White (1893–1955), civil rights leader. Born in Atlanta, White graduated from Atlanta University in 1916. In 1918, he became assistant to the chief administrative officer of the Atlanta NAACP and began reporting on race riots and lynchings in the South. In 1930, he became acting secretary of the national NAACP and began directing various legislation initiatives for anti-

lynching laws, voting rights, and the elimination of discrimination in the armed forces. He was instrumental in the formation of the Fair Employment Practices Committee in 1941. He also served as a consultant to the U.S. delegation to the United Nations founding convention. Low and Clift, *Encyclopedia of Black America,* 853–54.)

Eugene Kinckle Jones (1885–1954), civil rights leader. Born in Richmond, Virginia, Jones was the son of a slave father and freeborn mother. He received his BA from Virginia Union in 1906 and his MA from Cornell University in 1908. During his college days he helped found the Alpha Phi Alpha fraternity. He taught at Louisville University as well as Central High School in Louisville, Kentucky. For most of his life he worked for the National Urban League (NUL), expanding it to include more than forty branches across the nation. From 1911 to 1940, he was executive secretary of the New York branch of the NUL. Low and Clift, *Encyclopedia of Black America,* 477.

13. Mary McLeod Bethune (1875–1955), educator, civic leader. Born in South Carolina, Bethune attended Scotia College in North Carolina and the Moody Bible Institute in Chicago, where she was the only black student. In 1904, she founded the Daytona Normal and Industrial Institute for Negro Girls, which eventually became Bethune-Cookman College. She was president of Bethune-Cookman from 1904 to 1942 and from 1946 to 1947. She was the president of the National Association of Colored Women (1924–1928), the founder of the National Headquarters for the National Association of Colored Women (1926), and the founder-president of the National Council of Negro Women (1935–1949). She was heavily involved in the Hoover Committee for Child Welfare of the National Business League, the NUL, and the Commission on Interracial Cooperation. She was the first black woman to head a federal office (the Division of Negro Affairs for the National Youth Administration), and as such she created the informal Black Cabinet during the New Deal. In 1974, a national monument was erected in her honor in Washington, D.C.'s Lincoln Park.

14. "Dicty" is a pejorative term used with disdain for class snobbishness to describe striving and middle-class blacks who believe that they are more refined than those "beneath" them.

15. The Niagara Movement, cofounded in 1905 and then led by W. E. B. Du Bois, was a protest organization whose membership consisted of many northern black intellectuals including William Monroe Trotter. The Niagara Movement met annually until 1909, when a few of its members joined a group of progressive whites to establish the NAACP. Before its dissolution, the Niagara Movement issued manifestos that called for a broad array of civil- and human-rights reforms. The organization drew its name from the location of its founding conference: Niagara Falls, Canada. The group had been denied accommodations in nearby Niagara Falls, New York. Low and Clift, *Encyclopedia of Black America,* 327.

16. Robert Abbott (1868–1940), editor, philanthropist. Born to slave parents, Abbott attended Hampton Institute and Kent Law School in Chicago, where he graduated in 1898. Using his own funds, Abbott founded the *Chicago Defender* in 1905, which, under his direction, became the most widely disseminated and read black newspaper of its time. The *Defender* played a major role in influencing southern blacks to relocate to the North during the great migration. Abbott served on numerous civic committees including the Chicago Commission on Race Relations which produced the 1922 study *The Negro in Chicago*. Low and Clift, *Encyclopedia of Black America*, 3.

17. "High yellers," or "high yellows," was a term used to differentiate African Americans from each other on the basis of skin tone. Associated with higher socioeconomic standing, "high yellow" was often used as an exclusionary instrument by middle-class African Americans involved in fraternal organizations in the late nineteenth and early twentieth centuries. Skin color was measured in various ways such as matching skin color to brown paper bags and having visible blue veins, all of which were employed to survey who was allowed inclusion and who was not.

18. James E. Jackson, Jr. (1914–), writer, activist. Born in Richmond, Virginia, Jackson attended Howard University and studied with Ralph Bunche. Along with other black students and workers, he helped to found the Southern Negro Youth Congress in 1937 and in 1946 signed up black war veterans in Mississippi to vote for the first time. A year later, he became the chairman of the Communist Party in Louisiana and eventually became a leader in the national Communist Party USA (CPUSA). After CPUSA members were targeted for arrest under the Smith Act, Jackson went underground for five years, only to reemerge and stand trial. Although he received letters of defense from both Bunche and W. E. B. Du Bois, he was found guilty. Though convicted, the U.S. Supreme Court nullified the constitutionality of the Smith Act in 1957, before Jackson began serving his term. He traveled extensively and was the last U.S. reporter to interview Ho Chi Minh before his death in 1969.

19. *Grovey v. Townsend* was argued on March 11, 1935, and decided on April 1, 1935. Grovey, a black Democrat, argued that his Fourteenth and Fifteenth Amendment rights were violated when he was denied a ballot for the Texas Democratic primary because he was black. After deliberation, the court found that exclusion of blacks from the primary was not a state action and that such exclusion did not, in this case, abrogate Grovey's rights. The decision was reversed in 1944 in *Smith v. Allwright*.

20. Oscar DePriest (1871–1951), lawmaker, civil rights advocate. Born in Florence, Alabama, De Priest moved to Chicago in his childhood. He rose through the ranks of local elected offices until becoming a U.S. representative in 1928. With his election, he became the first African American elected to

Congress in the twentieth century. He served six terms in Congress, during which he fought for antilynching bills and a few civil rights measures. One of his more notable civil rights fights was for the right of his wife to have tea at the White House. He was defeated in 1934 by Democrat Arthur W. Mitchell. Chicago Tribute Web site, "Markers of Distinction," http://www.chicagotribute.org/Markers/DePriest.htm.

21. "Jackleg" is southern vernacular for someone who is untrained, incompetent, or unscrupulous.

22. Horace Roscoe Cayton, Jr. (1903–1970), sociologist, educator. Born in Seattle, Cayton dropped out of high school and entered the military. He returned to Seattle, finished high school, and graduated from the University of Washington with a degree in sociology. In 1934, he served as assistant to Harold Ickes, the U.S. Secretary of the Interior. In 1935, he became an instructor of economics and labor at Fisk University before heading to Chicago the following year for a job with the Works Progress Administration. During World War II, he refused to serve in the army because of its segregationist practices and enlisted instead in the merchant marines. He is best known for his study *Black Metropolis,* which he coauthored with St. Clair Drake in 1945. Appiah and Gates, *Africana,* 396.

23. George Stoney (1916–), filmmaker, educator. A graduate of the University of North Carolina and New York University, Stoney was working for the Henry Street Settlement in New York when he joined the *An American Dilemma* project. The only one of Bunche's three field assistants who was white, Stoney conducted a significant number of interviews, almost all of them in the South. After he completed his work for the project, he turned toward producing and directing documentary films. He joined the faculty at New York University in 1971. While there, he cofounded the Alternative Media Center, an organization dedicated to developing public access television. Brian Urquhart, *Ralph Bunche: An American Life* (New York: Norton, 1993), 84; New York University Web site, Public Affairs press release, "Tisch School's Kanbar Institute . . . to Honor Professor George Stoney," http://www.nyu.edu/publicaffairs/newsreleases/b_Tisch.shtml.

24. See editor's introduction for clarification on "Faber."

25. Lt. Lawrence Oxley was in the 1920s, director of the Division of Work among Negroes for the North Carolina Welfare Department. Franklin Roosevelt's Secretary of Labor, Frances Perkins, tapped Oxley as one of her assistants. Oxley's appointment dismayed many race liberals, who felt he was too adept at kowtowing to whites. He was one of the founding members of Roosevelt's unofficial Black Cabinet. His opinions, however, ran against the mainstream of that group of race advisers that included the likes of Mary McLeod Bethune, William Hastie, and Robert Weaver. John B. Kirby, *Black Americans in the Roosevelt Era: Liberalism and Race* (Knoxville: University of Tennessee Press, 1980), 16, 147.

26. Arthur Wergs Mitchell (1883–1968), politician. Born in rural Alabama, Mitchell studied briefly at the Tuskegee Institute under Booker T. Washington. After leaving Tuskegee, he served as president of Armstrong Agricultural School in West Butler, Alabama, for ten years. He studied law in Washington, D.C., and began to practice there in 1927. He became active in politics after the Republican Party sent him to Chicago in 1928 to campaign for Herbert Hoover. Mitchell changed party affiliation and ingratiated himself to the white establishment within the city. The Chicago Machine approved of his docile image and backed Mitchell's bid for a congressional seat, which he won, defeating black Republican congressman Oscar DePriest. Mitchell served four terms in the House of Representatives (1935–1943). He declined to run for a fifth term when he lost the support of the Chicago Machine. Biographical Directory of the United States Congress Web site, http://bioguide.congress.gov/scripts/biodisplay; African American Registry Web site, http://www.aaregistry.com/african_american_history/493/Arthur_W_Mitchell_political_pioneer.

27. Born in Florida, Ossian Sweet was a Howard University–trained physician who moved to Michigan in 1924 to take a job at Detroit's first black hospital. In order to avoid the poverty-stricken areas of Detroit's urban ghettos, Sweet and his wife bought a two-story bungalow in an all-white section of the city. Due to heavy anti-black sentiment in the neighborhood, including Ku Klux Klan attacks, Sweet prepared his family for the area by bringing along ten guns and one hundred rounds of ammunition. Sweet also asked his two brothers and several friends to stay in the house to defend the property. On the first night of the couple's stay in their new home, an angry white mob gathered outside and began to throw rocks at the residence. Detroit police did nothing in response. Trying to protect their family, Sweet, his brothers, and their friends fired their guns at the crowd. They missed their targets but hit a bystander across the street. All eleven occupants in the home were charged with conspiracy to commit murder. After two successful trial defenses by NAACP-hired attorney Clarence Darrow, the Sweets returned to their home. University of Massachusetts, Amherst, Campus Chronicle Web site, "Boyle Delves into Landmark Civil Rights Case from 1920s," www.umass.edu/chronicle/archives/01/02-23/Boyle.htm.

28. Doxey Alphonso Wilkerson (1905–1993), educator, radical. Born in Missouri, Wilkerson taught at various educational institutions including Howard University and New York's Yeshiva University. An outspoken advocate for black labor and civil rights, Wilkerson was a spokesperson for the Communist Party, eliciting investigations by the U.S. House Un-American Activities Committee. After resigning from the Communist Party in 1957, he continued to be prominent in the civil rights movement throughout the 1960s. He maintained his political engagement with civil rights issues and education until his retirement in 1984. Appiah and Gates, *Africana*, 1995.

29. No such appendix is found with the carbon copy held in the Bunche Papers at UCLA. It is likely that this appendix never was completed.

30. If the table headings are correct (See Appendix II), the leadership schedule was not distributed to students at Dillard, North Carolina State College, or Shaw.

31. This error has been fixed for publication.

Index

A note on terminology: When referring to Americans of African descent, "Negro" is predominantly used in the body of Bunche's memorandum and "black" is used in the editor's introduction. To avoid confusion when the different nomenclatures were used for the same individuals or groups they have been conflated in the index as "Negro/black." This convention is used merely for the reader's convenience. It is in no way a commentary on the changing self-naming practices of Americans of African descent.